THE DEVELOPMENT OF MINE WARFARE

THE DEVELOPMENT OF MINE WARFARE

A Most Murderous and Barbarous Conduct

Norman Youngblood

War, Technology, and History
Robert Citino, Series Editor

PRAEGER SECURITY INTERNATIONAL
Westport, Connecticut · London

Library of Congress Cataloging-in-Publication Data

Youngblood, Norman.
  The development of mine warfare : a most murderous and barbarous
    conduct / Norman Youngblood.
            p. cm. — (War, technology, and history, ISSN 1556-4924)
  Includes bibliographical references and index.
  ISBN 0–275–98419–2 (alk. paper)
  1. Mines (Military explosives)—History. 2. Submarine mines—History. 3.
    Land mines—History. I. Title. II. Series.
  UG490.Y68 2006
  355.8'25115—dc22   2006009800

British Library Cataloguing in Publication Data is available.

Library of Congress Catalog Card Number: 2006009800
ISBN: 0–275–98419–2
ISSN: 1556–4924

First published in 2006

Praeger Security International, 88 Post Road West, Westport, CT 06881
An imprint of Greenwood Publishing Group, Inc.
www.praeger.com

Printed in the United States of America

The paper used in this book complies with the
Permanent Paper Standard issued by the National
Information Standards Organization (Z39.48–1984).

10 9 8 7 6 5 4 3 2 1

Contents

Series Foreword

Military historians can be a contentious, feisty lot. There is little upon which they agree. The importance of attrition versus maneuver, the relative qualities of "deep battle" and "Blitzkrieg," the command abilities of Patton and Montgomery: put two military historians in a room, and you'll likely get three opinions on any of these questions. And yet, there is one thing that unites military historians across the spectrum. Virtually everyone within the field recognizes the crucial role that technology has played in the development of the military art. Indeed, this is almost axiomatic: the very first man who picked up a club against his neighbor was wielding "technology" of a sort. The outcomes of wars have been profoundly affected by the technological contexts in which they were fought. From spoke-wheeled chariots to the M1A1 tank, from blades of Toledo steel to the AK-47, from primitive "bombards" to the MOAB ("mother of all bombs"), the problem of technology has stood at the forefront of military history.

Beyond that unifying proposition, however, problems can still arise in analyzing the precise role of technology. Consider for a moment the impact of the Industrial Revolution. Just as it transformed society, economy, and culture, it changed the appearance of war beyond all recognition. It was the age of the mass army, "railroads and rifles," and the telegraph. The growth of industry allowed military forces to grow to unheard-of size. In 1757, Frederick the Great triumphed over the French at Rossbach with an army that totaled 22,000 men; at Königgrätz in 1866, well over 400,000 men contested the issue, and the Austrian casualties alone, some 44,000 men, totaled precisely twice as many as Frederick's victorious host at Rossbach. The railroad allowed these hordes to move, quite literally, 24 hours per day, and the problem of the slow-moving supply column that had bedeviled military operations from time out of mind seemed to have been solved. Moreover, the introduction of the telegraph meant that armies could be kept on a tight leash, even by commanders hundreds of miles away.

For each advantage of the new technology, however, there was a corresponding difficulty. It was soon clear that commanding and controlling the mass army was a huge, even insurmountable problem. It is generally agreed that Napoleon I had serious problems in this area in 1812 and that he was at his best with armies that totaled 85,000 men or less. It was foolish to expect an army of several hundred thousand men to maneuver nimbly across the countryside, wheel like a company, and whack the opponent a surprise blow in the flank. In fact, getting them to maneuver at all was a stretch. The telegraph was a modern marvel, true, but the vision it offered of total control of far-flung operations turned out to be a mirage. Tied to a static system of poles and wires, it was far more useful to the defender than to the attacker, and it was nearly useless in any kind of mobile campaign. The mass army, then, was a huge body with a small brain, and it had a very difficult time doing much more than marching straight ahead and crashing into whatever happened to be in front of it. At that point, a mutual slaughter would begin.

The other great technological advance of the era was the introduction of new firearms. The rifled musket, or simply the "rifle," dramatically improved the range and firepower of infantry. The 1860s saw another breakthrough, the breech-loader, which greatly increased rate of fire. With long-range rifles in the hands of the defenders, assault columns could theoretically be shot to pieces long before they struck home. In place of the old-style assault, there then arose the firefight, with extended skirmish lines on both sides replacing the formations of line and column. It was an "open order revolution," the logical culmination of the tactical developments since the French Revolution. Open order tactics, however, rarely allowed enough concentration of fighting power for a successful assault. Both sides lined up and fired. There were casualties—enormous casualties—often for little gain. It was the great conundrum of the era. Clearly, technology was not so much a solution to a problem on the nineteenth century battlefield; it was more like the problem itself.

These are the issues that will form the heart of Praeger's new *War, Technology, and History* series. Books in the series will focus on the crucial relationship between warmaking and technological advances in the past 200 years. During this period, new machines like the rifle, the railroad, and the telegraph (in the nineteenth century) and the machine gun, the airplane, and the tank (in the twentieth) have transformed the face of war. In the young twenty-first century, the U.S. Army has been emphasizing the ways in which information technology can have an even more radical transformative impact.

Historically, armies that have managed to integrate new technologies have found corresponding success on the battlefield, and their victories have as often as not come at the expense of those who have failed to ground their warmaking doctrine squarely in the available technology. The question is, therefore, much wider than a simple list of technical "specs" for various weapons. Books in the series will link technology and doctrine, that is, the weapons and the manner in which they were employed on actual battlefields of the day. The series is intended for a wide readership, from buffs and war-gamers to scholars and "operators"—military officers and policy makers.

It is hard to argue with the notion that technological change has held the key to understanding military history, and in our contemporary era of information management and smart weaponry, technology continues to change the face of battle. Questions remain, however. Is technology our master or our servant? Are there limits to its usefulness? Does it alter the nature of war, or is war based on timeless, unchanging principles? These are a few of the themes to be explored by the authors—recognized experts all—in this new series. It presents no party line or previously-agreed-upon point of view. Nor does it offer any simple answers to any of these questions. Welcome to *War, Technology, and History*.

Acknowledgments

As with many endeavors, this book could not have been completed without the help and support of many people. I particularly wish to thank those who guided me through my thesis, Dr. James Pohl (my chair), Dr. Dennis Dunn, and Dr. Michael Boone; and those who guided me through my dissertation, Dr. James Reckner (my chair), Dr. James Harper, Dr. Ronald Rainger, Dr. Ronald Frankum, and Dr. David Sneed. Both committees provided tremendous assistance on this project in its various stages. I would also like to thank James Reckner and Joe Kaufmann for their encouragement in turning my dissertation into a book, as well as for their review of the manuscript.

I was assisted in my work by a number of libraries and research centers. The Texas Tech University and Texas State University Inter-Library Loan Offices were both very helpful in tracking down hard-to-find works. In addition, some of the material was obtained during research conducted on a grant from the United States Air Force Historical Research Center at Maxwell Air Force Base, Alabama.

While many of the illustrations used in this book came from military manuals and other government documents, this was not always the case. The Vietnam Archive at Texas Tech University was a great help, not only in obtaining documents, but in providing several of the illustrations for the book. The University of Texas Perry-Castañeda Library's online map collection also provided some of the maps used in this work. Additionally, I would like to thank my friend Joel West for creating several of the maps used in this book on short notice.

I would also like to express my thanks to my family and friends and to the faculty and staff of the College of Mass Communications at Texas Tech University for their support over the years while I worked on this project.

Also, many thanks as well to the folks at Greenwood and Praeger for giving me the opportunity to write this, particularly Heather Staines. I also owe a debt to many of the other faculty I have studied under including Dr. Idris Traylor, Dr. John Leffler, Dr. Jan Dawson, Mr. Philip Babel, and many others.

Most importantly, I would like to thank my chief proofreader and my moral support during this project, my wife, Susan Youngblood. She has learned more than she ever wanted to about mine warfare, and this work could not have been completed without her help and support.

Introduction

The International Committee of the Red Cross estimates that landmines injure an average of 24,000 people every year. Most of these victims are civilians, many killed or injured by landmines planted during wars long over. During the past ten years, nongovernmental organizations across the world have worked to institute a ban on the manufacture and use of antipersonnel mines, bringing international attention to the weapon. The campaign came to fruition with the 1997 Ottawa Convention. As part of the convention, representatives from 122 countries promised to stop the manufacture, use, and stockpiling of antipersonnel mines by the year 2004. President Bill Clinton chose not to sign the convention, stating that he would not put American military personnel at risk by removing the weapon from American arsenals until a replacement has been found. Other key countries including China, India, and Pakistan also refused to sign the treaty. The use of sea mines created a similar outcry in the early twentieth century after mines left over from the Russo-Japanese War (1904–1905) threatened shipping along the Korean and Chinese coasts. The loss of civilian life coupled with a disruption of commerce brought calls for the regulation of mine warfare during the 1907 Hague Convention, culminating in the Convention Relative to the Laying of Automatic Submarine Contact Mines, an agreement that set the groundwork for how mines should be used.[1]

Land and sea mines share more than a history of inspiring international outrage. They are in many ways siblings, as many of the inventors of early sea mines were also involved in the design of landmines. Both weapons came into their own during the nineteenth century. Through the end of the century, it was uncommon for a book on mine warfare to address only one type of mine. Arguments against the use of mines began almost with their introduction. British naval officers complained bitterly about the American use of sea mines during both the American Revolution and the War of 1812. Union officers and soldiers protested equally as vehemently about Southern landmines during the American Civil War. By the end of the century, however, both types of mines were largely accepted as legitimate weapons, even if many in the military viewed them as weapons of the weak. Even when their paths diverged, the weapons still found common ground. Both became increasingly sophisticated in design, with inventors looking for more efficient ways to put out mines including dropping them from airplanes, as well as finding better ways to make sure they exploded at the right time.

Books on the development on mine warfare began to appear by the mid-nineteenth century, usually written by members of the military, often those involved in the development and use of mines. These works are a tremendous resource for those interested in the development of mine warfare. While there have been several studies in recent years on the development of mine warfare, most of them have concentrated on developments in the twentieth century. For works on sea mines, this usually means World War I. For works on landmines, this frequently means World War II. This study seeks to present a more balanced view of the development of mine warfare, and half of the book is dedicated just to developments in mine warfare before World War I. This study also tries to examine the development of mines from a variety of perspectives including technical, tactical, and strategic developments, as well as the people who developed mines and those who had to cope with mines on the battlefield.

The book is divided into seven chapters. The first looks at the origins of the mine from its beginning in the ancient Assyrian Empire through the end of the eighteenth century. Chapter 2, "The Age of Invention: From America to Russia," looks at the role of the individual in the development of the first modern land and sea mines, concluding with the development of the first modern sea mine and antipersonnel mine by Immanuel Nobel and their use in the Crimean War. Chapter 3, "The American Civil War," examines the development of mine warfare in the United States during the American Civil War. Of particular importance in this chapter is the transfer of technology from Russia to the United States and the debates by both Union and Confederate soldiers as to the ethics of using landmines. Chapter 4, "The Sea Mine Comes of Age," looks at the rapid developments in sea mines during the years after the Civil War and the eventual call for regulating the use of sea mines at the 1907 Hague Convention. The chapter also looks at the rise and fall of the landmine during these years, including its relatively unsuccessful use in the Russo-Japanese War.

The remainder of the book focuses on mine warfare in the twentieth century. Chapter 5, "The Great War," highlights the interplay of the role of submarines in the development of sea mines, both as a target of mines and as a way to lay minefields. Similarly, the chapter also discusses the role of the tank in resurrecting the landmine near the end of the war. Chapter 6, "World War II," looks at the use of mines during the next great war, a war in which the landmine emerged as an indispensable tool for the military and both land and sea mines grew increasingly sophisticated in their construction and in the way they were used. This chapter is of particular import as the development during the war of air-deployed landmines and inexpensive-to-produce landmines laid the groundwork for the problems that created the current international debate over the appropriateness of landmine warfare. The book's final chapter looks at developments in mine warfare since 1945, including technological changes and efforts to legislate the use of both land and sea mines, particularly the development of the International Campaign to Ban Landmines and the subsequent signing of the Ottawa Treaty limiting the use of antipersonnel mines.

1

The Origins of Mine Warfare

THE ANCIENT WORLD

THE BRITISH MUSEUM IN London houses one of the oldest records of landmine warfare—an Assyrian orthostat, or wall relief, depicting the breaching of a city wall by mining, or tunneling. The orthostat and its companions at the museum date from between 883 and 859 B.C.E. Taken together, the series provides details of the Assyrian art of war, including laying siege to a city, an activity in which the Assyrians excelled. Assyrian success in besieging cities lay in their ability to take advantage of a wide variety of tools and tactics, including psychological warfare, scaling the city walls, battering rams, sapping, and, of course, mining. The othostats show many of these being used in concert: men tunneling, warriors on ladders scaling city walls, and groups of archers mounted on great wheeled siege engines armed with battering rams. By coordinating these methods during an attack, the Assyrians denied the defenders the ability to concentrate their forces to stop any single attempt at breaching the walls. Historian Yigael Yadin presents the following compelling version of how an attack might have occurred:

> [O]ne or two wings are breached by groups of battering-rams; another wing is being stormed by warriors scaling the heights with ladders; beneath another section of the wall, units of enemy demolition sappers are tunneling cavities and undermining the foundation; elsewhere, part of the wall is beginning to crumble from the action of warriors using levers, spears, and swords to displace the bricks; and the doors of the gates are being set on fire by lighted torches.

Once they had taken the city, the Assyrians frequently killed or enslaved much of the remaining population.[1]

Laying siege to a city could be a time-consuming task. If the walls could not be breached quickly, the attacker was frequently faced with starving the inhabitants, an option that could take years. Not surprisingly, many commanders preferred to avoid this option. The Sicilian historian Diodorus Siculus's *The Library of History* provides an early European account of the breaching of a city wall by mining. He relates that when Hannibal of Carthage laid siege to the Sicilian city Himera in 409 B.C.E., he built siege engines to break down the city walls and "set about undermining the walls, which he then shored up with wooden supports and when these were set on fire, a large section of the wall fell." Once the wall collapsed, a fierce battle ensued as the Himerans attempted to keep the Carthaginians from entering the city. Despite putting up fierce resistance and briefly driving the Carthaginians from the field, the Himerans ultimately were defeated, losing half their population to death or slavery.[2]

The Carthaginians were not alone in their use of mines in the ancient world. Diodorus provides numerous accounts of the use of mines, including those by Greeks, Macedonians, and Romans, and even the use of countermines by the people of Rhodes in 304 B.C.E. Learning that the Greek leader Demetrius had begun to undermine the city walls, the Rhodians dug countermines to thwart their opponents. They also constructed defensive mines in areas where they thought the Greeks might use siege engines, so that the weakened earth would collapse when the heavy engines were rolled over it. These defensive mines anticipated modern antivehicular mines, albeit by collapsing rather than exploding.[3]

Countermines were used in a number of ways in the ancient world. The besieged sometimes dug a countermine in order to intercept their enemy's mine and bring battle to the miners. Another option was to introduce smoke, bees, hot pitch, or boiling water into the mine. Countermines—supported with timbers—could also be dug underneath the attacker's mine and fired in an effort to collapse the mine above.

The detection of an enemy's mine could be a complicated process. The Greek writer Aeneas Tacticus (fourth century B.C.E.) related that during the Persian siege of Barca in 510 B.C.E., a coppersmith hit upon the idea of placing a bronze shield against the ground and using it to amplify the sounds of the digging miners—much like an ear horn—allowing him to locate the attacker's mines. Once the mine was located, the Barcans dug a countermine and attacked the enemy miners. According to Aeneas, the use of a shield as a listening device remained a common technique for locating mines. The Greek architect Vitruvius described another technique for detecting mines. He relates that during the siege of Chios, the architect Trypho of Alexandria had shallow tunnels dug outside the city walls. He then had bronze vases hung inside the tunnels as sensors. The construction of other mines caused the vases to vibrate. When this happened, he had a number of the vessels in the area filled with "boiling water and pitch...along with human dung and sand roasted to a fiery heat." During the night, he instructed his men to pierce the floor of the tunnel and then flood the enemy mine underneath with the contents of the vessels. By the fourth century this was by far the most common way of causing city walls to collapse.[4]

The Greek writer Philo discusses mining and countermining in his second century B.C.E. manual on warfare, *Poliorketika*. Philo stresses the importance of mining as part of the overall siege of a city and cautions that mining parties must be armed in case mine and countermine intersect. He suggests the use of smoke to suffocate the opposing mining party. In his section on how to fortify a city, Philo discusses ways to stop the large siege engines and catapults used to break down city walls. He recommends that the defender dig at least three ditches outside the wall and advocates the use of a second century equivalent of an antivehicular mine: shallow-buried pots filled with seaweed in front of the outermost ditch protecting the city. Although people would still be able to walk over the area, the pots would collapse under the weight of a siege engine or catapult.[5]

The Roman military theorist Vegetius (circa 385–400 C.E.) offered similar advice for stopping siege engines, recommending the construction of a mine in the anticipated path of the siege engine. As the siege engine rolled over the mine, the ground would collapse, miring the engine so that it could not be moved. He also describes how to undermine the walls of a city:

> when they reach the foundations of the walls, they excavate the largest possible part of them, placing dry timber there and holding up the collapse of the wall by temporary works. They also add brushwood and other inflammable tinder. Then, when the soldiers are ready, fire is introduced to the work and, all the wooden props and boards having burned, the wall suddenly collapses, opening a way for invasive action.[6]

Mining was well known in western Europe as well as in the Roman Empire. In his history of the Gallic Wars (58–51 B.C.E.), Julius Caesar wrote about the Gaul's superb mining abilities against a Roman siege. Caesar also provided details on the state of Roman field fortifications. During his siege of Alesia in Gaul, his forces built extensive earthworks around the city. In front of these, Caesar employed a spectrum of obstacles. Among these were *cippus* and *lilia*. The former, loosely translated as border, or grave stone, was constructed by driving sharpened stakes into an uncovered five-foot ditch, so that anyone who stumbled upon them would be impaled. The latter, which translates as lilies, was made by digging a three-foot deep hole and setting three-inch sharpened stakes in it. The pit was then camouflaged with branches and twigs. The Romans placed eight rows of these pits at three-foot intervals in front of the *cippi* at Alesia.[7]

While the tactics for using area denial weapons were firmly in place by the beginning of the Middle Ages, the technology behind the development of land, and later sea mines, was still lacking. Siege mining, from which land-mines are an offshoot, remained much the same as it was centuries earlier. The goal was still to tunnel under the enemy wall, support the wall with dry timbers, and then collapse the wall by burning the timbers. The besieged still challenged mines with countermines. Roman and Greek military texts, such as Vegetius's *Epitome of Science,* remained standard reference works into the Renaissance. Siege craft remained at the heart of Western warfare, and mining remained a crucial part of the equation. Things changed tremendously, however, with the introduction of gunpowder.[8]

CHINA AND THE INTRODUCTION OF GUNPOWDER

While the first European record of gunpowder is Roger Bacon's 1267 work *Epistola de Secretis Operibus Arttiis et Nature,* the Chinese had known about the volatile mixture of saltpeter, charcoal, and sulfur for around 400 years. Ironically, Chinese alchemists discovered the deadly compound while looking for a serum for immortality. By the early tenth century, the Chinese had adapted their discovery for military purposes, first as a slow burning match to light an early flamethrower. Around mid-century, they developed the fire lance, a "proto-gun" similar to a modern Roman candle that shot out a five-minute blast of fire. Later the device was modified to shoot a variety of projectiles, including pieces of pottery, iron, and even poisonous material such as arsenic. Around 1050, the Chinese moved from using gunpowder as a burning device to using it as an explosive device: the thunderclap bomb. This weapon, named after the loud sound it created when it went off, was made of a combination of bamboo, pottery shards, and gunpowder, wrapped in a gunpowder-coated paper. It was usually thrown using a trebuchet and was designed primarily as an incendiary device. Contemporary accounts of the weapon recount not only the fire damage they caused, but the confusion and terror the noise generated when the bombs exploded. The Chinese also built smaller versions out of pottery that could be thrown like hand grenades.[9]

Two hundred years later, the Chinese developed the thundercrash bomb. A substantially more deadly weapon than its antecedent, the thundercrash bomb more closely resembles what we think of as a bomb—it had a metal exterior that yielded death-dealing shrapnel that could easily penetrate iron armor. Thirteenth-century accounts from the Chin Dynasty tell of the bombs being used as missiles from the decks of ships to repel an attack by Mongol forces and later of the bombs being lowered on chains from fortress walls during the Mongol siege of K'aifeng in 1232. The "heaven-shaking thundercrash bomb," essentially an iron vessel filled with gunpowder, was extremely effective and, according to Chin accounts, "the attacking soldiers were all blown to bits, not even a trace being left behind." The stage was set for the development of the modern landmine. All that remained was for someone to decide to create a device to detonate a bomb at a distance or to detonate it when it was disturbed.[10]

The first reference to the Chinese use of a device similar to a modern landmine dates from 1277. While the weapon was referred to as a bomb, it appears to have functioned more like a landmine, though details of the weapon are sketchy. Within 100 years, the use of landmines by the armies in China seems to have been relatively common and rather sophisticated. The *Fire-Drake Artillery Manual*, written in 1412, provides a detailed description of a command-detonated mine from the mid-1300s, a spherical cast iron container charged with around five pints of black powder. Each mine had three fuses in case one failed, and these were joined at a common touch hole. The author reports that

> [t]he mines are buried in places were the enemy is expected to come. When the enemy is induced to enter the mine-field the mines are exploded at a given signal, emitting flames and fragments and a tremendous noise.

The book also describes the use of a sophisticated network of mines, known as "the ground-thunder camp," which were primarily used around passes and frontier gates. The mines were built using nine-foot sections of bamboo. After being hollowed out, the bamboo was wrapped in leather tape, filled with boiling oil, and set aside to allow the oil to penetrate the bamboo, making it relatively water and insect proof. Once the oil was drained, the bamboo was filled with gunpowder for the first 80 percent of its length and then topped with iron or lead pellets. Groups of mines were then buried in a five-foot deep trench and connected to a disturbance-fused igniter.[11]

The manual also describes other landmine variants, including a "self-tripped trespass mine," which could be built using iron, rock, porcelain, or earthenware with a hollow inside for the gunpowder. These were put out in groups with a common fuse chain and appear to have had multiple detonators, any of which when tripped would set off the entire field. Another version is similar to the musket-based man-traps used in seventeenth and eighteenth century Britain and was constructed using a group of small guns set in different directions that all fired at once when the trigger was tripped. The triggers and detonators used for Chinese landmines were closely guarded secrets, and many were not revealed until the 1600s. Many were based on a flintlock type action, and several resembled early wheel locks. These detonators, which date back to around 1360, predate European weapons with similar locks by some 160 years.[12]

Not surprisingly, the Chinese were also the first to develop an explosive sea mine—the "submarine dragon-king." *The Fire Drake Artillery Manual* describes the mine as being made of a powder-filled wrought iron container carried on a submerged wooden board weighted with stones. The mine itself was put inside an ox bladder to keep it watertight. Unlike the Chinese land-mines, the sea mines were detonated using a delay action fuse. An incense stick, which acted as a timer, was placed inside a container that floated on the surface of the water and was attached to the mine by a section of goat intestine. Once the incense was lit, the mines were floated downstream toward the enemy ships. When the incense burned down, it ignited the mine's fuse, detonating the mine (hopefully) as it came alongside one of the ships.[13]

GUNPOWDER COMES TO EUROPE

Carried to Europe by Arabs around 1240, gunpowder changed the way European war was fought. Knights, already threatened by longbow and cross-bow, became even more vulnerable. Fortifications were threatened as well: walls that had survived centuries of attacks crumbled under cannon fire. In 1403, the Florentine military detonated a powder charge in the walls of Pisa. As military architects struggled to compensate for the changes in technology, fortification and siege craft developed into a science. The nature of war was also beginning to change. During the Middle Ages, the Catholic church pro-vided western Europe with strict religious rules as to how Christian countries should conduct themselves when fighting each other. Of paramount impor-tance was the concept of the just war—the idea of a war fought for justice rather than material gain—and the concept of chivalry, which helped govern the conduct of the knight on the field. Closely tied to this was a generally shared definition of noncombatants who were to be excluded from war, including children, women, clerics, and the elderly.[14]

The Chinese idea of using a rifle lock to detonate a landmine appears in Europe for the first time in 1573, around 26 years after the development of the European flintlock. Known as the *fladdermine* or "flying mine," it was developed by Samuel Zimmerman of Augsburg. H. Frieherr von Flemming described the mine in his 1726 work *Der vollkommene Deutsche Soldat,* or *The Perfect German Soldier,* as being a ceramic container filled with around two pounds of gunpowder. The clay used in making the container was mixed with shards of glass and pieces of metal to maximize the damage it could cause. The mines used a flintlock as a detonator, which usually fired after someone stepped on the mine or ran into a trip wire attached to the mine. The mines were buried in the area surrounding the *glacis*—the slope leading up to the walls of the fortification—in an effort to stop the advance of enemy soldiers. These early antipersonnel mines were likely unreliable at best as the gunpowder used in them was extremely vulnerable to moisture.[15]

Gunpowder changed the way war was fought on sea as well as on land. During the Roman era and before, battles at sea usually consisted of one ship attempting to ram another and then board it with infantry. By the mid-1500s, cannons were being used on ship, though often more to kill the men on the enemy ship rather than to sink the ship itself. The cannon came into its own at the Battle of Lepanto in 1571, when the weapon helped bring victory to the forces of the European Holy League over the Ottoman navy. Fourteen years later, Frederico Gianibelli, an Italian engineer, developed another way to harness the combustible substance at sea: a floating time-detonated mine.

In 1585, Gianibelli was living in Amsterdam in the Spanish Netherlands. The city was in the midst of a siege by Spanish forces under the Duke of Parma. The Duke blockaded the city by building a 2,400-foot wooden bridge across the Scheldt River, which effectively blocked off the city's access to the sea and to English reinforcements. Destroying the bridge would be complicated. Half of the bridge rested on piles and the other half on boats that were chained together. Gianibelli hit on the idea of sending a fleet of ships filled with explosives to blow up the bridge. The local government proved unconvinced by his plan and limited his resources to two exploding ships and 32 small fireboats. Gianibelli's plan was to fill the holds of two exploding ships, *Fortune* and *Hope*, with 7000 pounds of gunpowder each. *Fortune* was armed with a slow burning fuse and *Hope* with a clockwork timer, both designed so that the ships would explode when they arrived at the bridge. On top of each ship's hold, he placed a six-foot-deep layer of tombstones that he covered with "a pyramid, made of heavy marble slabs." He filled the inside of the pyramid with mill stones, cannon balls, and various other metal and stone objects. The debris on top of the ship helped maximize the force of the explosion by directing the charge toward the bridge, though it is uncertain whether Gianibelli knew that it would do that. It also became lethal fragments flying through the air, cutting down hundreds of Spanish soldiers, which is likely what Gianibelli intended it to do.[16]

The fireboats arrived at the rafts supporting the bridge first. Most became entangled in the hooks and spearheads of the bridge's defenses or simply ran aground. The failure of these boats to cause any real damage drew cries of derision from the Spaniards on the bridge. The exploding ships followed shortly and drew up against the side of the bridge. The *Fortune* was the first to arrive. A small explosion was heard, but it produced no damage to either ship or bridge. A group of Spanish soldiers boarded the vessel and put out the few small fires they found. The party quickly left the ship. The *Hope* arrived shortly, coming to rest near the juncture of the stationary and floating sections of the bridge. Smoke trailed upwards from small fires on the deck of the ship. The Duke ordered a group of soldiers aboard to investigate and watched from nearby as the men explored the ship. Somehow sensing trouble, a young ensign name De Vega managed with great effort to convince the Duke to move away from the ship. Moments after the Duke left, the clockwork timer on *Hope* detonated, blowing a 200-foot hole in the bridge and killing between 800 and 1000 Spaniards.[17]

In the end, however, the commander of the Dutch naval forces, Admiral Jacobzoon, failed to take advantage of the breech, and Spaniards were able to repair the bridge during the night. The Duke of Parma captured Antwerp later in the year, and Gianibelli left for England. The maquinas de minas, or mine machines, left a long-lasting impression on the Spanish military. Three years later, when the Spanish Armada drew near the English fleet near Calais, a group of eight English fire ships were able to break up the Spanish fleet without actually coming into contact with it. The Spanish fear of the "hell-ships of Antwerp" were all the more heightened as they knew Gianibelli was in the employ of England. Many of the Spanish ships simply cut their anchors when they fled, making it difficult to regroup and ultimately setting the stage for an English victory.[18]

Gianibelli's successes at the bridge in Antwerp and England left a tremendous mark in naval warfare. The English used similar ships against the French at St. Malo a hundred years later, and Major General Benjamin Butler tried a similar attack against southern forces at Fort Fisher during the American Civil War. Butler, however, failed to learn Gianibelli's lessons completely and placed nothing on top of the powder holds. When the ship detonated, there was nothing to shape the force of the explosion. Consequently, while there was a tremendous explosion, the ship did little damage to the fortifications. Gianibelli's idea of setting off a large explosive charge against a floating target also paved the way for a new generation of inventors in the eighteenth and nineteenth centuries, helping to lead to the development of the modern sea mine. He was not without his moral critics, however. As mentioned above, the Spanish of the time called his ships the hell-burners of Antwerp. Three hundred years later, the American historian John Motley, while not openly critical, repeatedly refers to Gianibelli's ships as "infernal machines," a phrase that had taken on a particularly negative connotation during the American Civil War.[19]

On land, the French engineer, Sebastien LePrestre de Vauban, was at the forefront of the use of gunpowder in siege mining. After entering military service at age 17 in 1651, his aptitude for mathematics and fortification landed him a position as a draughtsman. In 1655, he received a commission as Engineer in Ordinary to the King. His star rose rapidly during the war with Spain in 1669, when he successfully coordinated the sieges of Tournai, Douai, and Lille. Vauban's successes were not limited to offensive actions; his responsibilities included designing a series of fortresses to secure the French frontier, and he ultimately rose to the rank of marshal.[20]

Vauban spent several pages on the conduct of mine warfare in his treatise *A Manual of Siege Craft and Fortification.* The mines of the era were composed of a series of galleries and a chamber in which the explosive charge was placed. He divided offensive mines into three types: a simple mine, consisting of a single gallery and chamber; the double or T-shaped mine, with two chambers; and the triple or trefoil mine, made up of three chambers. Of the three types, he found the latter the most effective in its devastation. He cautioned the reader to make sure that the galleries contain at least two right-angled turns to ensure that the chamber could be properly sealed when it was time to detonate the mine. He added that the importance of the seal was not to be underestimated, because a poor seal would diminish the power of the explosion.

The floor of the chamber was lined with wooden planks and covered in straw to a depth of one inch. The straw was then covered with a coarse cloth and the gunpowder placed atop the cloth. Next, the fuse, a cloth tube filled with gunpowder, was extended to the entrance of the gallery in a wooden trough. The opening to the chamber was then sealed with wooden beams, cemented with dung, and caulked to fill the gaps.

Vauban also recommended the use of mines in the defense of a fortification. His suggestions were updated versions of the defensive mines used by the ancients and included countermines designed to destroy an attacker's mine as well as defensive mines designed to destroy potential enemy positions outside the fortification.[21]

By Vauban's death in 1707, the French were well known for their expertise in siege warfare, particularly in the field of mining. The French military engineer, Simon Francis Gay de Vernon, provided a detailed look at the science of mining in his 1805 work *A Treatise on the Science of War and Fortification.* He defined a mine as "a hollow made in a mass of earth or masonry, and filled with powder." Not surprisingly, his description of gallery style mines is very similar to that of Vauban; however, Gay de Vernon also included a more thorough discussion of defensive mines, including the fougasse and the camouflet.[22]

The fougasse was established in a manner similar to the large mines, except that it did not require the digging of an underground gallery. Instead, one dug a hole in the ground and placed the mine—a box of gunpowder—in a small chamber in one side of the hole. A box containing one or more bombs was then placed atop the mine. Connected to the mine was a small wooden trough, which held the fuse. The trough led to a sheltered site, generally a trench or a place within the fortification itself, from which a soldier could light the fuse in safety. As with the larger mines, it was necessary to brace the back of the mine to prevent the explosion from being directed backward. Gay de Vernon suggested that a typical fougasse would create a crater of 13.5 feet in diameter. The camouflet was closely related to the fougasse, differing only in that it was hastily constructed and used against an enemy mine or to prevent an attempted enemy advance through the crater created by a recently sprung mine.[23]

Gay de Vernon described fougasses as most useful when "they are used to defend large posts, and in advance of the front of attack of a fortress that has no permanent defensive galleries [countermines]." He added, however, that the fougasse had some disadvantages in that

> the besieged must have time and means to prepare this kind of defense between the opening of the trenches and the arrival of the besiegers at the foot of the glacis.[24]

He noted that although one might establish these mines in the same area, it is better to set them off individually. By way of an example, he discussed the use of fougasses in the destruction of an enemy battery. Although four mines set off together would surely destroy the battery, each mine set off independently would render the battery "unserviceable" four times. Thus, the enemy would be forced to waste more time and effort than if the mines had been used in concert. He added that care must be taken to prevent the explosion of one mine from setting off another and that, consequently, the distances between the mines must be laid out carefully.[25]

Gay de Vernon's work was influential outside of Europe. His work was a standard text for cadets at the United States Military Academy at West Point. Although in 1817 Major John O'Conner translated the book into English, it is likely that it was first used in its original language.[26]

In the 1830s, West Point instructor Dennis Hart Mahan compiled his own text on the art of fortification that quickly supplanted that of Gay de Vernon. In addition to drawing upon the latter's work, which Mahan must have studied as a cadet at the Academy, it is likely that he drew upon his experiences, gained during his sojourn in France in the years between his graduation from the Academy and his assumption of a teaching position there. While in France, Mahan studied at the French military schools, especially in the fields of artillery and engineering. In his 1836 book, *A Complete Treatise on Field Fortification,* Mahan discounted most defensive mines as useless "due to the rapid character of the assault which generally causes the mines to be sprung too late." He then added that the main effects of the mines are psychological, derived "from the panic they may inspire."[27]

The only exception to this rule, according to Mahan, was the fougasse, whose use and construction he outlined:

> To make this mine, an inclined funnel shaped excavation is made, to the depth of five or six feet, at the bottom of the funnel a box containing fifty-five pounds of powder is placed, with which a powder-hose [fuse] communicates. A strong shield of wood, formed of battens well nailed together, is placed in front of the box; and three or four cubic yards of pebbles...or other materials, are filled in against the shield. Earth is then rammed around the shield on top and behind, to prevent the explosion from taking place in the wrong direction.

Mahan added that when the mine is exploded, its contents cut a swath about 60 yards in length and 70 yards in width. Mahan stated that the stone fougasse could be effectively used in the defense of the ditches and salients of field works, probably because of the large area that the mine covered when it exploded.[28]

The American Army continued to use Mahan's work on field fortifications through the 1870s. Although Mahan revised his manual several times, the alterations were minor, and his section on mines remained unchanged even in the post-Civil War edition of the book. Mahan's work was used to instruct virtually all West Point cadets from 1836 through the Civil War. Indeed, Mahan taught many of the future generals on both sides of the Civil War. In 1862, an edition of Mahan's work on field fortification was even published in Richmond, Virginia, for the use of the Confederate military.[29]

Despite the American Army's emphasis on engineering and siege mining, it used siege mines only occasionally and seldom, if ever, with great success. The Americans' first attempt at mining came early, during the American Revolution (1775–1783). In late May and June 1781, colonial forces under Major General Nathanael Greene invested Fort Ninety-Six, about 60 miles northeast of Columbia, South Carolina. One of the first actions by the Chief Engineer, Colonel Tadeusz Kosciuszko, a Polish émigré, was to establish a mine that aimed to destroy one of the fort's satellites, the Star Redoubt. Unfortunately, the British were aware of their efforts and ambushed the colonial forces working on the mine, killing many of those involved and wounding the Colonel.

The mine was not ready in time for the planned attack. The Americans tried siege mining again at the Battle of Petersburg during the American Civil War (1861–1865). As will be discussed later, this effort proved disastrous. Regardless, siege mining remained a standard part of an engineers training through the early twentieth century.[30]

As the century turned from the eighteenth to the nineteenth, the world entered a new age, the Industrial Revolution. Over the course of the next century, inventors assumed the task of designing more effective ways to kill and maim. Mines on both land and sea became a controversial part of their legacy, and by mid-century people began to question whether it was time to establish a law of war. The opening chapter of this new age of war was written in the Americas.

2

The Age of Invention: From America to Russia

ON JUNE 25, 1815, HIS Majesty's ship (HMS) *Ramillies* captured an American schooner near New London, Connecticut, after a brief gun battle. By the time they reached the ship, the American crew had abandoned it. When British sailors attempted to furl the vessel's sails, they unknowingly pulled a cord attached to a gun lock, setting off a large charge of powder. The resulting explosion killed an officer and ten seamen. Admiral Sir John B. Warren of the Royal Navy (RN) lamented the loss to First Secretary of the Admiralty John W. Croker as "a most Melancholy event" caused "by a Diabolical and Cowardly contrivance of the Enemy" who sought to combat the British blockade "by means of Torpedoes [mines] Fire Vessels and other Infernal Machines…beyond conception."[1] While torpedoes were not a standard tool of the American Navy, attempts to employ them in defense of America's coasts were far from uncommon during the War of 1812.

While the booby-trapping of a ship may have caused the British some consternation, they should not have been surprised at the Americans' reliance on torpedoes. Robert Fulton, one of the pioneers of mine warfare, had demonstrated his sea mines to the British a scant eight years earlier.[2] Furthermore, the Americans had used primitive sea mines during the American Revolution—a first for a western nation. America's development of these mines reflected the public's desire to avoid a large navy and to rely instead on an almost porcupine-like coastal defense. In addition, the torpedo represented a great equalizer, allowing men to band together in a militia and defeat even a man-of-war.[3]

American interest in the use of sea mines dates from the very beginning of the Republic with David Bushnell's efforts during the Revolution. Bushnell's idea was to develop a device that could be delivered next to an enemy ship and exploded either by contact or by a clockwork device. His earliest efforts used a small submersible vessel, the *Turtle,* generally considered to be the first military submarine. Bushnell describes the vessel as bearing "some resemblance to two upper tortise [sic] shells of equal size, joined together; the place of entrance…being represented by the opening, made by the swell of the shells, at the head of the animal." The interior held enough air for the operator to remain submerged for 30 minutes, and propulsion was achieved through a pair of oars, one for forward and backward motion and one for ascent and descent. The operator would approach the target at night while surfaced and then submerge near the enemy. Working with very little light, the operator would then come up underneath the ship and secure a screw attached to a mine containing 150 pounds of gunpowder. Once the operator had attached the mine to the ship, he would release the mine from its position over the submarine's rudder. A clockwork device would determine when the mine would explode.[4]

On the night of September 6, 1776, Sergeant Ezra Lee piloted *Turtle* underneath HMS *Eagle* anchored above Staten Island in New York. His efforts came to naught, however, when he realized he had positioned himself under an iron bar and could not attach the screw to the ship. In the process of repositioning, Lee surfaced and discovered the sun was coming up. As he had no desire to let himself or the submarine come into British hands, he felt "the best generalship, was to retreat" and reach American lines. The British discovered him near Governors Island, causing him to release the mine so that if they caught him "[they] should all be blown up together." Happily for Lee, the British appeared to have been more afraid of the strange craft than curious and chose to leave him unmolested. The mine discharged as he passed the island, and American forces recovered both Lee and his vessel. Before *Turtle* could set out again, however, American forces retreated from New York.[5]

Two attempts on the Hudson River proved similarly unproductive. Soon after, the British sank the boat carrying the submarine. While Bushnell was able to recover *Turtle,* he abandoned the project as he said he was in "a bad state of health" and "despaired of obtaining the public attention, and the assistance necessary" and was thus "unable to support [him]self." In addition, he was unsure that he could develop the cadre of trained operators needed for such operations. Having left the submarine behind, he now sought less expensive and complicated ways of delivering his mines to the enemy.[6]

In April 1777, David Bushnell and Colonel William Worthington exhibited "a specimen of a new invention for annoying ships" to the Connecticut Council of Safety. Bushnell's work duly impressed the Council, and it voted to order "officers, agents, commissarys [sic], to afford him assistance of men, boats, powder, lead &c. as he shall call &c. &c."[7] Presumably, this was the type of support Bushnell had been looking for. The "new invention" was a pair of sea mines to be delivered by the tide rather than submarine.

The new weapon was composed of two barrels of gunpowder connected by a length of rope. The barrels were to be released upstream from the enemy ships and carried to them by the current. When the rope snagged on a ship, one or more of the barrels would be brought alongside the ship making the rope taut. This would in turn release the hammer of a gunlock, setting off the charge and, hopefully, sinking the ship.[8]

Bushnell's first attempt to employ his device was on the night of August 13, 1777, when he released several of his weapons from a small boat against HMS *Cerebus* on the Connecticut River near New London, Connecticut. In his official report, Captain John Symons of the *Cerebus* recounted that his men discovered the line about eleven o'clock on the evening of the August 13. Mistaking it for a fishing line, the men commenced to haul it aboard the *Cerebus*'s tender. After bringing in between 70 and 100 fathoms of rope, the men found the barrel which, "Mistaken for something Valuable," they tried to examine. The mine promptly exploded, killing three of the four men onboard and sinking the tender.[9]

Symons immediately ordered the rest of the cord cut away lest there be a torpedo attached to the other end as well, an assumption that proved to be correct. In his report to his superiors, he expressed concern that these attacks might continue. As this was "their first essay," he concludes, "I have thought it indispensably my duty to return and give you the earliest information of the circumstances, to prevent the like fatal happening to any of the advanced ships." Symons was not as harsh on the Americans as was the captain of the *Ramillies* in the War of 1812. While he used the term "villains" once to describe his adversaries, he is amazingly restrained and avoids the heavy rhetoric of his later colleagues.[10]

Bushnell continued his efforts through the year, undaunted by having missed his primary target in August. His next attempt came in December 1777. A British fleet lay anchored off Philadelphia, little suspecting they were to become the next targets of Bushnell's machines. Late in the evening, Bushnell launched a series of barrels filled with gunpowder upstream from the British fleet. As before, he equipped each keg with a gunlock that would ignite the powder if the barrel were disturbed. This time, however, the inventor relied on a buoy to hold the barrel under water so that it would explode under the ship's waterline. While Bushnell hoped the floating mines would reach the fleet before sunrise, his calculations proved imperfect due to his dependence on "a Gentleman" he later discovered to be "very imperfectly acquainted with that part of it [the river]." Thus, the mines were released too far away, and the British discovered the buoys in the morning. While Bushnell did not succeed in sinking any of the ships, the mines killed a number of sailors on a small boat when they attempted to haul the device onboard. During the ensuing panic, the British began firing at the remaining barrels in what American poet Francis Hopkinson in a 1778 poem christened "The Battle of the Kegs."[11]

The Battle of the Kegs was to be Bushnell's last major effort at mine warfare, in large part because funding for the project had dried up. The British captured Bushnell in 1779 during a coastal raid and released him two weeks later. He spent the remainder of the war as an officer in a company of miners and sappers in the newly formed engineering corps and left the military in 1783 at war's end. By 1790, Bushnell had been lured to France by the hope of gaining fame and fortune with his submersible. His efforts to sell his plans to the French government were ultimately rebuffed, and he returned to the United States. While in Paris, however, he met a young American named Robert Fulton whose name was soon known for a variety of accomplishments, including one of the first successful demonstrations of a sea mine against a ship. Bushnell finished out his life in Georgia, living anonymously under the name David Bush, and died in 1826.[12]

In the years after the American Revolution, American naval policy was caught between two camps, the Navalists and the Antinavalists. The former called for a strong navy that could protect the United States and increase American prestige in Europe. The Antinavalists argued that the country faced no real threat of invasion and could ill afford the cost of maintaining a large navy, particularly as it would open the door for involvement in foreign wars and might bring about the equivalent of an arms race with Great Britain. The Antinavalist idea of a largely defensive navy hit its zenith under the presidency of Thomas Jefferson, who encouraged Congress to authorize the construction of over 250 gunboats in 1807. While the gunboats were needed to protect the Mississippi from being closed by the Spanish as well as for other coastal operations, they also fit in with the Antinavalist idea of building a navy that was largely defensive in nature. Furthermore, the gunboats proved easy to operate, allowing the ships to be maintained by militia seamen, an idea that appealed to Jefferson's predilection for a militia-oriented military. Unfortunately, the gunboats proved largely ineffective in the War of 1812, a war in which they were largely used in a role they were never intended to fulfill.[13]

Sea mines were a perfect mate to Jefferson's idea of a militia-based military, and Robert Fulton pursued this tack with zeal in promoting his work. Like Bushnell, much of Fulton's early work concentrated on the development of submarine warfare, and Fulton also courted the favor of the French

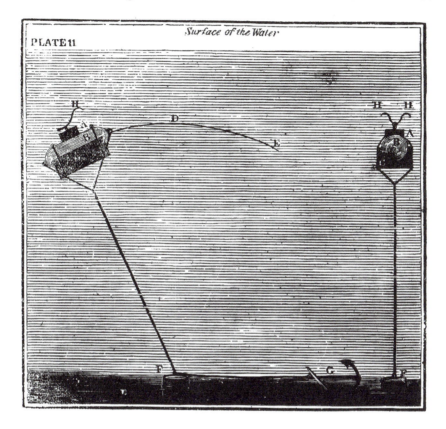

Design of one of Robert Fulton's sea mines. (Thomas C. Cochran, *The New American State Papers 1780–1860,* vol. 9 [Wilmington, DE, 1973], 24.)

government. In 1797, Fulton began negotiations with the French government to build a submarine-like vessel. While the French government initially seemed positive about his proposal, the plans were rejected, quite possibly because of Fulton's insistence on a large commission for each vessel his machines destroyed. Further complicating the issue, the French had ethical concerns about this type of warfare. Over the next six years, Fulton's fortunes in France ebbed and flowed along with the ever-changing government. In the end, Fulton's arrogance may have cost him as much as any ethical problems his proposals raised. His early proposals included statements to the effect that his plans would be too difficult for the average reviewer, including the Minister of the Marine, to understand. He successfully demonstrated a submarine, *Nautilus,* in June 1800, but was unable to attack the English fleet. In November, he modified his plans so that *Nautilus* now was meant to carry mines to the enemy fleet rather than attach an explosive charge to the bottom of a ship. Despite several attempts to attack the English fleet, he was never able to carry the battle to them. By 1804, he was ready to give up on the French and cast his eyes west to England, the very country whose ships he had hoped to target with *Nautilus*.[14]

Fulton conducted his most momentous experiment with torpedoes in Great Britain rather than the United States. On October 15, 1805, Fulton demonstrated his torpedo to the British government on the Danish brig *Dorthea*. After training a boat crew in the skill of deploying the weapon, Fulton suspended a torpedo filled with 180 pounds of gunpowder under a buoy. Rather than relying on a concussion fuse, Fulton used a clockwork device set for 18 minutes. The crew put out the mine, and it successfully snagged the brig's cable, bringing the device underneath the ship's hull. The ensuing explosion brought the ship six feet out of the water and broke the ship in half.[15]

The experiment's success appears to have shocked at least one observer who, according to Fulton, declared shortly before the explosion that, "if a torpedo were placed under his cabin while he was at dinner, he should feel no concern for the consequence." Another, Earl St. Vincent, found the devices a waste of time and stated that Prime Minister Pitt "was the greatest fool that ever existed, to encourage a mode of war which they who controlled the seas did not want, and which, if successful, would deprive them of it." While the end of the war between France and England caused the British to lose interest in Fulton's work, the inventor felt sure that the British observers "would feel much disposed to respect the rights, nor enter the waters, of a nation who should use such engines with energy and effect."[16]

Based on his work in Great Britain, Fulton petitioned Congress and President James Madison to provide him with funds to continue his work. The Senate approved his request on February 26, 1810 and awarded him $5,000. The committee stated that Fulton's work demonstrated the country could escape "the necessity of a navy to protect commerce on the ocean, and to extricate a suffering world from, that system of oppression, now exercised by the great maritime belligerents on the high seas." While the committee deemed it premature to make any decisions about the structure of the military, it felt that continued success would "merit the attention of every Government, who at present d[id] not exercise, or d[id] not hope to exercise an undue influence on the seas."[17]

Fulton's report to the President and Congress included plans for two basic types of torpedoes. The first was a static device geared for harbor defense. The mine was to be attached to the harbor floors by means of a weight and an anchor. The explosive charge would be set when a ship came into contact with

Woodcut of the brig *Dorothea* being blown up by one of Robert Fulton's sea mines on October 15, 1805. (Thomas C. Cochran, *The New American State Papers 1780–1860,* vol. 9 [Wilmington, DE, 1973], 21.)

a lever releasing a gun lock contained in a brass box. Fulton chose to fork the lever in order to increase its service area. To facilitate the retrieval of the devices following the end of hostilities, Fulton recommended fitting the mines with a clockwork release mechanism that would cause them to rise to the surface at a preset interval.[18]

The second type of mine was also geared toward harbor defense and relied on a harpoon gun to deliver the mine to the enemy. The harbor defender would close with the enemy and fire a harpoon into the enemy's bow. A mine attached to the harpoon by a rope would then be drawn next to the hull of the moving ship. A clockwork device would then release the gunlock several minutes after the harpoon had been fired, igniting the charge and sending the enemy ship to the harbor bottom. Fulton anticipated that boats armed with these devices would be employed *en masse* against the enemy, representing an overwhelming force.[19]

Fulton credited both types of mines as representing a sound defensive investment, particularly when compared to the cost of a frigate. Fulton estimated the cost of an anchored torpedo at $84 and a clockwork torpedo at $150. He further speculated that defending Boston, New York, the Delaware River, the Chesapeake, Charleston, and New Orleans would require a total of 650 boats, 1,400 anchored torpedoes, and 1,300 clockwork torpedoes at a total cost of $531,000. While no small sum, according to Fulton, it was still less than the cost of a frigate which could not be in all ports at once and could be lost in an instant.[20]

Of the $5,000 approved by Congress, $1,500 went to preparing a display of Fulton's designs in September 1810. In addition to models of various designs, the inventor was prepared to demonstrate his cable cutting devices, anchored torpedoes, and harpoon gun mines. Demonstrations with the first two devices seem to have gone well. Members of the evaluation committee were duly impressed with the weapons, particularly the durability of the anchored torpedo. His success with the harpoon gun mines proved marginal at best. Having challenged one of the navy representatives to prepare a defensive perimeter, Fulton proved unable to design a way around the series of nets around the USS *Argus*. Even this was adjudged a mild success by some members who pointed out that the netting used around the ship would encumber its movement. While the committee was skeptical about harpoon gun torpedoes and spar mounted torpedoes, most considered the anchored torpedo particularly useful and recommended its adoption.[21]

On June 22, 1812, four days after the beginning of the War of 1812 (1812–1814), Robert Fulton offered his services to the American government. He pointed out there was still $2,500 remaining in the funds for experiments with torpedoes and suggested he be allowed to construct 10 or 12 of the devices and "make preparations for their use." In an effort to assuage any doubts as to his plans, he included the caveat, "If you think proper to send it to me [the funds], and I do not use it in a manner satisfactory to Congress, I will always be responsible to return it." He also requested that Secretary of the Navy Paul Hamilton have his torpedo-making equipment and boats sent to New York.[22]

In a more characteristic tone, he added that it would prove beneficial if the government established a reward system for the destruction of British ships by private individuals equaling $2,000 per gun rated. In addition, he recommended publishing a reward policy for the delivery of British ships by their crew into American hands. He defended potential criticism that this is "not honorable war" by pointing out that the British policy of impressing

American citizens forced Americans to "fight against their Brethren." Fulton sent a similar letter to Hamilton's successor, William Jones, shortly after Congress approved a reward policy in March 1813. A second letter to Jones followed two weeks later. Jones responded by sending Jacob Lewis to assist Fulton and provided a fire ship and small crew. The Secretary added, however, that the Navy must "incur no expense whatever on account of these experiments."[23]

Fulton's principal endeavor during the summer was the development of an underwater gun that could be fired from the surface. Jacob Lewis wrote several promising reports to the secretary of the navy, but there is little evidence the device ever saw use against the British. By the end of the summer, Fulton abandoned the project in favor of developing a steam-powered ship.[24]

Fulton's abandonment of the torpedo did not mean the end of its use during the war. More than one American sought to take advantage of the government's lucrative offer to reward anyone sinking a British warship. In addition to the *Ramillies* incident cited earlier, Elijah Mix attempted to employ drift torpedoes against the British. Despite government assistance, Mix proved unsuccessful in materially damaging the enemy. Several of Mix's attempts were noticed by the British. Rear Admiral George Cockburn reported on the American use of mines to Admiral Sir John B. Warren. Cockburn stated that a boat from HMS *Victorious* picked up one of the mines, which he refers to as "Fulton's," and that others had likely passed the fleet unobserved. As the mine was picked up on its way out to sea, Cockburn expressed concern that the Americans' efforts to "dispose of us wholesale Six Hundred at a time" would, in fact, lead to the injury of neutrals or other ships in open waters. His concerns proved prophetic. As the practice of mining became commonplace in the early twentieth century, more than a few civilian ships became unintended victims of mines meant for someone else. As his ships were now closing on Hampton Roads, American efforts could now be made "with much more facility…and much less Risk to the Public at large." In the end, however, American mining efforts proved to be at best a nuisance to the British.[25]

The construction of sea mines was taken up in the 1820s by yet another American, Samuel Colt, later famous for his revolver. Colt conducted his first experiment at age 15 on July 4, 1829 when he succeeded in blowing up a small raft using a submerged explosive charge. He continued his experiments in private over the next 12 years. In June 1841, Colt wrote President John Tyler requesting government assistance in putting on an exhibition demonstrating that "a sailing vessel…cannot pass (without permission) either in or out of a harbor where…[his] engines of destruction are employed."[26]

By March 1842, Colt had succeeded in using the electricity generated from a galvanic battery to explode a torpedo from a distance of over ten miles. On July 4, Colt drew public attention by destroying the gunboat *Boxer* in the New York harbor with a mine. The following month, he demonstrated his device to the President, cabinet, and other government officials including Major General Winfield Scott, destroying a schooner with an electric mine from a distance of five miles. Following this demonstration, Congress voted to provide Colt with $17,000 to continue his work. Colt's work continued to draw public attention, and, in April 1844, he demonstrated his mine system to Congress. Two days after the demonstration, Congress commissioned an inquiry into the method Colt used to detonate his system and its applicability to harbor defenses. Colonel Joseph Totten, Chief Engineer of the Army, wrote the principal report.[27]

Totten's report was particularly harsh and labeled Colt's work as lacking in originality, stating that Colt had merely combined the work of other people. In addition, Totten did not recommend the government purchase Colt's system or rely on it, as the mines could easily be located by small ships pulling dredges. In addition, he expressed great concern about the ability of the operator to explode the mine at the correct time, particularly at night. Instead, he recommended the use of mines similar to Fulton's anchored torpedoes, which detonated on contact. Sadly, target acquisition was the only truly unique aspect of Colt's system, and he was steadfast in providing that information to as few people as possible. Colt relied on a camera obscura, a device that projects an image of the outside world through a lens onto the wall of a darkened room, and mirrors to tell the operator when to set off the mines. Had he been more open, the military might have proved less intransigent. In addition, Colt failed to stay within the financial bounds set by Congress for his project, overspent by $9,000, and refused to adequately document all his expenses. The combined effect ultimately cost Colt government support.[28]

While Colt's torpedo was not adopted by the United States, the idea of using electricity to detonate mines spread. As with Colt, many of the scientists involved in these activities were also involved in the development of the telegraph. Among these was Prussian artillerist and scientist Werner von Siemens. Born in 1816 in Hanover, he left the Kingdom when he was 17 and moved to Prussia, where he trained as an artillerist in the Prussian army. Siemens was also of a scientific mind and developed a keen interest in chemistry, acquiring patents for a number of processes and devices including an improved guncotton, metal plating techniques, printing equipment, and telegraphy devices. It is for his work in this last field that he is perhaps best known. In 1846, the chief of the telegraphy service ordered Siemens to assist a commission developing a national electric telegraphy system in

Prussia. As the commission was concerned that aboveground wires could be easily damaged, they felt it prudent that the wires be buried. This decision meant that the wires had to be waterproof—much like lines that could be used to detonate mines. Siemens's younger brother William had sent him a sample of gutta-percha, a by-product of the Malaysian *Isonandra Gutta* tree similar to rubber. Siemens found the resin worked well as a wire insulator; however, it tended to eventually separate from the wires. To solve this problem, Siemens used a screw press to apply the gutta-percha to the wire under high pressure. The results proved very satisfactory, and Siemens's wire and several of his other inventions became standard equipment in the Prussian telegraph system. In 1847, Siemens resolved to leave the military and set up a telegraph manufacturing plant. He decided, however, to delay his exit from the military until the telegraph commission finished its work. In March 1848, Siemens convinced the commission to hold a competition for telegraphic devices, a competition he felt he would certainly place in. To his surprise, on March 18, both the competition and the commission, in his words, "came to an abrupt end." The 1848 revolutions that had begun in France had reached Berlin. While the Berlin revolution was brief, the work of the commission came to a halt. Within days of the revolution in Berlin, Schleswig-Holstein broke with Denmark, a move that eventually drew Prussian support and landed Siemens in charge of the defense of Kiel during the Danish-Prussian War of 1864.[29]

Siemens's sister Mathilde and her husband, Karl Himly, had moved to Kiel a year before the revolution when Karl had taken a position at the local university. While the rebellion against the Danes in Kiel had been successful, the Danes still controlled the mouth of the city harbor and were rumored to be preparing to retake the city. In a letter to her brother, Mathilde expressed grave concerns about the possibility of an attack, particularly as she and her husband lived close to the harbor. Troubled about the plight of his sister, Werner hit upon what he referred to as the "then entirely novel idea of defending the harbor with submarine mines fired by electricity" using the gutta-percha coated wires he had developed for the telegraph. Siemens wrote his brother-in-law about his idea, who forwarded it to the country's provisional government, who in turn petitioned the Prussian government to allow Siemens to travel to Kiel and put his plan into action. While the Prussian government initially demurred because they were not at war with Denmark, Siemens was unofficially told that he should be prepared to leave at once should war break out between the two countries, and it was not long before Siemens received his marching orders.[30]

Upon Siemens's arrival in Kiel, he and Karl Himly set to work assembling the mines. Siemens had originally planned to use watertight bags to hold the charges, but as he had not yet completed them, he modified the design and replaced the bags with waterproofed wooden casks. The powder-filled casks were fused and anchored 20 feet below the surface in a narrow channel leading into the harbor. Gutta-percha coated wires were then run back to watch two points near the banks, where sentries were posted to watch for the Danish fleet. When a ship was observed coming over one of the mines, a sentry would raise a pole to activate the mine. The sentries were instructed to keep the circuit on the mine open until the enemy ship moved out of range. One of the unique aspects of Siemens's design was that the switches at both observation points had to be activated for the mine to detonate, allowing the sentries to detonate the mine when a ship was directly over it.

Siemens also took over the command of local forces and occupied the nearby fort at Friedrichsort to prevent the Danes from anchoring there and then shelling Kiel. When some casks were freed up by the arrival of waterproof bags from Prussia, Siemens reconfigured one as a landmine in front of the fort entrance. When some Danish ships appeared outside the fort, Siemens ordered his brother Friedrich to arm the mine. The result was almost disastrous when Friedrich accidentally detonated the device as he finished arming it, wounding himself and two others and blowing the roof tiles off much of the fort. The action also altered the Danish fleet, which chose not to proceed further because they thought the explosion was one of the sea mines. In the end, the Danes did not attack the city, a decision Siemens, at least, credited to the presence of his mines. In his memoirs, he added that, when the waterproof bags were retrieved two years later, the powder was still dry and the mines still functional.[31]

While Siemens's mines had not been put to the test, they were perhaps the first command-detonated sea mines to be deployed in wartime. The first successful use of mines during wartime, however, was not far away and came to be closely tied to the development and deployment of the first successful landmine during the Crimean War. As such, it is worth noting how the sea mine's cousin was developing during these years.

LANDMINES IN PRACTICAL USE

Most armies remained focused on traditional siege mining. The only real antipersonnel mine in use was the fougasse, and it was seen as having only limited value. Eventually the American military began to use galvanic batteries to detonate mines, and the technique was incorporated into American military manuals. Henry Wagner Halleck's *Elements of Military Art and Science* was among the earliest of these. First published in 1846, Halleck's work was written for training volunteers and militia and became one of the most widely read books among the army's officer corps. Dennis Hart Mahan's work on field fortification heavily influenced Halleck's work. Indeed, Halleck referred to Mahan's text as "the very best work that has ever been written on field fortifications," adding that "every officer going into the field should supply himself with a copy." Between the two of them, Mahan and Halleck played a major role in educating the officers who fought in the Civil War.[32]

Mahan's influence is particularly apparent in Halleck's discussion of the stone fougasse, which bears remarkable similarity to Mahan's. Halleck's discussion, however, reflects the advancements made in mine warfare between Mahan's work and his, and added that a galvanic battery, rather than the traditional powder hose, could be used to detonate the fougasse. Halleck also discussed the shell fougasse, a device not found in Mahan's work. The construction of the shell fougasse is similar to that of the stone fougasse. The main difference is that, with the shell fougasse, a box of shells is placed over the explosive charge in such a manner that, when the fougasse is ignited, the shells are thrown into the air before they explode, thus increasing the chance for devastation and, to an extent, foreshadowing modern bounding munitions.[33]

Halleck, like Mahan, was skeptical of the advantage mines provided in the defense of a position, especially one in a relatively flat area. Despite his concerns, Halleck stated that, if the mines are "judiciously arranged in the plan of their [the fortification's] construction, and well managed during the operations of the siege, they contribute very materially to the length of the defense." While Halleck and Mahan provided guidance to young officers as to how to fortify a position, as Captain Gabriel Rains proved during the Seminole Wars, actions in the field were not always in accordance with the manuals.[34]

During the Seminole Wars (1835–1842), Gabriel Rains began experimenting with disturbance fuses. His work had a lasting effect on the development of both land and sea mines. Barely 20 years later, he designed variants of both weapons for the Confederacy during the American Civil War. Rains was graduated from the United States Military Academy at West Point in 1827, 13th of a class of 36. Following graduation, Rains was commissioned a second lieutenant in the Seventh Infantry. He spent his early Army years on frontier duty in Arkansas. In 1839, Rains, by then a captain, was sent to the Florida Territory to participate in the Second Seminole Indian War.[35] Stationed in north-central Florida, the young captain embarked upon a war that seems to have left an indelible impression upon him, providing the seeds for his development of mines during the American Civil War.

Rains's first assignment upon reaching the Florida Territory was as a company commander in charge of Fort Micanopy in the north-central part of the territory, an area that shortly became a hotbed of Seminole activity. Fort King, 25 miles to the north and in an area with a large Seminole presence, had been assigned several companies under the command of Colonel William Whistler. As it became apparent that the Seminoles were concentrating their efforts on the smaller force at Fort Micanopy, the decision was made to swap the garrisons of the two forts; Whistler's troops were transferred to Fort Micanopy, and Rains and his troops were sent to Fort King. This shift placed Rains at a substantial numerical disadvantage to the surrounding Indians, who had probably avoided attacking Fort King because of the large number of troops there. The Seminoles soon realized that Fort King now had the smaller force and moved quickly to exploit the situation. Soon, according to Rains, "it became dangerous to walk even around the post, and finally two…men were waylaid and murdered in full view thereof."[36]

In order to counter the aforementioned inequality, Rains hit upon the idea of the subterra mine. As described by Rains, in its initial incarnation, the device consisted of a shell covered by the clothing of the two dead soldiers and set to explode when the clothing was removed. The idea behind this appears to have been that, by using the torpedo, Rains would force the Seminoles to cease their brazen attacks upon the Fort because of fear of such devices. The torpedo exploded several days later, but upon reaching the device, Rains and his detachment of 16 men found naught but a dead opossum. Lurking nearby, however, were some 100 Seminoles who descended upon the small group, killing and wounding seven of the men, including Rains.[37]

Rains's wounds were severe enough that he was not expected to live. In fact, several newspapers published erroneous accounts of his death. He was promoted to the rank of brevet major for "Gallant and Meritorious Conduct in the Action with the Seminole Indians." Rains went on to place a second torpedo near Fort King but was ordered to remove it due to the fear it created among the fort's soldiers.[38]

Although Rains received a promotion for his actions, he also achieved a certain degree of infamy within the ranks of the United States military. Twenty-two years later, following Rains's mining activities during the Confederate retreat from Yorktown, U.S. Brigadier General William Berry, recalling Rains's exploits at Fort King, denounced "this dastardly business" and the "similar mode of warfare inaugurated by him [Rains] while disgracing the uniform of the American army in the Seminole war in Florida." During the years between the Second Seminole War and the Civil War, it appears that Rains made little use of his invention.[39]

Although the cadets of West Point appear to have made little use of the fougasse, the manuals must have had an impact upon them. The manuals provided a tactical framework that emphasized the use of the mine in the defense of a fortification. This tactical framework, however, did not include the mining of roads or buildings. Those innovations came later, during the Seminole Indian Wars and the Civil War, and aroused tremendous controversy within the American military.

Perhaps the only practical experience the American military had with the use of the fougasse came during the Mexican-American War. As American forces, commanded by Major General Winfield Scott, prepared for their assault on the capital of Mexico in September 1847, they were faced with the task of taking the Mexican fortress, Chapultepec. The fortress, situated on a hill that dominated the surrounding terrain, was well fortified by Mexican forces under the command of Major General D. Nicolas Bravo. Anticipating that the Americans would attack from the west, General Bravo attempted to secure the area with a series of parapets placed midway up the hill. In front of these, he placed a series of six fougasses, only three of which were charged.[40]

When the Americans attacked, their assault came so quickly that the Mexican officer in charge of setting off the mines was unable to accomplish his mission. The Americans did not discover the fougasses until after the battle. In his memoirs, Lieutenant Pierre Gustave Toutant Beauregard, recalled:

> Rodgers and myself having heard the order to charge, left the Voltigeurs and ran across the space which separated us from it. In doing so we passed over a certain number of mounds of earth and stone, which I mistook at the time for graves, but afterwards to my horror, found they were mines or fougasses, which they had prepared to blow us up with—but fortunately did not or could not explode them in time!

Some 20 years later, Beauregard served as a general officer in the Confederate Army. The list of officers serving at Chapultepec who later rose to prominence during the American Civil War was surprisingly long. Among these officers were George Pickett, James Longstreet, George B. McClellan, Ulysses S. Grant, and Robert E. Lee. Surprisingly, neither Lee nor McClellan mentions the fougasses at Chapultepec in their Mexican War writings.[41]

The fougasse at this point, of course, had its drawbacks. As shown at Chapultepec, the mine had to be set off manually and, in the event of an attack, might not be set off at the appropriate moment. In addition, its powder hose, or fuse, was susceptible to moisture. Nevertheless, the fougasse set the precedent for the use of landmines as a defensive rather than an offensive weapon and, perhaps most important, as a legitimate weapon of war. All that now remained was the discovery of an efficient and timely means of exploding the device for the fougasse to take on a form similar to that of modern land mines.

IMMANUEL NOBEL: THE FATHER OF MINE WARFARE

The experiments with sea mines in the West drew considerable attention in the Russian Empire. In October 1839, Tsar Nicholas I formed the Russian Committee on Underwater Mines. The committee was composed of four army officers, one naval officer, and a scientist, a Prussian émigré Herman Jacobi. The committee was the first of its kind, and it conducted the only organized and systematic research program on underwater warfare before the American Civil War. The group's original focus was on the use of galvanic batteries to set off the mines. This focus changed with the chance meeting of two members of the committee, General Karl Andreyevich Schilder and Professor Jacobi, with Swedish émigré Immanuel Nobel in 1839.[42]

After going to sea at age 13, Nobel had apprenticed with a builder and then enrolled in the Stockholm Academy of Arts, where he studied architecture. His time as an architect was short-lived, however, and he was forced to file for bankruptcy within a few years after starting his career. Rebounding from his failures, he established one of Sweden's first rubber factories and approached the Swedish military with plans for an inflatable backpack and contact-detonated land and sea mines. The Swedish military proved uninterested in any of his ideas and Nobel, now married with three children, left Sweden for the Russian Empire, going first to Finland and then to the Russian capital, St. Petersburg.

Shortly after his arrival in St. Petersburg, Nobel attended a reception held by a friend, where he overheard Schilder and Jacobi discussing a planned demonstration of the latter's electrically fired sea mines. Nobel quickly joined in and informed the pair that he had designed a mine requiring neither batteries nor an observer. Within a few days, Nobel successfully demonstrated his contact mine to the astonishment of both Andreyevich and Jacobi. The general danced in delight at Nobel's success and kissed him on the cheek, informing Nobel that the committee had been under tremendous pressure to present a new device. In September 1840, the committee recommended Nobel's device to the tsar, and in 1841, Nobel demonstrated his weapon to Tsar Nicholas and was subsequently awarded 3,000 silver rubles.

Nobel used the award to establish a factory in which he continued his research. In 1842, he demonstrated a production sea mine to Grand Duke Michael, blowing up a three-masted ship and earning an additional 25,000 rubles. Flush with success, Nobel sent for his family. All three of his sons ultimately joined the family business, including Alfred, the inventor of dynamite and the founder of the Nobel Prize.[43]

The elder Nobel's work on mines sparked a storm of controversy within the Committee on Underwater Mines as members of the army and navy vied to see which branch of the service would be responsible for sea mines. In the midst of the squabbles, Nobel's plans and models were lost. When the clouds of war gathered in 1853, Nobel had to reconstruct his invention without the plans.[44]

The Nobel sea mine of 1853 had a zinc body, two-feet long and 15-inches wide at the top. The device had a charge of eight pounds of powder. Later mines may have used as much as 25 pounds. The mine had a chemical fuse that protruded from the device. The fuse consisted of a pencil-sized glass tube filled with sulfuric acid and suspended over a combination of potassium and sugar. Around the tube were two metal slide bars. The entire arrangement was encased in a lead tube extending from the top of the mine, moored several feet below the surface of the water. When the glass broke, either by the movement of the slide bars or by the crushing of the lead casing, the acid released into the potassium and sugar, creating a violent chemical reaction and setting off the main charge. Variations on the Nobel mine, along with electrically fired observation mines, became a common part of Russian defenses in the coming war.[45]

The Crimean War (1854–1856) was the first war to see the successful use of land and sea mines, both of which were the work of Immanuel Nobel. One of the Russians' first concerns as the war began was improving the defenses surrounding the island fortresses of Sveaborg and Kronstadt, which guarded the approaches to the Russian capital, St. Petersburg. When a British and French fleet under the command of Vice Admiral Sir Charles Napier arrived at Kronstadt in June 1854, they found the fortress impossible to take by sea without suffering heavy losses. To reduce the fortress, Napier was faced with the choice of loosing his barrage from his capital ships in shallow water and in full range of the Russian batteries on shore or using smaller ships that could come in closer to the fortress—and these vessels were few in number. Furthermore, the Russians had deployed a number of Nobel's mines in the waters surrounding the fortress. Napier had been warned about the mines before leaving England but had initially dismissed their existence almost out of hand. Intelligence received by Napier en route, however, confirmed the presence of the Nobel mines at Sveaborg and Kronstadt. The British were able to retrieve one of the mines at Kronstadt and soon conducted a trial with it at Riga. After doubling the powder charge, the British were able to destroy the target ship. In the end, the admiral decided not to risk his fleet and left Kronstadt. Sveaborg too proved unattainable due to a combination of large shore batteries and the use of mines. The English public had held high hopes for Napier and his forces. Disappointed by his failure to take Sveaborg or Kronstadt and unwilling to accept the realities of the situation, the British government relieved Napier of his command.[46]

An Anglo-French fleet arriving in the Baltic the next summer faired little better and found that the Russians had only strengthened the defenses at Kronstadt and Sveaborg. After surveying the defenses at Kronstadt, Admiral R. S. Dundas reported, "no serious attack appears to me to be practicable, with the means at my disposal." Among other changes, British reconnaissance forces reported the presence of 44 observation mines and 950 pressure-fused mines. At least four English ships were damaged by mines in the waters off Kronstadt that summer. An officer onboard one of the vessels, the *Merlin,* recalled that

> The ship was steaming slowly along, when a tremendous shock was felt; the portion of the crew below rushed wildly on deck, and for some moments great confusion prevailed. Bulkheads were thrown down, the ship's side was bulged in, girders and beams were broken, crockery smashed, and the contents of the hold inextricably mixed together. The vessel was nearly dismasted, and escaped destruction as by a miracle.[47]

Admiral Dundas also reported one instance of a near miss by an electrically fired mine off the coast of the island. British forces were then forced to begin what was perhaps the first effort at mine sweeping—in this case retrieving the mines from the water and bringing them aboard to disarm them. In all, they raised around 50 of the devices, many of which they took apart to see how they worked. This process could be a tricky business and, on one occasion, Admiral Dundas was wounded when one of the captured mines exploded. While the material effect of the mines may have been limited, the effect on morale was greater. In his 1882 study, *History of Torpedo Warfare,* Royal Bradford opines that the mines "probably prevented the attack on Cronstadt," and the only reason the mines did as little damage as they did was that the powder charge was too small (around 8–12 pounds). Bradford also provides some insight into the arrangement of the Russian mines and relates that the mines were not used as a formal barrier, but were used more as a harassment weapon in potential anchorages. Still, the mines had accomplished their mission, and their success led the Russian government to sign an 116,000-ruble contract for over 1,000 of Nobel's sea mines. Sveaborg proved less fortunate in the 1855 summer campaign and, mines or no mines, was leveled by a combined Anglo-French fleet.[48]

The Russians also used a number of sea mines in the Crimean campaign with limited success. They established a large field of electrically fired observation mines in the straits between the Azov and Black Seas, which might have proved a hindrance to Allied naval forces had the shore-based observation points not been captured. The Russians also used sea mines elsewhere in Black Sea, but again with only negligible success, in part due to the use of improvised material. On the other hand, the Russian use of landmines in their defenses at Sebastopol proved at least inconvenient to the Allied forces.[49]

Faced with the problem of quickly constructing a strong defensive position at Sebastopol, the Russians threw up a number of earthen works near the city. These works, combined with a vigorous defense by the Russian soldiers, helped stave off the attacking French and British for quite some time. In order to strengthen their defenses, the Russians planted landmines throughout their positions. These mines proved not only a hindrance to the allies during their assaults on the Russian positions, but also a nuisance to the Allies when they finally occupied the Russian defensive works.[50]

The use of mines as an obstacle to one's attackers was nothing new. The fougasse, as discussed by Simon Frances Gay de Vernon and Dennis Hart Mahan, had been known to the armies of Europe for centuries. The new Russian mines, however, were designed to explode when stepped upon. This design removed the problem posed by the fougasse—that, in the event of an attack, an operator might set them off too soon or too late. The design also made the mines dangerous even after the Russians had been driven back. Unlike Rains, who relied on a friction primer for a fuse, the Russians used the Nobel fuse. Most sources, including some from the time, erroneously credit the fuse to Jacobi, probably due to his prominence in the Committee on Underwater Mines.[51]

Major Richard Delafield, an American observer, provided a detailed description of the Russian mines at Mast Bastion in his 1860 report on the war.

> They [the mines] consisted of a box of powder eight inches cube, (a, fig 101,) [see illustration] contained within another box, leaving a space of two inches between them, filled with pitch, rendering the powder in the inner box secure from wet and moisture, when buried under ground. The top of the exterior box was placed about eight inches below the surface, and upon it rested a piece of board of six inches wide, twelve inches long, and one inch thick, resting on four legs of thin sheet iron, (o,) apparently pieces of old hoops, about four inches long. The top of this piece of board was near the surface of the earth covered slightly, so as not to be perceived. On any slight pressure upon the board, such as a man treading upon it, the thin iron supports yielded, when the board came into contact with a glass tube (n) containing sulphuric [sic] acid, breaking it, and liberating the acid, which diffused within the box, coming in contact with chloride of potassa [sic], causing instant combustion, and, as a consequence, explosion of the powder.[52]

An alternate arrangement used by the Russians entailed placing the glass tube of sulfuric acid inside a metal tube (see illustration). The metal tube rested on two supports (b, d) over the powder box. A branch (c) extended down into the powder box, communicating the fuse. When the mine was stepped on, the metal tube would bend, breaking the glass tube. The acid would then run into the potassium, combust, and detonate the powder. A description of this second type of fuse also appeared in the writings of London *Times*'s correspondent William Howard Russell. In addition to describing the construction of the mine, Russell also presented a brief description of the effects of the mine which, when exploded,

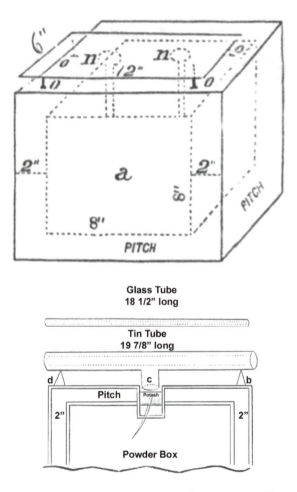

Russian landmines and fuses used during the Crimean War. (Richard Delafield, *Report on the Art of War in Europe 1854, 1855, and 1856* [Washington, D.C.: George W. Bowman, 1860], 109, 110.)

not only destroyed everything near it, but threw out a quantity of bitumen [probably pitch], with which it was coated, in a state of ignition, so as to burn whatever it rested upon.[53]

The Russian land and sea mines did not change the course of the war. Sebastopol was captured, and the island fortress Sveaborg was leveled. Kronstadt was the weapon's greatest success. There, the Russians had used the mines in large numbers and as part of a strong overall defense. As mentioned earlier, the Russian military judged the mines a success and continued to place orders for them. The British, while not having lost many ships to the Russian mines, saw the mine's potential and commissioned the engineer William Armstrong to develop the weapon. Nobel's devices also gained converts across the ocean in the United States.[54]

The war in the Crimea soon attracted the attention of the American Secretary of War, Jefferson Davis, and, in 1855, Davis organized the "Military Commission to the Theater of War in Europe." Davis instructed the commission to study the art of war as practiced by the nations of Europe and appointed three officers to the commission: Major Richard Delafield (engineering), Major Alfred Mordecai (ordnance), and Captain George B. McClellan (cavalry). Unfortunately, the commission was unable to reach the Crimea until after the fall of Sebastopol. With the aid of the British and the French, however, the commission still conducted a thorough study of the battlefields. Of the commission's three officers, Major Delafield was by far the most interested in the Russian mines. Delafield heartily recommended the adoption of torpedoes, both on land and sea, by the American military. He was particularly impressed with Jacobi's (Nobel's) fuse, which he states, "recommends itself to our attention." Indeed, in his report to Congress, Delafield spent some time on the subject of the mines, including detailed drawings of the Russian invention.[55]

Major Mordecai had little if anything to say in his official report about the Russian mines. In part, Mordecai's omission of the mines may well be due to his position in ordnance, given that mining at this juncture was generally considered within the realm of engineering. In addition, Mordecai was confined to camp by illness while in the Crimea, and his report was the last to come out. Captain McClellan also had little to say about the Russian mines. His commentary consists of a description of the field fortifications at the Malakoff about which he notes, "Explosive machines, on the Jacobi principle were also employed." It should, of course, be added that McClellan's main concern was with the operation and organization of the European cavalry.[56]

Another man whose attention was caught by the war in the Crimea was First Lieutenant James Saint Claire Morton, a young engineering officer.

Morton had a long-standing interest in marine torpedoes (mines) and their application in coastal defenses. Reading about the results of the war in the Crimea, especially the siege of Sebastopol, only served to increase his interest. By 1859, he had written a number of works on coastal defense, including a set of plans for the New York City harbor defenses. In his 1859 work, *Memoir on American Fortifications,* Morton conveyed his concern about the poor state of readiness in America's coastal fortifications and stated: "If a war should break out this year, or the next, or within five years, our masonry forts would probably be found incomplete or unarmed." Furthermore, he believed that the regular army was too small to effectively man even the existing fortifications. In addition, Morton felt that the militia units upon which the army would have to rely were ill-trained and definitely not of a soldierly caliber equal to the European forces. In order to compensate for these problems, Morton advocated the use of marine torpedoes and other obstructions in the harbors, and

> well disposed earthworks, ditches, abattis, and other cheap field fortifications, including the use of fougasses and mines . . . as equal to the task of repelling the attack of any foreign armies, whatever be their reputation.[57]

The use of torpedoes was no small thing to Morton, and he devoted two chapters (6 and 7) to the subject. Morton places Fulton's torpedoes in an almost romantic light:

> That invention was of a highly philanthropic character. It aimed to place into the hands of the maritime States, whose domestic institutions, as well as their integral wealth and prosperity, demand a peaceful foreign policy, and forbade the maintenance of great standing navies or armies which…would almost alone suffice for the defense of their ports from the overwhelming squadrons of Britain.

Morton goes on to dismiss claims that the weapon was an "unmanly, uncivilized, unchivalrous, inhuman, wholesale, unfair &c., means of destruction" by pointing out the weapon was of a wholly defensive nature; i.e., if the enemy would not try to invade in the first place, they would not have this problem. He also addresses the issue of the American military's failure to adopt the device stating, "Professional men are rarely the ones to invent, or the first to adopt…an invention," adding that all new weapons are viewed with scorn at first. Finally, he points to the hierarchical nature of the military and the possibility that torpedoes may

> seem calculated to diminish the importance of the military profession, as a profession.…[It] does not require a lifetime spent in the ranks of an army, nor an education at a military academy. It is essentially popular in nature.[58]

Morton acknowledged the shortcomings of the fougasse and other mines, especially with regard to effectiveness and timely detonation. However, he felt that "mines will probably be much more used in future defenses, since the application of voltaic electricity, to the purpose of firing them, has given the defenders the power of exploding them at any instant, and as many at the same moment as may be desired." When war came, however, it was with the South, not Europe. While Morton gained the ear of Secretary of War John B. Floyd, his ideas do not seem to have been readily accepted by the mainstream military. During the Civil War, Morton served as chief engineer of the Army of the Ohio and chief engineer of the Army of the Cumberland. In June 1864, Morton was killed by a stray bullet while laying out the Union defenses at the battle of Petersburg.[59]

The real impact of both the Russian mines in the Crimean War and the reports of the Military Commission to Europe was not found within the United States Regular Army but rather within the Army of the Confederacy. The early fuses for landmines used by the rebels bore a close resemblance to those of Nobel. Furthermore, Jefferson Davis had initiated the Military Commission to Europe headed by Delafield. Less than five years later, as President of the Confederate States of America, Davis must have remembered Delafield's recommendations when confronted with a heated debate over the use of landmines by Southern forces.

By the beginning of the Civil War in 1861, the landmine had evolved from the fougasse, an outgrowth of traditional mining, into something resembling its modern form: a pressure-sensitive device that could be buried in front of fortifications and elsewhere to prevent enemy incursions. On a tactical level, the Russian mines owed a debt to both siege mining and area denial weapons. On a technological level, however, the development of the new mines was closely tied to that of naval mines—a trend that continued during the American Civil War. The mine in its new form aroused no controversy. Its use mimicked that of its predecessors: a weapon to be placed in front of one's fortification. Within a few years, however, the use of mines caused a storm of controversy. The way the weapon was used changed during the Civil War. No longer was the mine used only to secure a defensive position. Now it was used to slow an enemy's advance along a road and to prevent the enemy from occupying abandoned positions. This change in tactics and the accompanying ethical debates foreshadowed the modern debates on the use of landmines.

3

The American Civil War

WHILE MEMBERS OF THE American military were familiar with both land and sea mines by the beginning of the Civil War, the weapons had not been integrated into the psyche of the American military. Officers in both branches of the service still questioned the ethics of using mines as well as whether or not they would prove effective in battle. The Civil War forced the consideration of both issues. While the North developed a few mines late in the war, it was the South that truly saw the advantages offered by mine warfare. Confederate forces were on the defensive for much of the war, particularly at sea and on the rivers where the Union navy had a tremendous advantage in size. Like others before them, Southern military commanders turned to mines to help compensate for being outnumbered and outgunned by their opponents. While land and sea mines did not save the South, mines frequently proved their worth in slowing Union forces. Shades of the work of David Bushnell, Karl Himly, Robert Fulton, Samuel Colt, Immanuel Nobel, and others are evident in many of the mines developed by Southern inventors. Confederate mines ranged from defensive observation and contact mines to current-driven offensive sea mines. This was a war driven in part by technology and industry and is often considered the first modern war.[1]

Commander Matthew Fontaine Maury, late of the United States Navy, was one of the first members of the Southern military to become involved in mine warfare. His work on sea mines led to the earliest use of landmines during the war. Maury is better known, however, for his oceanographic work, particularly his 1855 work, *The Physical Geography of the Sea*, generally considered the first major textbook on oceanography. His work mapping the floor of the Atlantic ocean between Ireland and the United States set the stage for the laying of the first transatlantic telegraph cable in 1858. It is likely that

Maury was familiar with Colt's experiments with sea mines in the 1840s, as he knew Colt and had connections with several of Colt's associates. When the Civil War broke out, Maury, a Virginian, resigned his commission in the American Navy in favor of one in the Confederate Navy.[2]

In April 1861, Maury was appointed to the advisory council of the Governor of Virginia to help make plans for the protection of the state's waterways. Given the South's shortage of naval vessels, Maury recommended torpedoes to protect Southern waterways. Most members of the committee, however, were unconvinced and considered the use of a hidden weapon, such as the torpedo, uncivilized. After conducting several experiments, Maury presented his plans to the governor who in turn arranged for Maury to conduct a demonstration of his weapon.[3]

The demonstration took place in June. His audience included the governor, the secretary of the Navy, and the Congressional Committee on Naval Affairs. Maury used a rope lanyard attached to a percussion fuse to explode a torpedo, generating "a column of water fifteen or twenty feet." Government observers were more than satisfied and provided Maury with $50,000 to carry out his plans.[4]

Maury now geared up for an attack on the Union fleet. He prepared pairs of oak casks each containing 200 pounds of gunpowder, connected by a rope attached to primers so that the kegs would explode should the cord be pulled. His plan was to float the mines downriver toward Union vessels so that the rope would be caught by the bow of a ship and a keg be pulled to each side, exploding the mines and, hopefully, sinking the ship. On the night of July 7, 1861, he attacked several Union ships anchored at Hampton Roads, Virginia. His effort failed, however, and federal forces found the torpedoes adrift two weeks later, the powder damp from an imperfect seal. Other efforts in the same vein also failed, but Confederate interest in torpedo warfare had been piqued, and Maury had laid the groundwork for the establishment of the Submarine Battery Service, a branch of the Confederate navy tasked with the development and use of sea mines.[5]

In the meantime, Maury had been ordered to England in June 1862 to purchase supplies for the Confederate military and conduct further research on mine warfare. As part of his research effort, Maury entered into the service of the British government and conducted numerous experiments with landmines, which proved helpful later with his work on sea mines. In collaboration with British scientist Sir Charles Wheatstone, Maury rented a field near Bowden, England, which they then blew up. On May 2, 1865, Maury, equipped with several sets of new torpedoes, set sail to return to the Confederate States with hopes of using his mines to keep open the port of Galveston, Texas.[6]

While en route to the South, Maury discovered that the Confederacy had fallen. Like many veterans of the lost cause, he turned his sights toward Mexico, where he hoped to enter into the service of Emperor Maximillian. Maury's work in England had not been as fruitful as Jefferson Davis might have liked, and there is little evidence that the Confederate government profited from Maury's work on landmines. Nevertheless, several of Maury's naval mines found their way through the Union blockade during the war. Furthermore, Maury succeeded in procuring much needed war materials including Wheatstone exploders. Rebel mining activity did not end when Maury left for England. If anything, the Southerners grew bolder and more successful.[7]

One of the first officers to act on Maury's ideas was Lieutenant Isaac Brown of the Confederate States Navy, the officer in charge of establishing Confederate defenses on the Mississippi. Brown, a 20-year veteran of the American Navy, had discussed the idea of torpedo warfare with Maury in the summer of 1861. Faced with a large area to defend, he established torpedo stations to coordinate defensive actions, the first of these stations located at Randolph Bluff, just above Columbus, Kentucky. Brown employed electrically detonated land and sea mines in his defenses. The landmines were made of cast iron containers with handles, similar in appearance to pots, filled with gunpowder, with wires coming out from underneath bolted on covers. Brown had the mines planted along the two roads leading into Columbus from the North. The mines were never fired, however, and the Union army captured the entire system intact in March 1862. Brown remained a driving force in the South's mining programs for the remainder of the war and continued his work with mines in Latin America after the war.[8]

While there were a number of Southerners involved in designing land and sea mines, General Gabriel Rains was the most successful of the group. His torpedo designs, particularly his fuses, were the most commonly used of the war on both land and sea. Rains, of course, had already shown an interest in mines during the Second Seminole War, and this interest only increased during the Civil War. On September 20, 1861, Jefferson Davis recommended Rains for induction into the Confederate army as a brigadier general in the artillery. Ten days later, Rains was ordered to report to Major General John B. Magruder at Yorktown, Virginia. In May 1862, Rains, now a division commander, prepared to use mines to protect the Confederate retreat from Yorktown, which for almost a month had been invested by Federal forces under the command of Major General George McClellan.[9]

Shortly after McClellan's arrival at Yorktown in early April 1862, the Pinkerton Detective Agency presented him with an estimate of Confederate strength. Relying on this report, the ever-cautious McClellan placed the strength of the defenders at almost 100,000 and decided to lay siege to the city rather than risk an open confrontation. In reality, the rebels had only around 31,000 men by April 11. McClellan's decision may well have been motivated by his background as an engineer and his experiences in the Crimea. In undertaking the siege, he confided to his wife, "I *do* believe that I am avoiding the faults of the Allies at Sebastopol & quietly preparing the way for a great success."[10]

It took almost a month for McClellan to implement his siege plans. Confederate troops maintained their positions until the night of May 3, when it became apparent that McClellan planned to use his siege guns to blast them from their positions. Under cover of darkness, the Confederates slipped away and headed down the road to Williamsburg. When the Union forces entered the city and its surrounding works, they found their way obstructed by rebel mines. A young enlisted man wrote in his diary, "Wherever a torpedo had been buried, a short stick or branch was standing up, and woe to the man or animal who tread on it or kicked it." More mines were found on the road leading out of Yorktown to Williamsburg.[11]

While historians place McClellan's numerical advantage at Yorktown at almost three to one, at the time, General Rains placed it at almost ten to one. Drawing on his experiences at Fort King, Rains mined parts of the Confederate defenses in an effort to even the odds and prevent enemy incursions. In his report of May 14, 1862 to Major General Daniel H. Hill, Rains states that "at a salient angle, an accessible point of our works, as part of the defenses thereof, I had the land mined with the weapons alluded to, to destroy assailants."

Union sources describe the mines as being made from either mortar or columbiad shells armed with friction primer fuses and buried a few inches below the ground so that "they exploded by being trod upon or otherwise disturbed."[12]

In his memoirs, Union Colonel Charles Wainwright gave a more detailed description of the rebel shells:

> All that was visible was a foot or two of telegraph wire sticking out of the ground, the idea seeming to be that men or horses would get entangled, and so pull the wire, which was to fire the torpedo.

Confederate veteran S. A. Cunningham described the mines as being capped with a Rains-developed fuse so sensitive that "to drop it on the floor or any slight concussion would explode it."[13]

The mines Rains described to General Hill were not, however, the only ones encountered by Union soldiers when they entered Yorktown. Union sources report that the Confederates had placed torpedoes (landmines) all over, "in any place that was likely to be visited by our men." A Union telegraph operator died soon after he set off a mine planted at the base of a telegraph pole. Other mines were found buried in the streets of the city and attached to tools and other items likely to be picked up by the soldiers. McClellan quickly denounced the mining and, in a May 4, 1862, letter to Secretary of State Edwin Stanton, declared,

> The rebels have been guilty of the most murderous & barbarous conduct in placing torpedoes within the abandoned works, near flag-staffs, magazines, and telegraph offices, in carpet-bags, barrels of flour &c.

He added, "I shall make the prisoners remove them at their own peril." McClellan's policy of using prisoners to clear rebel mines was adopted by other Union officers and continued throughout the war.[14]

An excerpt of McClellan's letter appeared in the New York *Herald* and found its way to the Confederate commander, General Joseph E. Johnston. Johnston initiated an investigation into the matter, and contacted Rains's superior, Major General D. H. Hill. When questioned about his role in the incident, Rains denied any complicity and stated that he knew nothing about the use of torpedoes in the manner described by McClellan, nor did he believe it, as "wells, springs of water, barrels of flour, carpet-bags, &c. are places incompatible with the invention." While Rains denied any knowledge of the torpedoes to which McClellan referred, soldiers on both sides linked him with the torpedoes, and it appears Rains was briefly arrested for his activities, though he was released without trial. In all, the torpedoes at Yorktown cost McClellan almost 30 casualties.[15]

There were Confederate losses from mines as well. The Reverend Nicholas A. Davis of the Fourth Texas Infantry Regiment, the last infantry unit to leave Yorktown, recalled that the evacuation

> might have been accomplished with some degree of secrecy had not the whiskey drinking propensities of some of our cavalry led them into a trap which had been arranged for the reception of the Yankees. Secret mines had been placed in several houses, to explode on entrance. Ignorant of that fact, our enterprising troopers burst open a door, and though unsuccessful in their search for liquor, came out of the house considerably "elevated" themselves.

Val C. Giles, a soldier in the same regiment, presented an almost identical version of the story adding, "This premature explosion notified the enemy that the Confederates were in full retreat and the Yankees came in legions."[16]

After fighting a delaying battle at Williamsburg, the Confederates again retreated and headed toward Richmond. On May 5, heavy rains slowed the retreat, bogging down artillery and ambulances. Rains, commanding the rear guard during this action, found an abandoned ammunition wagon loaded with artillery shells. Rains had four of these shells armed with pressure-sensitive primers and planted in the roadway near a fallen tree to have a "moral effect in checking the advance of the enemy."[17]

As the Union cavalry moved up the road to Richmond, the ground suddenly shook from the force of an explosion. The result was "the horrible mangling by one of these shells of a cavalryman and his horse."[18] Despite incurring less than a score of casualties, the subterras caused such terror among the Union troops that they refused to move forward until the roads from Williamsburg had been cleared, slowing the Union pursuit by at least three days and allowing Rains's forces time to escape. On the success of his efforts, Rains remarked,

> Thus our rear was relieved of the enemy. No soldier will march over mined land, and a corps of sappers, each man having two ten-inch shells, two primers, and a mule to carry them, could stop any army.[19]

Rains's actions were met with mixed reviews by his fellow officers. Major General James Longstreet instructed his subordinate Brigadier General G. Moxley Sorrel to write Rains:

> It is the desire of the major-general commanding that you put out no shells or torpedoes behind you, as he does not recognize it as a proper or effective method of war.

In his memoirs, Sorrel added that he told Rains that "if he would put them [the subterras] aside and pay some attention to his brigade his march would be better and his stragglers not so numerous."[20] At the same time, however, Major General D. H. Hill of the Confederate States Army (CSA), wrote the Confederate Secretary of War G. W. Randolph, "In my opinion all means of destroying our brutal enemies are lawful and proper."[21] Surprisingly, opinions among the Union commanders, while less diverse, proved in some cases at least conciliatory, and none of the Union generals seem to have had quite the disdain for Rains's mines as General Longstreet.

While General McClellan claimed, "The rebels have been guilty of the most murderous & barbarous conduct," his objection was not to the use of the weapon *per se,* but to the method in which the Confederates had employed the device at Yorktown, namely booby traps. The use of landmines was not new to McClellan. In his memoirs written after the Civil War, McClellan discussed the Confederate use of landmines at Yorktown, stating, "To place mines in the path of assaulting columns is admissible under the customs of war, but, such use of them as was made here is barbarous in the extreme." He added that the mines "much delayed" the progress of the Union troops as they entered Yorktown, a statement that in Rains's opinion would certainly have vindicated his mining activities, but in McClellan's case may have also served as a convenient explanation for his failure to act in a timely manner.[22]

Other Union generals took a view similar to McClellan, as did many of the rank and file on both sides. In his report on the capture of Yorktown, Brigadier General William Berry, while bitterly complaining about the rebel use of mines, stated that the situation would have been altogether different had the mines been "placed on the glasis at the bottom of the ditch, &c., which, in view of the anticipated assault, might possibly be considered a legitimate use of them." As one might expect, the Union rank and file had little good to say about the rebel mines. Their officers' philosophical distinctions meant little to them, and the men often referred to the mines derogatorily as "infernal machines." Many Confederate enlisted men held views similar to those of their Union counterparts. After being led through the mines on the road leaving Yorktown, one rebel soldier stated, "This is barbarism."[23]

Rains had little trouble justifying the use of the subterra. In his May 14, 1862, letter to General Hill explaining the happenings at Yorktown, Rains presented four justifications for his actions. First, he argued that the placement of the subterra shells in the defenses of Yorktown was necessary to help even the odds between the Northern and Southern forces. Second, Rains pointed out that McClellan had intended to use a mine to destroy part of the defenses at Yorktown, Fort Magruder, which he felt legitimized the use of his smaller mines. Third, Rains felt that the mines on the road to Williamsburg were necessary to save his men. Finally, Rains justified his actions by pointing out that Union forces had already broken the rules of civilized war. When the Union forces began the siege of Yorktown in April 1862, they began their bombardment "without a word of warning to innocent women and children, as at New Berne, North Carolina, my native place," and sent "death-dealing fragments among the innocent and unoffending." It is this last point, perhaps more than any other, that enabled Rains to rationalize his actions. During the course of the war, Rains seems to have developed a hatred of the North. War Department clerk J. B. Jones writes in his diary that Rains told him in private that he "would not use such a weapon in ordinary warfare; but has no scruples in resorting to any means of defense against an Army of Abolitionists, invading our country for the purpose avowed, of extermination."[24]

The dispute between Rains and his superiors was arbitrated by Secretary of War G. W. Randolph. After considering correspondence from both sides of the issue, Randolph decided that the legitimacy of the landmine "depends upon the purpose with which they are used." He found it "inadmissible" to kill merely for the sake of killing and thus prohibited the use of mines "with no other design than that of depriving your enemy of a few men, without materially injuring him." On the other hand, he allowed that it was "admissible to plant shells in a parapet to repel an assault or on a road to check pursuit" because there was a greater goal than merely killing the enemy's men. As General Longstreet was Rains's superior, Randolph felt that Rains "should give way, or, if he prefers it, he may be assigned to the river defenses, where such things are clearly admissible."[25]

Rains chose the latter of Randolph's options. On June 18, 1862, Rains was given command of the submarine torpedo defenses of the James River, and all area commands were ordered to render whatever assistance they could. Rains's command proved short-lived. On September 9, 1862, Rains was ordered to turn over his command to Lieutenant Hunter Davidson of the Confederate navy, an associate of Matthew Maury, the head of the newly created Submarine Battery Service. Rains, in turn, was given command of the Service's sister organization, the Torpedo Bureau. Three months later, on December 15, the secretary of war appointed Rains general superintendent of the Confederate Conscription Service. With Maury on his way to Europe, Lieutenant Davidson soon took over the Submarine Battery Service. While the Navy created the two organizations in September 1862, the Confederate congress did not provide them with specific funding for almost a year. In May 1863, the congress appropriated $20,000 for the construction of submarine batteries. The following year, appropriations were increased to $350,000. In the last year of the war, appropriations for torpedo warfare reached $6,000,000.[26]

In view of the dangerous work required of the men in the Torpedo Bureau and the Confederate Submarine Battery Service, those men received healthy bonuses. Not only was there the possibility that the mines they were laying might explode prematurely, but Union officials frequently threatened to hang anyone caught putting out torpedoes. The men in these organizations were highly valued by the government, a fact best illustrated by a document carried by torpedo electrician R. O. Crowley through the course of the war, stating that should he be captured by the Union, "he will be exchanged for any general officer of their army who may be in our hands."[27]

Members of both the Torpedo Bureau and Submarine Battery Service took oaths of secrecy about their activities. While the following quote is a part of the enlisting articles for the Submarine Battery Service, it is likely that the Torpedo Bureau used a similar format.

> We, the undersigned…do agree, individually—
> Article 1. To enter the C. S. Naval Submarine Battery Service.
> Article 2. To do our duty in said service loyally and faithfully.
> Article 3. To obey all lawful orders of those set above us in authority.

Article 4. Under no circumstances, now or hereafter, to make known to any one not employed in this service, anything regarding the methods used for arranging or exploding the submarine batteries, excepting only by permission of the honorable Secretary of the Navy or the commanding officer of said service.[28]

Lieutenant Isaac Brown was among the men who signed up for the Torpedo Bureau, the man responsible for establishing mine defenses along the Mississippi River in early 1862. December 1862 found him in charge of the Confederate defenses on the Yazoo River after his ship, the Confederate ram *Arkansas,* had been destroyed. Brown and his associates, Masters Zedekiah McDaniel and Francis Ewing, decided to put out mines to slow the Union advance down the river. They acquired five-gallon glass demijohns (glass containers) from the army, filled them with gunpowder, and armed each with an artillery friction primer. For each mine, Brown then had McDaniel and Ewing run an iron wire across the river and attach it to the demijohn's friction primer so that when a ship hit the wire, the mine, several feet below the water, would detonate.[29]

On December 12, the ironclads *Cairo, Queen of the West,* and *Pittsburg,* together with the steamers *Marmora* and *Signal,* headed down the Yazoo to clear the area of torpedoes and destroy rebel shore batteries. As sailors on boats from *Cairo* and *Marmora* cleared mines from the river, the *Cairo* drifted into the cable strung by Brown's men. The mine detonated underneath the ship, sending the ship's anchor flying through the air. Within 12 minutes the ship had sunk in 30 feet of water. Surprisingly, while the ship was a complete loss, there were no deaths, and most of the baggage was salvaged. *Cairo* was the first of 29 Union ships to be sunk by Southern mines during the course of the war.

In his report on the incident, Rear Admiral David Porter of the United States Navy reported that *Cairo* had "proceeded too far ahead," but he observed that her captain was guilty only of being "incautious" and said he had assigned him a new command. Porter blamed the incident in part on the large number of dud torpedoes the ships had already encountered. The mines elicited no ire in the official reports from the Union officers involved. Porter, while lamenting that it might cost him three or four more ships, steadfastly maintained that the presence of the torpedoes would "not prevent [him] from carrying out [his] original intentions" and that he would "succeed in carrying out the plan for the capture of Vicksburg." The last comment proved overly optimistic because Vicksburg held out for another year and a half.[30]

While the main emphasis at these stations was on establishing harbor defenses, the stations also used subterras. Rains arrived in Mobile in early

August 1863 and met with the local commander, Major General Dabney H. Maury, to discuss establishing torpedo defenses at Mobile. Despite the success of mines in other areas, Maury remained unconvinced and wrote that "General Rains has gone away with his gimcracks; he was not at all practical; everything I received from him was vague and visionary."[31] Rains prevailed, however, and both land and sea mines were put out at Mobile. These mines proved to be a formidable obstacle for Union forces.[32]

Shortly before the end of his tenure at the Conscript Bureau, Rains sent President Jefferson Davis a book he authored extolling the virtues of the sub-terra shell. Soon after, Rains wrote General Hill, "It caused him [Davis] to enter with zest into the schemes, and behold, I found myself ousted from my position…and ordered to Vicksburg." In May 1863, three months before his trip to Mobile, Rains was removed from command of the Conscript Bureau and sent to Vicksburg to employ his mines in the city's defenses.[33]

On May 27, Secretary of War James Seddon informed General Joseph Johnston, the commanding officer at Vicksburg, of the imminent arrival of General Rains and added,

> The President has complete confidence in his inventions, and is desirous that they should be employed both on land and river.…Such means of offense against the enemy are approved and recognized by the Department as legitimate weapons of warfare.[34]

Despite Rains's enthusiasm toward his devices, he was skeptical that he could turn the tide of a battle already in progress and delayed his departure for some weeks by writing appeals to President Davis, stating that Vicksburg was not necessarily the ideal test ground for his inventions. By the time Rains left Richmond, Johnston had already begun his retreat from Vicksburg to Jackson, Mississippi, and had only a few mines to plant on the roadways behind him. In his writings after the war, President Davis made clear his displeasure in Rains's delay, stating, "There could scarcely have been presented a better opportunity for their use than that offered by the heavy [Union] column marching against Jackson."[35]

With the South facing chronic shortages in the raw materials necessary to carry on war, it was imperative that Rains make his subterras reliable before they could be used *en masse*. At Yorktown the subterra consisted merely of an artillery shell capped with a friction primer buried in the ground. While the basics of this design—a pressure-sensitive fuse connected to a powder-filled shell—remained the same throughout the war, Rains made substantial modifications to the individual components. Among the first changes was the design of a more effective fuse.

While the friction primer was designed to explode the artillery shell on impact with the ground, it could not be assured that such force would be generated by the pressure of a walking human or horse. To counter this problem, Rains replaced the old artillery style friction primers with a sulfuric acid fuse similar to those used by the Russians during the Crimean War. The fuse (top right of the illustrations of mines designed by Rains) was composed of a soft lead cap (b) that covered a small glass tube containing sulfuric acid (a) resting in a mixture of chlorate of potash and white sugar (c). When the cap was dented, the glass tube would break and the acid would combine with the potash mixture, igniting the main fuse.[36]

Rains later developed a more effective fuse (middle right). While the formula for the device was kept a secret during the war, Confederate Engineer Viktor Von Scheliha, an Austrian officer, later revealed that it was made from a mixture of 50 percent potassium chlorate, 30 percent sulfuret of antimony, and 20 percent pulverized glass. The fuse (d) was then covered by a thin copper cap (e), which helped keep the fuse from becoming damp. When the cap was crushed, the mixture detonated, igniting a fuse of gunpowder dissolved in alcohol, setting off the main charge via a tube of gunpowder (d). Only seven pounds of pressure were needed to detonate the fuse. To help prevent accidents, a safety guard (f) was screwed in over the copper cap. Rains used the same type of fuse in manufacturing hand grenades.[37]

Rains began building shells of his own design to improve the effectiveness of his mines. The keg torpedo was among the more commonly used of his mines. Designed to be used as both a land and a sea mine, the device consisted of a small wooden keg to which cones of wood were secured to either end. The keg was then filled with gunpowder, covered in pitch, and fitted with a primer.

Numerous variations on this design were used during the war. For example, the top two mines on the left are of the type of mine used in the defenses of Mobile, Alabama. As with earlier mines, when used on land, a board was often placed above the primer to widen the area of coverage. The third mine was probably used exclusively as a water mine and had multiple fuses to provide maximum coverage. The bottom mine is of particular interest in that it uses a modified fuse assembly (shown in detail next to it). Instead of relying upon a copper cap, the mine used a plunger (f) suspended by a spring (h) to break a standard Rains fuse. A stuffing nut (e) and Indian rubber packing (i) were used around the plunger to prevent the fuse from becoming damp. As a safeguard during transport, a spike or wire was placed in a hole in the plunger (k), thus preventing the accidental explosion of the mine. This variation proved readily applicable to land use. Its use around Charleston, South Carolina, particularly at Battery Wagner, is discussed in more detail below.[38]

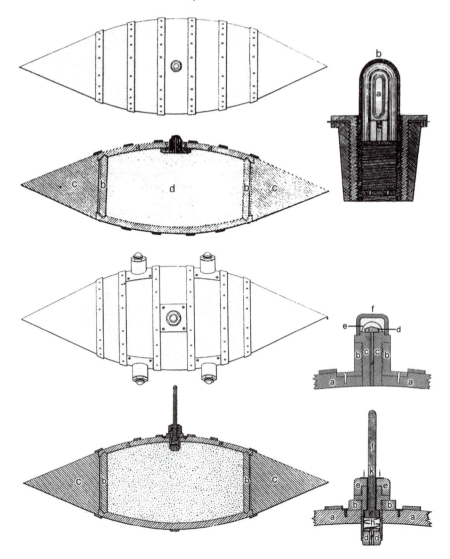

Examples of mines designed by Brigadier General Gabriel Rains during the American Civil War. (J. S. Barnes, *Submarine Warfare, Offensive and Defensive* [New York: D. Van Nostrand, 1869], P1. IV, Fig. 2. Viktor Ernest Karl Rudolph Von Scheliha, *A Treatise on Coast-Defense* [London: E. and F. N. Spoon, 1868], Pl. IX, Figs. 2, 4, 5, 6, 8.)

In addition to the keg torpedo, Rains also developed a second type of torpedo, the "frame" or "shell" torpedo, for use as a sea mine. This rather simple design placed a series of explosive shells on a wooden frame that could be raised and lowered in the water. Rains and others often modified existing artillery shells as subterras by installing a Rains fuse. To prevent moisture from ruining the shells, Rains added a tin shield that covered the primer and subterra. This shield protected the subterra and primer from moisture and enlarged the surface area exposed to the primer.[39]

While Rains's book, which caused Jefferson Davis "to enter with zest into the schemes," was lost during the war, some of Rains's wartime writings on the subterra survived. Among these writings is a letter to James Seddon dated November 18, 1864, detailing the use of the subterra in establishing a defensive position for artillery batteries at Charleston and including a diagram illustrating his ideas. Rains recommended using mines for the first line of defense of the position, followed by *chevaux-de-frise*.[40]

Part and parcel of Rains's defensive strategy was a system of markers designed to allow the Confederate troops to move through the field of subterras without endangering themselves. Rains outlined this system in the letter mentioned above. A small red flag was placed three feet behind each subterra and was to be removed if an enemy attack was eminent. In addition to the flags, several pathways were to be marked through the minefield by long streamers. At night, the streamers were replaced by glass lanterns, covered in red flannel on one side, and dark on the other three. Placed in pairs, the lanterns marked the edges of the path through the subterras at night.[41]

As the war progressed and the Southern position grew more desperate, opposition to Rains's devices within the ranks of the Confederate officer corps began to melt. The Confederacy established torpedo stations throughout much of the South, with large stations located at Charleston, South Carolina; Savannah, Georgia; Richmond, Virginia; Mobile, Alabama; and Wilmington, North Carolina. All five of these stations employed both land and sea mines. By the end of the war, Southern troops had planted landmines in most theaters of operation.

One of the better-known examples of Rains's tactics in action occurred during the battle for Battery Wagner in 1863. Battery Wagner was an earthwork that defended the entrance to Charleston harbor. On approaching the battery, Union troops speculated greatly as to why neither *chevaux-de-frise* nor other obstacles had been placed in front of the rebel defenses. They received their answer on August 26. Near 6:30 that evening, the 24th Massachusetts Volunteers captured a Confederate position known as "the ridge," near what became the fifth parallel, some 245 yards from Battery Wagner. They took 67 prisoners. The prisoners stated that they had been unable to retreat for fear of setting off their own mines. The Confederate story was confirmed when a corporal of the Third United States Colored Troops stepped upon one of the mines and was thrown over 25 yards and deposited naked

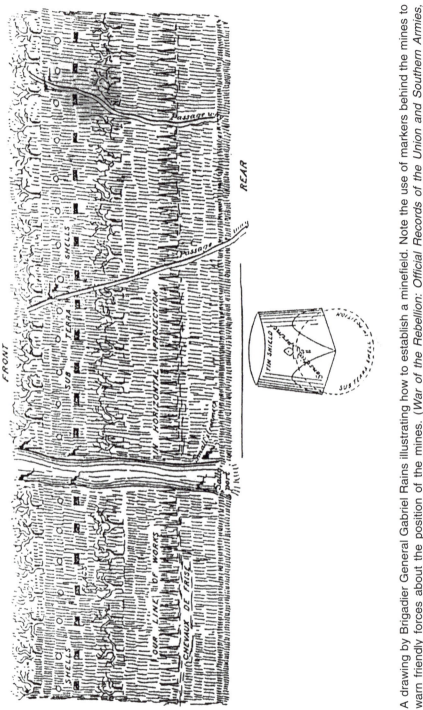

A drawing by Brigadier General Gabriel Rains illustrating how to establish a minefield. Note the use of markers behind the mines to warn friendly forces about the position of the mines. (*War of the Rebellion: Official Records of the Union and Southern Armies*, series I, vol. 42, pt. 3 [Washington, D.C.: Government Printing Office, 1897–1900], 1221.)

with his arm resting on the plunger of another torpedo. When his body was discovered the next morning, his position gave rise to claims that the rebels had tied him to the torpedo as a decoy.[42]

The South used a variety of mines at Battery Wagner, and these devices hindered advancing Union troops all the way through the Southern evacuation of Battery Wagner on September 6. In all, the rebels employed some

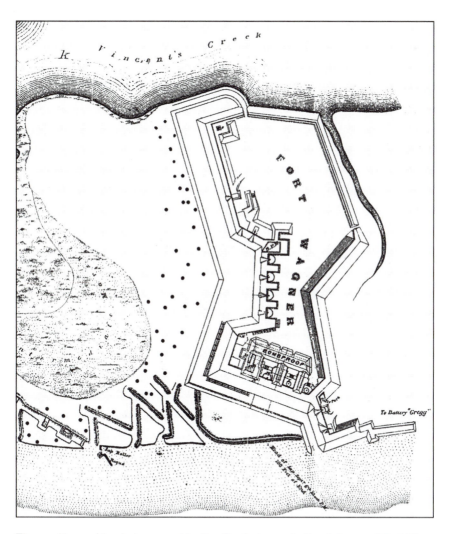

The positions of landmines used by the Confederacy in the defense of Fort Wagner. (Q. A. Gilmore, *Engineering and Artillery Operations Against the Defenses of Charleston Harbor in 1863* [New York: D. Van Nostrand, 1865], Pl. 3. Map has been altered by the author.)

60 mines scattered along the most likely path of the advancing enemy. The approximate positions of these shells are marked on the map of Battery Wagner. The rebels used two types of mines in the area. The first, numbering about 37, were of keg type mines fitted with a wooden plunger. The most common method of disarming these torpedoes was by drilling a hole in the keg and pouring water inside, thus ruining the powder. Over 30 keg torpedoes were disarmed this way. In addition to using boards on top of the mines to increase the area of coverage, the Southerners also employed a cap formed of three iron arms, 15 inches long. The second category of mine, made from artillery shells, fall into two types. The first type of shell mine, of which there were about 20, was made from 24-pound shells covered with tin shields. The second type, of which there were only three, was made of 15-inch navy shells topped with the three-pronged caps used on the keg torpedoes. Each of these shells was fitted with a standard Rains fuse.[43]

While the rebel mines did not prevent the fall of Battery Wagner, they slowed the advance of the Union forces and occupied Union troops in searching for and disarming the devices. Captured Confederate troops were also used to find mines. The mines at Battery Wagner appear to have caused none of the outrage raised by earlier mining efforts, though the presence of the mines must have weighed heavily on the minds of the Union soldiers.[44]

On August 31, 1863, Rains informed the War Department "that the hand grenades, described in the enemy's press as so terrible in repelling their assaults on Battery Wagner, were subterra shells." President Davis added to the letter, "Acknowledge with gratification, the success of General Rains' subterra shells." General Beauregard, the commander of the Confederate forces in Charleston, was also particularly pleased with the success of the landmines at Battery Wagner, and found them effective in slowing the enemy's advance and in warning of an enemy attack.[45]

As Charleston was one of the South's major ports, it became a proving ground of sorts for an array of harbor defenses including mines. Among these innovations were the introduction of the torpedo boat and the first successful use of the submarine. The torpedo boats at Charleston, sometimes referred to as cigar boats because of their shape, were small, fast, steam-driven boats with a contact-fused mine attached to a spar on the front of the boat. The concept was relatively simple: ram the enemy boat with enough speed to detonate the mine without coming close enough to be caught in the explosion. A number of these boats were used in Southern harbors, and they were responsible for damaging several Union ships including the ironclad *New Ironsides.* Charleston was also home to *Hunley,* the first submarine to sink a ship during a war. Based on a 25-foot boiler made for a ship, the submarine carried a crew of eight and was hand powered. *Hunley* made its only successful attack on

February 17, 1864, ramming home a spar torpedo into the Union corvette *Housatonic,* sinking it. Unfortunately for the crew of the submarine, it too was caught in the explosion and sank along with its victim.[46]

While Rains's keg torpedoes were the most common mines used by the South, other varieties also saw heavy use. The second most common were those developed by E. C. Singer and J. R. Fretwell of Texas. The large cylindrical mines were relatively simplistic and relied upon a mechanical, rather than a chemical, fuse. The main body was built of light boiler iron or tin and held between 50 and 100 pounds of gunpowder. The mines were designed to float under the surface of the water, anchored in place by a large weight. When a ship brushed against the trigger rod (e), it bent back, releasing the hammer (b) and sending it crashing down on a percussion cap (f), which detonated the main charge. Evaluators from the Engineering Headquarters Department were particularly impressed with Singer's plans and had high praise for the "simple" nature of the lock mechanism that they suggested might be adapted for use on land. They also saw a great advantage in the lack of human operator as it lessened the chance for the mine being set off too early or too late. In practice, the mines had some marked deficiencies. When left in the water too long—as little as a month in the ocean—the spring that propelled the hammer decayed and failed to provide enough force to set off the percussion cap. In other cases, marine worms were found lodged between the hammer and the percussion caps, likewise deadening the hammer's impact.[47]

The Singer torpedo proved particularly popular in the Confederate defenses along the Gulf coast. In May 1863, Captain D. Bradbury, CSA, began a concerted effort to block Union access to the Texas coast. His first assignment was to put out a series of 18 mines to block the channel between Fort Esperanza and the sandbar at Pass Cavallo. While he expressed little faith in the effectiveness of the mines if Union ships had tried to get past them, he credited the presence of the mines as having been a great deterrent in having kept the fleet out of the pass. Bradbury also put out mines in the entrance to the Guadalupe River at Aransas Pass and in the channel between Powder Horn and Port Lavaca. While the mines on the Texas coast never damaged Union ships, Bradbury believed strongly in the Singer torpedoes he put out and pointed out to his superiors that "knowing of these torpedoes is what has kept their gun-boats from coming up long before this," adding "if they will not try them we cannot expect to destroy them." Bradbury also adapted the Singer mines for use on land.[48]

As Confederate fears of an impending Union attack grew, Bradbury was ordered to return to Fort Esperanza with all his remaining torpedoes and mine the area surrounding the fort. In response, Bradbury planted some 24 modified Singer sea mines in the trenches around the fort. Rather than

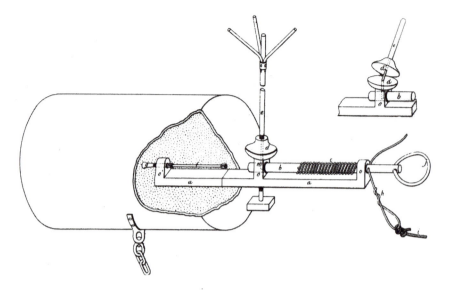

A Singer sea mine. (Viktor Ernest Karl Rudolph Von Scheliha, *A Treatise on Coast-Defense* [London: E. and F. N. Spoon, 1868], Pl. VIII, Figs. 1–2.)

setting up the mines to explode on contact, he attached lengths of rawhide rope to the safety pins so that pulling the rope would set off the mines, allowing the Fort's defenders to set them off when they would do the most damage. While Captain Bradbury felt that the mines would have "been very effective" if the Union troops had attempted to storm the fort, the Confederates abandoned Esperanza in the face of an impending Union assault.[49]

Singer mines also played a role in perhaps the best known use of sea mines during the Civil War, Union Rear Admiral David Farragut's assault on Mobile Bay in Alabama. By August 1864, Mobile was one of the South's last remaining ports, and blockade runners still ran in and out of the bay. The Confederates had established a series of forts to guard the bay entrances and supplemented these with a line of obstructions and torpedoes across most of the main channel, save for a small break to allow the blockade runners through. Farragut, a veteran of the assaults on Port Hudson and Vicksburg, was convinced he could take advantage of this gap to force his way past the rebel gun emplacements at Fort Morgan and gain entrance to the bay. His goal was to seal off the harbor and to capture the Confederate ram *Tennessee*. His attack fleet included 14 steamers and four ironclad monitors: *Tecumseh, Manhattan, Winnebago,* and *Chickasaw.*

The fleet headed for Fort Morgan early on the morning of August 5 with the monitors in the lead. The steamers were cabled together in pairs and traveled in a line behind. As the exchange between the ships and Fort Morgan drew to a fevered pitch and the column approached the line of torpedoes, the lead steamer, *Brooklyn,* faltered, its captain apparently worried that he was moving too quickly and about to come alongside the rear monitor, *Tecumseh.* The rest of the fleet came to a halt amidst a hail of cannon fire from the fort. Farragut signaled for *Brooklyn* to move forward, but the ship remained still. As Farragut tried to sort out the column, *Tecumseh* ignored the buoy marking the edge of the gap in the torpedoes. The resulting explosion startled both sides. Within minutes, the monitor was gone along with 120 souls, almost the entire crew. As *Brooklyn* continued to hesitate, Farragut, who had climbed into the rigging for a more commanding view of the fight, decided to move his flagship into the lead—directly into a suspected minefield. As the story goes, when he was warned of the mines, he replied simply, "Damn the torpedoes!" and ordered the ship forward.

As the ships passed through the line of torpedoes the crews could hear the hammers of the Singer torpedoes striking the percussion caps. Fortunately for Farragut and his men, the torpedoes they hit proved to be duds. The Admiral's assessment that the mines had been in the water too long proved correct. In the end, the day belonged to Farragut. The fleet secured the bay and, after a long fight, the *Tennessee* surrendered. Fort Morgan lasted a few more weeks, but it too succumbed. Mobile itself was not captured until 1865, but with the entrance to the bay in Union hands and the *Tennessee* and much of the rest of the Southern fleet in the bay captured, its importance as a sea port diminished.[50]

Farragut's victory far from ended the use of mines in the bay area. Many of the Union navy's smaller ships were tied up trying to locate and disarm the mines. The steamer *Metacomet* under the command of Pierce Crosby removed 150 of them just in the days leading up to battle of Spanish Fort, in April 1865. Southern mines proved deadly, sinking six Union vessels in the bay area between March 12 and April 14, including the monitors *Milwaukee* and *Osage.*

Nor did the Torpedo Bureau ignore landmines. One of the better examples is Spanish Fort where they planted the mines outside the fort's general works and in front of the abattis and other obstacles but within range of fire from the fort. In addition, many of the nearby roads were mined. The mines were placed about six feet apart and marked with small forked twigs instead of the customary red flags. While the twigs may have been more difficult for the rebel infantry to see, the twigs did not need to be taken up prior to an enemy advance.[51]

The mines at Spanish Fort were constructed of modified 12-pound artillery shells. Contrary to standard practice, the rebels did not use a device to increase the surface area exposed to the primer. Another surprising aspect of the mining at Spanish Fort is that the Confederates mined the approaches to water holes likely to be frequented by Union soldiers, an act not generally seen outside of the battle at Yorktown. The mines proved to be, in the words of one Union officer, "a source of considerable annoyance," due more, however, to the "moral effect produced upon the troops, than from their destructive power."[52]

Mining roads with torpedoes became standard practice in many areas, and Union forces encountered them from the roads of Mississippi, through South Carolina, and into Richmond itself. Among the developments making the mining of the roads practicable was the use of a primer that could be activated after the subterra had been planted, allowing the local citizenry to pass safely on the road and requiring only little notice to arm the shell.[53]

Mining roads could have severe repercussions. In May 1864, Federal forces under the command of Major General Philip H. Sheridan encountered mines on the roads near Richmond. The mines—apparently modified artillery shells—were planted "on each side of the road, and so connected by wires attached to friction-tubes in the shells, that when a horse's hoof struck a wire the shell was exploded." The mines "exploded as the column passed over them, killing several horses and wounding a few men." That evening, Sheridan ordered a group of some 25 prisoners to get down on their hands and knees, search for the wires of the subterras in the darkness, and then dig up the shells. Upon finding that a nearby resident had been involved in planting the shells, Sheridan ordered the man and his family taken away and a number of the mines arranged in the man's house so that they would explode should a rebel column come by.[54]

Union troops entering South Carolina in January 1865 also encountered mines. Several Union soldiers were killed by mines when Northern troops under Major General William T. Sherman crossed into South Carolina at Sister's Ferry. Major General Henry Slocum wrote of the incident,

> This was unfortunate for that section of the State. Planting torpedoes for the defense of a position is legitimate warfare, but our soldiers regarded the act of placing them in a highway…as something akin to poisoning a stream. If that section of South Carolina suffered more than any other, it was due to the blundering of people who were more zealous than wise.[55]

American soldiers would react similarly to mined areas during the Vietnam War.

Other Union generals reacted similarly when they encountered subterras planted in the roads. Although Sherman initially declared the rebel use of mines illegal and used Confederate prisoners to find and remove the mines, by June 1864, Sherman rethought his position, writing:

> I now decide that the use of the torpedo is justifiable in war in the advance of an army so as to make his advance up a river or over a road more dangerous. But after the adversary has gained the country by fair warlike means, then the case changes entirely. The use of torpedoes in blowing up our cars and the road after they are in our possession is simply malicious.

He added that,

> if torpedoes are found in the possession of an enemy to our rear, you may cause them to be put on the ground and tested by wagon-loads of prisoners, or, if need be, citizens implicated in their use…if a torpedo is suspected on any part of a road, order the point to be tested by a cart-load of prisoners, or citizens implicated, drawn by a long rope. Of course an enemy cannot complain of his own traps.[56]

In October 1864, a Federal agent in Richmond reported, "[o]n all the roads approaching the city torpedoes are being laid and covered in dust. Cords 400 feet long are attached to the torpedoes and men secreted in the bushes pull the cord on the approach of the enemy." A Confederate report from the Torpedo Bureau adds that, after being "indoctrinated" on the use of the subterra, many of the general officers in the area "now gladly avail themselves of this means of defense," and that some 600 torpedoes had been planted around Fort Gilmer and Battery Harrison.[57]

The use of torpedoes also gained currency within rebel partisan groups, and by 1864, even General Robert E. Lee advocated arming partisans with mines. While Rains did not introduce the use of subterras by partisans, he seems to have wholeheartedly supported it. The originator of the idea seems to have been A. R. Boteler who, in August 1863, discussed with Colonel John Mosby the possibility of using Rains's subterras against the Orange and Alexandria Railroads in Virginia. Confederate Chief of Ordnance Josiah Gorgas expressed doubts as to the use of the subterras by Mosby "unless these torpedoes can be continually replaced," and added that, "To use them once only is to irritate, not intimidate." His concerns were justified, because Mosby and other partisans' actions often served merely to infuriate the enemy into taking harsh actions against area civilians.[58]

The South also used command-detonated mines, similar to those discussed by James Saint Claire Morton in the late 1850s. A good example of this type of defense is that used by Colonel William Lamb at Fort Fisher near Wilmington, North Carolina.

Faced with defenses that "amounted to nothing," his troops built an earthwork fortification he describes as being of "[s]uch magnitude that it could withstand the heaviest fire of any guns in the American navy." Lamb relied on torpedoes as part of his defenses, establishing three lines of modified electric sea mines buried along the land face of the fort placed in such a manner that they could be set off independently and "blow up consecutively three advancing columns." According to R. O. Crowley, an electrician assigned to the fort, the mines were "copper tanks of a capacity of several hundred pounds of powder" armed with English made Abel fuses and Wheatstone exploders that had recently come through the blockade. The tanks were buried at a depth of three feet about 300 yards in front of the fort, and their wires connected to detonators in trenches near the fort.[59] Inside the line of subterras was "a heavy palisade of sharpened logs nine feet high, pierced for musketry, and so laid out as to have an enfilading [raking] field of fire on the centre." In addition, the fort had a large number of heavily entrenched artillery pieces.[60]

In December 1864, following what James McPherson describes as the "heaviest bombardment of the war," Union Major General Benjamin Butler landed a group of infantry on the beaches surrounding Fort Fisher. Despite the pummeling the Confederates received, Union troops took heavy artillery fire and discovered the area in front of the fort had been mined. Butler was soon forced to withdraw his men. In his memoirs, Butler refers to Fort Fisher as "the strongest earthwork built by the Confederacy" and speaks of its strong defense, including "subterran torpedoes," which were placed "so as to blow up any assaulting column coming down the beach to attack the fort." In January 1865, the second assault succeeded, in part, because the wires leading to the land torpedoes were destroyed during the bombardment, as were many of the fort's guns.[61]

In general, the Union army did not use landmines during the war as by the time mines came into widespread use, the North was not in a defensive position. They did, however, conduct the more traditional form of siege mine warfare taught by Sebastien LePrestre de Vauban and Simon Francis Gay de Vernon and attempted to explode charges under rebel positions. Perhaps the best known, and most disastrous, of these attempts was the ill-fated Battle of the Crater at Petersburg, Virginia, where Union miners attempted to use a traditional mine filled with some four tons of explosives to blow a gap in the Confederate lines. Unfortunately for the Union, the attack was poorly planned, and Union troops were pushed back into the crater and made easy targets for the Southern defenders.[62] While the Union army may not have readily adopted the subterra, most of its officers seem to have come to terms with the weapon by the war's end. However, there remained a steadfast resistance to accepting the weapon's use behind their lines or as booby traps.

Despite this resistance, by mid-1864, subterra units began to appear in the Union army. While only scant mention is made of the mines in the *Official Records,* Captain W. R. King sheds some light on the subject in his post-Civil War work, *Torpedoes.*[63]

According to a letter to King from Lieutenant Charles A. Suter, Engineering Corps, one of the most common Union mines was a railway mine designed by Captain Charles S. Smith. It consisted of one or more mines attached to a percussion fuse. The mine was composed of a tarred box containing a charge of black powder. The firing device consisted of a lever attached to a rifle lock. When the lever was tripped, the rifle lock was released, igniting a powder train that led to the mine.[64]

To lay one of Smith's mines, the spikes from a section of rail were removed so that the rail could be lifted and one or more timbers removed. A hole was then dug underneath the removed timber and the mine placed in the hole. The timber was then returned to its original position. Another hole was dug several timbers away and the lock placed so that its trigger rested on the timber. The rail was then carefully replaced so that it rested lightly on the firing lever, and the mine connected to the lock. The weight of a passing train would trigger the firing lock and detonate the mine. To prevent the mine from being detected, Suter recommended that the earth dug up during the planting of the mine be carried off so that it would not be seen.[65]

Each part of the mine was designed to be carried by one person, with only one man needed to carry each mine and one man needed to carry the lock. The squad was to be sent out behind enemy lines, work at night, and rest during the day. By varying the lengths of the fuses, they could choose which car would be destroyed. Their primary targets were the irreplaceable southern locomotives. Success could be achieved with a charge of as little as 18 pounds of powder, though the inventor recommended a charge of between 20 and 30 pounds. While the Federals conducted numerous tests of Smith's invention, it appears they did not employ it in the field.[66]

The North also appears to have had its own subterra shell, though it was basically a copy of Rains's modified artillery shell. King describes the Union land torpedo as "essentially the same as the [rebel] 'ground torpedo.'" Unfortunately, King offers no description of how, when, or even if Union forces ever applied the weapon.[67]

By the time of Lee's surrender at Appomattox, most of the officers in the Confederate military had fully accepted the use of mines in warfare, though the booby traps of Yorktown remained unpopular. Around November 1864, Rains wrote Secretary of War Seddon that the Torpedo Bureau had already planted 1,298 subterras and emphasized that mines "seem to be popular with our officers and are planted as fast as our limited means will permit, say 100 per diem."[68] By 1865, the Confederates had employed landmines in almost every theater of the war, from Virginia to Texas, albeit with varying degrees of success. President Davis's postwar writings reveal a continued faith in the use of landmines, particularly pressure-sensitive mines.[69]

The North meted out no punishment to the men responsible for either the Torpedo Bureau or the Submarine Battery Service. The end of the war found Rains in Richmond. He spent the next ten years in semiretirement in Augusta, and Atlanta, Georgia. In 1877, Rains became a civilian employee of the United States Government in Charleston, where the one-time general served as a clerk at the United States Quartermaster Depot until the year before his death in 1881.[70] Hunter Davidson, on the other hand, served in the military of several foreign governments, including Venezuela and Argentina, and entered into a running argument with Jefferson Davis as to the history of torpedo warfare during the Civil War. A degree of mystery still surrounds the Torpedo Bureau. The majority of its records were destroyed at the end of the war, and few members of the Torpedo Bureau or Submarine Battery Service ever published accounts of their activities.[71]

By the end of the Civil War, the idea of landmine warfare had taken root in the American military. The new weapon had been used in all theaters of operations and, with the exception of remotely delivered mines, had been used in most of its modern forms: in the traditional form of an area denial weapon designed to secure a perimeter; as a way to block pursuit; as a means to deny the enemy easy use of transportation routes; and as a command-detonated defensive weapon. The American military had been forced to address ethical issues of landmine warfare as well, particularly the question of when it was allowable to use mines. General Berry's feeling that mining should be conducted only in areas obviously prepared for defense held sway in the American military through World War I.

The effect of landmines on civilian populations and friendly troops also became an issue during this period. Rains devised systems that allowed mines to be put in place and not armed until needed, allowing civilian traffic to pass over them safely, though this system was successful only in areas with a sympathetic civilian population. With his lantern system, Rains anticipated the need for friendly forces to be able to safely navigate a minefield during operations. In addition, the Union reaction to landmines during their advance into South Carolina showed the potential for retaliation by soldiers against civilians in areas that had been mined and foreshadowed problems the American military would face in the war in Vietnam. Sea mines too had proved their worth during the war. On the coasts and in the rivers, the presence of mines slowed and sometimes prevented an enemy advance into an area, particularly if the mines were covered by artillery fire. Southern sea mines were responsible for sinking 29 Union ships and damaging another 14. In the years after the war, the success of rebel sea mines helped encourage calls for the use of defensive mines to guard the American coast. Southern mining efforts did not go unnoticed in Europe either, and they encouraged fresh mining efforts even before the Civil War was over.[72]

4

The Sea Mine Comes of Age

AT THE SAME TIME that the United States was embroiled in civil war, countries in Europe were entering into agreements on the conduct of war. The groundwork for these agreements was laid in the Resolutions of the Geneva International Conference held in Geneva, Switzerland, October 26–29, 1863. The conference resolutions called for the formation of civilian committees to assist in caring for wounded soldiers and recommended that "belligerent nations should proclaim the neutrality of ambulances and military hospitals." A year later, on August 22, 1864, twelve West European countries signed the Convention for the Amelioration of the Condition of the Wounded in Armies in the Field, based in large part on the conference of the previous year. In 1868, an international military commission took the process of regulating war a step further with the Declaration Renouncing the Use, in Time of War, of Certain Explosive Projectiles, banning the use of explosive or inflammable projectiles under 400 grams. Anticipating the rapidly changing nature of war, the treaty also called for further meetings "in view of future improvements which science may effect in the armament of troops...to conciliate the necessities of war with the laws of humanity." With the Industrial Revolution in full swing, science would bring a host of new weapons for future conferences to deal with, including new and improved types of mines.[1]

Sea mines drew increasing attention worldwide in the years during and after the American Civil War. The Danes, having encountered Prussian mines during their 1848 war in Schleswig-Holstein and having observed the success of Confederate mines, now used the weapon against the Prussians in their 1864 war over Schleswig-Holstein. On the island of Funen, the Danes relied on electric observation mines. On the island of Als (Alsen), they used contact mines with a unique potassium-based fuse. A large glass bottle was fitted inside a 20 inch x 20 inch x 24 inch wooden box. The bottle was then filled with around 25 pounds of powder—about halfway—which left enough air so that bottle would still float. The fuse was made from a J-shaped glass tub, closed on the long end and open at the other. A small amount of naphtha, a petroleum distillate, and three or four tablets of potassium were then put into the tube, and the open end sealed with parchment paper. The bottom of the tube was then put into a rubber bag of gunpowder, and the whole affair was placed into the glass bottle such that the long end was still sticking out. A cork was then slipped over the tube and cemented into place to seal the mine. Once the mine was anchored in place, the protruding glass was liable to be broken by a passing ship. When this happened, water poured into the tube, mixing with the potassium as it displaced the naphtha to the end of the J and causing an almost instantaneous ignition of the potassium, which in turn set off the naphtha, blowing out the parchment, firing the surrounding powder and the mine as a whole. The beauty of the design was that if the tube broke in the air while the mine was being transported, the mine was perfectly safe. In the end, however, the Prussians did not attack in the mined area. With the exception of a large pontoon, the mines caused no casualties.[2]

Torpedoes saw service again in Europe two years later during the 1866 Seven Weeks' War between Austria and Prussia, as the Austrians attempted to protect their cities in Italy, including Venice, from Italian incursions. The Austrian mines initially were similar to those they used in the 1859 Italian War for Independence. While their previous efforts had relied on observation stations equipped with a camera obscura, it was evident from the beginning that Venice and some of the other ports lacked good places for observation posts. The solution was to build contact-fused mines that used an electrical detonator, allowing the minefield to be turned on and off as needed. A narrow channel was left in the minefield to lessen the chance that a passing friendly ship might damage one of the deactivated mines. The three-foot long cylindrical mine casing was made of iron and was 3.5 feet in diameter. Each mine held around 300 pounds of powder and had multiple contact points. While the Austrian mines caused few if any casualties among the enemy, the new design was considered to be one of the best of its time.[3]

In 1868, Prussian scientist Dr. Albert Hertz developed a new fuse for sea mines. Known as the Hertz Horn, the fuse was made by placing a carbon plate, a zinc plate, and a glass vial of bichromate in a bulge on the side of the mine. When a ship hit the bulge, it crushed the vial of bichromate that then mixed with the metal plates. The result created a battery and an electric charge that detonated the mine. Ultimately, the Prussian mines and their German successors had a number of these fuses on each mine, much like the multifused keg mines of the American Civil War. The Hertz Horn ended up being one of the most successful designs in the development of sea mines, and variants of it are still in use.[4]

The militaries of Latin America had also paid attention to the Confederate mining efforts during the Civil War. As the war drew to a close, a number of Confederate officers and government officials left the South and formed émigré communities or entered into the service of other governments. Latin America was a common destination. Some of those fleeing had a background in mine warfare, most notably Hunter Davidson who served with both the Argentinean and Venezuelan militaries. Not surprisingly, many of the men involved in mining carried on their work with their new employers. In 1866, a group of these veterans helped establish a series of command-detonated sea mines to guard the Peruvian city Callao against Spanish efforts to take the city during the Spanish-Peruvian War (1864–1866). The Paraguayan military also employed mines in their ill-fated war with Brazil, Argentina, and Uruguay, the War of the Triple Alliance (1864–1870). Fought in part over Brazilian intervention in Uruguay, much of the fighting occurred on the Paraguay and Paraná Rivers, areas ideally suited for mine warfare. Some of the mines were the work of a former member of the American Navy, Thomas H. Bell. Ironically, the man hired by the Brazil navy to counter these mines was the former Confederate chief engineer, James H. Tomb, a veteran of the torpedo service in Charleston and other areas.[5]

When Tomb arrived in Brazil in 1866, the country's army and navy were stalled on the Paraguay River as they tried to decide what to do about the mines put out by the Paraguayan military. Tomb soon gained entry into the Brazilian navy and, given his background, was asked if he could do something about the torpedoes. He soon produced plans for a device designed to be mounted on the front of a ship to snag the mines. Upon presenting his plans, he was asked if he would be confident enough in the device to "go up on the ship when the attachment was in place?" When he replied that he would, he was given the needed resources and sent to the front. He fitted his mine sweeper onto the ironclad *Tamandaré* and soon was sleeping soundly below deck—the only officer comfortable enough to do so.[6]

The Paraguayans used a variety of mines on the river. One arrangement, often used at night, was similar to David Bushnell's and Matthew Fontaine Maury's early mines but used two canoes instead of barrels. One canoe was fitted with a box filled with 200 to 500 pounds of gunpowder and a gun as a firing device. A cord was attached to the gun and to a second canoe further upstream. When the cord was pulled taut, the gun would discharge, detonating the main charge. In at least some cases, an observer in the second canoe would pull the cord to detonate the charges. According to Tomb, these could be seen fairly easily and "never did any damage to us." Other mines were anchored to the bottom of the river and used a sulfuric acid-based contact fuse similar to the ones developed by Immanuel Nobel and Gabriel Rains. Containing 100 to 300 pounds of powder in a long cylindrical zinc body, these mines used a long metal bar as a trigger and were usually set to hover three to five feet below the surface of the water. The Paraguayans also used observation mines, which tended to be rather large. Upon discovering one of these mines, Tomb found it to be filled with 700 pounds of powder; a second one held 500 pounds. These also used a sulfuric acid fuse. In this case, the mine was designed to be set off when a cord was pulled from shore, forcing a small piston into the glass vial holding the acid. As in many instances, the powder in the mines was fouled with water, in part due to shoddy construction. This discovery, however, did little to assuage the minds of the Brazilian officers—nor should it have.[7]

As the Brazilian navy moved up the river toward Asuncion, the Paraguayan capital, they found the way partially blocked by a series of piles. Admiral Tamandaré ordered Tomb to reconnoiter the area and search for torpedoes. Armed with a set of cutters and a grapnel, Tomb and his men found an 80-foot gap in the obstruction. They also found a shore battery and what appeared to be at least three torpedoes just under the surface of the water. On their way back, they met with the ironclad *Rio de Janeiro* and alerted her commander, Captain Americo Silvado, to both the gap and to the presence of mines. In the morning, *Rio de Janeiro* and two other ironclads, *Brazil* and *Bahia,* moved up the river to engage the enemy battery. As *Rio* exchanged fire with the shore battery, the Captain apparently forgot about the mines and allowed his stern to drift over one of the torpedoes. Tomb relates that what followed was "an instantaneous explosion and a great column of water…in a few minutes the ship went down with most of the officers and crew." The Brazilians found other mines as they made their way up the river to Asuncion. While the devices slowed the Brazilian advance, the destruction of *Rio de Janeiro* was Paraguay's only major success in its mining efforts.[8]

As evidenced by the success of the Paraguayan mines in slowing the advance of Brazilian forces, naval mines by this stage did not have to cause many casualties to be successful. This idea was reinforced by the Prussian use of sea mines in the Franco-Prussian War (1870–1871). As the war began, the Prussians found themselves short of supplies and quickly announced in the press that they had mined the approaches to their harbors. The warnings were soon picked up by the French press and republished. In the meantime, the Prussians began putting out as many mines as they could, including dummy mines in cases when they did not have enough live ones. The Prussians employed both electrically and chemically fused contact mines. The latter variety relied on a sulfuric acid based fuse, and the former relied on a metal plate sealed inside glass. When the glass was broken by a passing ship, the influx of sea water completed the circuit, setting off the mine. Ironically, the chemically fused mines probably injured more Prussians than French as they proved difficult to transport and killed 30–40 men in accidents. That said, despite Prussia not having a navy, its ports were never invaded, nor were they effectively blockaded, as the French navy dared not risk the minefields, particularly in view of the rising cost of building ships, which accompanied the introduction of the ironclad. The Russians had similar successes with mines in the Black Sea during the Russo-Turkish War (1877–1878). Despite having virtually no navy in the region, Russian mines helped prevent Turkish sea attacks on anything larger than a small village.[9]

The popularity of the sea mine was not, however, unchallenged. By the mid-nineteenth century, the term torpedo had been synonymous with what is now considered a mine. During the American Civil War, with the introduction of the spar torpedo, the word began to take on another meaning. The definition of torpedo was further expanded when the Royal Navy's Captain John Harvey designed a torpedo in the 1860s that could be towed from the bow of a ship so that it would pass underneath its victim. Robert Whitehead's development of the automobile or fish torpedo further complicated the definition. Whitehead's invention, a self-powered, unmanned explosive device that could be fired at the enemy from a tube ultimately became the definition for a torpedo. It also gained tremendous popularity and, by the 1870s and 1880s, began to eclipse the sea mine as the weapon that people felt would change the nature of naval warfare. By the 1890s, what had previously been referred to as stationary torpedoes were now simply called mines. Despite the surge in interest in the automobile torpedo, sea mines still drew a following, particularly in the United States.[10]

While navies around the world were modernizing in the 1870s, the United States was looking inward, struggling through the process of rebuilding after the Civil War. Expenditures on new naval vessels and the development of new military technology in general were limited. As the nation began to look outward again in the early 1880s, it found its military technology lacking, and members of the public began clamoring for an increase in military spending. One of the biggest concerns in the debate was the safety of the American coastline, and it became a frequent topic in mainstream publications. Many of the writers concerned with national security tied their hopes at least in part on the use of sea mines.

A common question was what effect mines would have on the balance of power at sea. In 1877, an American author writing under the name Isaac Newton poised the question, "Has the Day of the Great Navies Passed?" as the title of his article. The article, published in *The Galaxy,* contrasted the expense of a new ironclad, around $2.5 million, as being comparable to the cost of providing sea mines for most of the American coast, stating that "Less than the cost of one of these ships would supply abundant submarine defenses such as the skill of our engineers have produced to destroy a fleet of these monster iron-clads...." Much like Confederate officers the previous decade, the author stressed the importance of developing the submarine torpedo given the small size of the American Navy and the nation's long coastline, adding that the weapon could "neutralize the greatest navies of the world, and all of them put together." The debate continued in the 1880s as the public became increasingly concerned with the state of the country's defenses. Articles such as "Our Defenseless Coasts" and "Our Sea-Defenses" clamored for an increase in defense spending, pointing out that spending on new fortifications had ended in 1875 and that only a few hundred thousand dollars a year were allotted for maintenance. In their eyes, American defenses were a full generation behind those of Europe, America having decided "to do absolutely nothing...while other nations are spending millions." The articles, citing reports from both the army and navy, called for establishing new fortifications, updating shore batteries, building torpedo boats, and putting out extensive submarine minefields. Given the desperate state the authors felt the country's coastal fortifications were in, "it seems impossible that Congress should still neglect to make provisions for our defenseless coast."[11]

Ironically, the country's next experience with the threat of mines, which came during the Spanish-American War, came not in using them in defense of the American coast, but rather as a pretext for going to war. In January 1898, the battleship USS *Maine* arrived in the port of Havana, Cuba, to protect American interests in the wake of proindependence riots against the Spanish government. Tensions between Spain and the United States were high, as the American government was bringing increasing pressure on the Spanish government to give the colony autonomy if not outright independence. To lessen the chance of incidents ashore, the *Maine's* commander, Captain Charles Sigsbee, chose not to let the crew take liberty in port. Only officers were allowed to go ashore. At 9:40 on the night of February 15, the ship exploded, killing 266 of the ship's crew of 354. Immediately after the explosion, Captain Sigsbee ordered his men to prepare to repel borders. Sigsbee was convinced the explosion had come from outside the ship. Most Americans agreed with Sigsbee, and the press in the United States began calling for war with Spain. A Spanish inquiry found that the *Maine* had been destroyed by an internal explosion. In March, an American commission disagreed, finding that at least one of the two explosions that sank the *Maine* had been caused by a mine planted under the ship. The country was now ready for war, rallying around the battle cry "Remember the Maine." Almost 90 years later, Admiral Hyman Rickover ordered a group of naval historians to revisit the incident. They found the explosion had been internal, probably caused by an accident in the ship's coal bunkers.[12]

While the mine blamed for destroying the *Maine* proved illusionary, Spanish mines in other areas proved much more real, even if often ineffective. America's military buildup of the mid-1880s left her with a modern navy much superior to that of Spain, particularly the Spanish fleet deployed in the Americas and in the Philippines, and Spanish commanders often turned to mines as a way to try to offset the odds. In the Philippines, Admiral Patricio Montojo argued for forming his defensive of the west side of the island in Subic Bay. His plan was to block the harbor's eastern entrance by sinking ships in the channel and then group his ships behind a line of 14 sea mines—the total that he had available—and use land batteries to help rebuff an American attack. Motojo had little faith that his ragtag fleet would be much of a match for the American fleet headed to the islands from Hong Kong and made frequent requests to the minister of the marines for men and equipment. He was met only with calls for using "zeal and activity" to make up for the shortcomings in supply. At one point the minister ordered the admiral to seal off the ports with mines. Montojo mournfully replied "You know I have not torpedoes. I will do it when I can." The minister sent 70 mines, none of which arrived before the American fleet.[13]

When Montojo arrived in Subic Bay with the Spanish fleet on April 26, he found the defenses in shambles. Little had been accomplished. Guns remained unmounted, and only five of the mines were in place. Faced with the impending arrival of the American fleet under Admiral George Dewey, the Spanish admiral decided to regroup his forces and make his stand in Manila Bay. What few mines were available were placed in the channels leading into the bay, Boca Chica and Boca Grande. These were covered by gun emplacements. Unfortunately for the Spanish, nine of the 17 guns covering the channels were muzzle loaders. These were characteristic of the problems Montojo faced in general: not only was his fleet outgunned by Dewey's, it was also outclassed. While the American fleet was composed largely of modern vessels, the Spanish fleet was composed of older vessels, none of which had armored decks to protect them from plunging fire. The largest of the Spanish ships, *Castilla*, was not even made of steel and iron: it was wooden.[14]

While Dewey had received intelligence that the channels leading into the bay were mined, he felt the devices posed little threat to his fleet, particularly if the fleet entered the harbor through Boca Grande where the water was deep enough that the anchored mines would not be effective. He also had doubts that the mines themselves would even work because he felt the mines would probably prove unreliable once they had been exposed to the tropical waters and environment for very long. He was partially correct. Dewey began his attack on the morning of May 1. As the Spanish batteries began firing on the American fleet, the Spanish detonated two observation mines in front of the lead ship, the battleship *Olympia.* Accounts are unclear as to why the mines were fired when they were, but rumors soon circulated that the Spanish torpedo boat captains had refused to mount an attack if they were forced to go over active mines. The battle of Manila Bay itself was decisive and relatively short. By 2:00 P.M. the Spanish had surrendered. None of the Spanish mines claimed an American ship. The mines in Boca Chica did, however, cause the men onboard *Raleigh* some consternation a few days after the battle as the ship returned from picking up Spanish prisoners on the island of Corregidor. As the ship began drifting into the channel, a Spanish officer onboard began begging to be sent ashore. *Raleigh,* he informed the Americans, was drifting into a minefield. He was, of course, correct. Happily for all concerned, the contact mines had been placed in water too deep for them to be effective.[15]

The Spanish had more success with their mining efforts at Santiago in Cuba. Santiago was an obvious target for the Americans because the Spanish fleet under Admiral Pascual Cervera y Topete was based there. The Spanish position was complicated by the presence of Cuban insurgents. In April, General Jose Toral began looking at ways to strengthen the city's defenses and decided to deploy a series of mines across the entrance to the channel leading to the city. The passage was an ideal place to use mines. The entrance to the four mile channel was long and narrow and difficult to navigate under normal circumstances. In addition, the mines could be covered with guns placed on the bluffs above the entrance. The Spanish placed two lines of observation mines in the channel: a row of seven on April 21 and a row of six on April 27. Combined with covering fire from above, the mines posed a serious obstacle as, unless the Americans secured the heights, anyone trying to clear the mines would be under constant fire.[16]

When the American fleet under Rear Admiral William Sampson arrived on the Cuban coast off Santiago in June, he expressed reservations about trying to force his way through the minefield under fire and called for the army to take the heights above the channel and blockade the port, lest the Spanish fleet escape. Sampson had asked the army to land close by the heights and storm the fortifications quickly. The army commander, Major General William Shafter, however, had other ideas. Concerned that the Spanish defensive positions were too strong, he decided to land his forces at Daiquiri and attack the city itself. The campaign, which began on June 22, proved more arduous than Shafter had thought. In addition to the Spanish, the army had to deal with supply problems and disease, both of which took a heavy toll. On July 2, Sampson pressed him to take the heights. Shafter responded harshly, "If they are as difficult to seize as those we have already been pitted against, it will require some time and many casualties. I am at a loss to understand why the navy cannot work as well under destructive fire as the army. My losses yesterday were more than 500." Sampson, frustrated by the lack of progress, resigned himself to the fact that the heights would not be taken. He sent for mine clearing equipment at Guantanamo and prepared to force his way through the channel. Fortunately for the Americans, Admiral Cervera decided to try to break the blockade the following day. His ships were hunted down and destroyed. After hearing of Cervera's defeat, the city sued for peace. The mines, while never used, had kept the American fleet at bay and forced the American Army to undertake a costly campaign.[17]

American forces had fared better at the battle for Guantanamo the month before where they were able to undertake mine-sweeping efforts. Initial attempts were made under cover darkness with a steam launch using grappling lines. After dragging across the channel several times, the boat ran aground and only narrowly escaped detection before it made its way back to the fleet. Later operations relied on pairs of boats—a steam launch and a whaleboat—to drag for the mines. The boats ran a rope between them with a chain drag in the middle. When the pair grappled onto a mine, they moved together, and the mine was pulled to the surface where it was disarmed. In all, two pairs of boats recovered 14 of the Spanish mines—in some cases while under fire from shore.[18]

Despite the mixed success of the Spanish mines, it was clear the weapon held great potential. While Dewey was not slowed by the Spanish mines at Manila, the mines were poorly placed. When used correctly, the mines kept the Sampson fleet from entering Santiago and tied up a large American force onshore trying to seize the heights covering the channel entrance. Sea mines proved their worth again a few years later in the Russo-Japanese War. While the Russo-Japanese War brought attention to the sea mine as an effective weapon, it also drew attention to failings of another weapon, the landmine.

In the United States and elsewhere, the landmine was much less celebrated than its sibling. When the weapon was discussed, it was usually as part of a discourse on mine warfare in general. In the United States, naval officers were responsible for many of the early studies on torpedo warfare. Among the more prominent of the works during this period were Lieutenant Commander J. S. Barnes's *Submarine Warfare, Offensive and Defensive* (1869) and Lieutenant Commander Royal Bradford's *A History of Torpedo Warfare* (1882). Both officers were particularly interested in the fuses used by the Russians during the Crimean War and those developed by Gabriel

Rains during the Civil War. Much of their information on mine warfare in the later war was drawn from one of the few Army reports on mine warfare, Major W. R. King's work, *Torpedoes: Their Invention and Use, from the First Application to the Art of War to the Present Time.* Interestingly, the work was commissioned by the Chief of the Army Engineers, Major General Richard Delafield, whose writings on mine warfare during the Crimean War had been so persuasive to then Secretary of War Jefferson Davis. *Torpedoes* proved to be one of the most influential studies on mine warfare published in the years after the American Civil War, even if its influence was mainly felt in naval circles.[19]

King made four main observations on the use of landmines. First, he pointed out that mines tended not to be exploded at the time planned. Second, he said that the mines damaged only a small area. His third observation was that accidents seemed to be commonplace among people using torpedoes. Finally, he stated that these accidents made the mines, "aside from moral effect...nearly as dangerous to friends as foes." King added in a footnote that, while one cannot determine the exact psychological value of subterras, "the knowledge or even suspicion, of the presence of torpedoes, has doubtless prevented many an attack on both land and sea." King's statements were far from a resounding endorsement of the landmine.[20]

Concerned about the dangers of handling the "sensitive shell," mines that explode upon contact, and the problems posed by firing an observation mine, King designed his own mine, which he felt incorporated the best features of both types. The improvised mine was based on a 15-inch artillery shell. To increase the number of fragments when the shell exploded, King recommended cutting two-inch squares into the shell's surface. While the mine could function as a command-detonated mine, it also worked as a contact mine when someone pressed down a spring by stepping on the ground above the mine. King suggested placing a large flat stone under the mine to direct the force of the explosion upwards and enhance the effectiveness of the mine. A trio of wooden beams on the side of the mine facing away from the target served a similar purpose.[21] The principal advantage of King's creation was that it could be fired from a distance or automatically. As King relied on electricity in both instances to fire his mine, the mine could be turned on and off at will and was harmless when not connected to a battery, making its transportation and deployment much safer than the mines designed by Rains and others during the Civil War. In many ways, King's plan anticipated the ideas that were adopted for sea mines. His design, however, had a distinct drawback as the Russians discovered when deploying a similar style mine in the Russo-Japanese War. In the event the wires to the mine were cut during an artillery barrage, the mine would be rendered useless.[22]

King's design remained a staple in the American Army's discussion of landmines for the next ten years and was included in Captain O. H. Ernest's 1873 work, *A Manual of Practical Military Engineering*. Ernest expressed reservations about both contact- and observation-fired mines and recommended King's design because it allowed the arming of the weapon from a distance, "thus combining the advantages of both methods of explosion." All of the above weapons were to be constructed in the field rather than mass produced.[23]

By the time of Captain William D. Beach's 1894 edition of *A Manual of Field Engineering for the Use of Officers and Troops of the Line,* the term torpedo had been dropped and the term landmine had become part of the American military vocabulary. Beach defined landmines as "small mines placed in the line of advance of the enemy and exploded either by electricity or fuze from the defense." The mines Beach discussed, however, were not as sophisticated as those discussed by his predecessor Ernest. Surprisingly, Beach did not recommend or even mention the possibilities presented by the pressure-sensitive fuse. The landmine he discussed resembled a fougasse more than anything else. Constructing the mine consisted of digging a hole two to three yards deep and placing a box containing a 25- to 80-pound charge in a shallow hole dug in one corner. Wires were attached to the charge, and the hole filled in. After the wires were run back to the main works, they were attached to a battery. There is little evidence, however, that any of these designs were frequently used in practice by the American Army.[24]

Landmines did appear occasionally in European wars. The British used them in their colonial wars, particularly during the Boer War where they found mines helpful in stopping Boer raiding parties from destroying bridges and railroads. In addition, the British used makeshift mines in their wars in Sudan and against the Zulu. In general, however, the British mines lacked the sophistication of the earlier Confederate landmines of the Civil War and relied on rifle trigger mechanisms. One European power, Russia, did invest in continuing the development of landmines.[25]

The American and international militaries' view of landmines in the early twentieth century was, at least in part, influenced by the Russian use of landmines during the Russo-Japanese War (1904–1905) a war that ironically was fought neither in Japan nor in Russia, but rather on the Liaodong Peninsula of China over Russian influence in China. Most major countries, including the United States, sent observers to study the war. The war was seen as a significant chance to observe new weapons and techniques, particularly the role of the general staff. One American observer, Major Joseph Kuhn, described the war as the "first great war between nations having modern arms and training since 1877." In his report, he also expressed a degree of disappointment, adding that most aspects of the war "savor strongly of the text-book."[26]

The Russians fought a primarily defensive war against the Japanese. As such, they relied heavily on obstacles to help secure their positions. These included barbed wire fences, wire entanglements, *troup-de-loups,* fougasses, and landmines. The Russians usually placed their mines between 50 and 200 meters from the main defensive works. In works protecting hills, mines were often buried in the ravines leading up to the hills, thus denying the Japanese easy access to a covered attack route. At the Battle of Nanshan, 35 miles northeast of Port Arthur (now Lushun), the Russian defensive perimeter

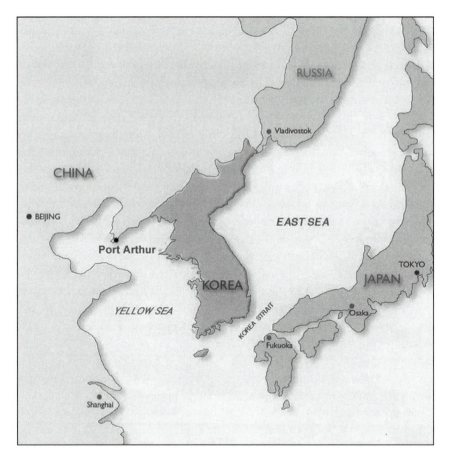

The location of the theater of operations in the Russo-Japanese War. (Courtesy of the University of Texas Libraries, The University of Texas at Austin. The map has been adapted by the author.)

included three miles of wire entanglements and some 84 mines and fougasses. The Russians used both contact- and command-detonated mines. The mines were generally iron containers or wooden boxes, each containing up to a 25-kilogram charge. Command-detonated mines were usually connected in series, allowing the mines to be detonated at the same time.[27]

During the Crimean War, the Russians had relied on a chemical fuse to detonate their contact mines. By 1904, they had replaced this with an electrical fuse. Major Kuhn described the mines as being "for the most part wooden boxes, 24 by 20 by 16 inches, soaked in tar or asphalt to make them waterproof and filled with powder and made to fire automatically by means of... [an] electric closer circuit." The closer circuit was attached to the top of the mine, and a board supported on the corners by coiled springs was placed on top of it. When someone stepped on the board, a metal ball (B) would complete the detonation circuit by touching a metal ring (C).[28] Much like the mine Major King recommended, the Russian mine had the advantage of being rendered harmless when not needed by simply turning off the electrical current to the minefield.

In addition to standard landmines, the Russians also relied on electrically detonated stone fougasses, similar to those described by Sebastien LePrestre de Vauban 100 years earlier. Neither fougasses nor landmines, however, caused heavy Japanese casualties. Overall, the Russian's principal success with

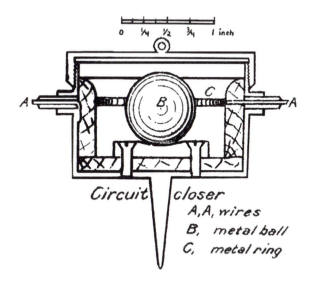

The fuse used on the Russian landmines in the Russo-Japanese War. (Joseph E. Kuhn, *Reports of Military Observers Attached to the Armies in Manchuria during the Russo-Japanese War,* Pt. 3: Report of Major Joseph E. Kuhn, Corps of Engineers [Washington, D.C.: Government Printing Office, 1906], Plate XXXIV.)

the weapon was in generating fear and in tying up their adversary's engineering troops. Tadayoshi Sakurai, a lieutenant in the Japanese army during the siege of Port Arthur, mentioned the problems posed by landmines several times in his memoirs, *Human Bullets*. In his general discussion of the strength of Port Arthur's defenses, he commented, "Each spot was made still more unapproachable by ground-mines, pitfalls, wire-entanglements, etc. There was hardly any space where even an ant could get in unmolested." Japanese engineers spent a considerable amount of time clearing the Russian obstacles, locating and cutting the electrical wires for the mines, and trying to cut through the mass of wire entanglements. While Russian obstacles slowed the Japanese advance, it was the new machine gun that caused heavy casualties and drew the attention of international observers.[29]

Sakurai described the machine gun as a "terrible engine of destruction" and related how the Russians would wait until the Japanese were almost to the defensive works and, "just at the moment we proposed to shout a triumphant *Banzai*, the dreadful machine would begin to sweep over us as if with the besom of destruction, the result being hills and mounds of dead." Major Kuhn, in his report to the War Department, pointed out the "telling success" the Russians had in using machine guns against the advancing Japanese. Of the landmines, Kuhn said that the Japanese reported "no noteworthy losses." Captain Carl Toepfer in a 1910 article on the war for the U.S. Army Corps of Engineers's *Professional Memoirs* added, "On the whole the moral effect which the detonation of the mine produces has, like always heretofore, been greater than the material loss." The British seemed unimpressed with the landmines as well, stating in their official history of the war that the landmines at Port Arthur "inflicted little or no loss upon the assailants." Overall, the landmine seemed ineffective and unnecessary. The failure of landmines to contribute significantly to the defense of Port Arthur, coupled with the success of the machine gun, left the militaries of the world relatively uninterested in the landmine.[30]

In contrast to their subterranean brethren, sea mines played an important role in the Russo-Japanese War. The Japanese surprise attack on the Russian fleet at Port Arthur on February 8, 1904, proved less of a success than the Japanese had hoped. Despite having successfully breached the harbor, Japanese torpedo boats were able to damage only three of the Russian ships, the cruiser *Pallada* and the battleships *Retvizan* and *Tsarevich*. All three soon returned to active service. This presented the Japanese with a question of how to neutralize the Russian fleet and blockade the port. When efforts to block the harbor entrance by sinking ships in the channel failed, the Japanese turned to mines, turning the tables on how the weapon should be used. Naval mines were now being used to keep the enemy in rather than to keep the enemy out. Japanese torpedo boats made frequent nocturnal visits to lay new minefields, some-times laying over 30 mines in a night. Their efforts proved effective, and the Russians were soon forced to expend a tremendous amount of effort dragging for Japanese mines, particularly when moving their larger ships.

Failing to clear the mines could have serious consequences. On the evening of April 12, Admiral Stepan Makaroff, the commander of the Russian squad-ron, noted the silhouettes of Japanese ships outside the harbor—presumably laying mines. These he said would have to be dragged for in the morning. During the night, however, the Russian destroyer *Strashni* became separated from a group of destroyers headed out on a scouting expedition. At daybreak, her captain found that the ships he had regrouped with during the night were part of the Japanese fleet. Upon discovering each other's identities, shots were exchanged. The Japanese cruisers unleashed a broadside. *Strashni* countered by firing a torpedo and wisely trying to beat a hasty retreat. Her run was quickly cut short and the ship sunk. In the meantime, Makaroff, alerted to the ship's plight, ordered the fleet to arms and joined the battleship *Petropav-lovsk,* one of the first ships to get underway. Makaroff and the rest of the fleet crossed the freshly laid field of some 30 mines without incident and arrived in time to support the Russian cruisers *Baian* and *Diana* in battle with the Jap-anese. The Russians began to gain the upper hand and the Japanese withdrew. As the Russian fleet returned to Port Arthur, it had to once again cross the minefield put in by the Japanese the previous night. Makaroff was not so for-tunate the second time. At 9:30 a.m., *Petropavlovsk* hit a mine and was rocked by a series of three explosions: the detonation of the mine followed quickly by the ship's magazine and then its boilers. In addition to a supply of 12-inch shells, the magazine held 15 mines, each holding around 180 pounds of gun-cotton. The magazine explosion destroyed the front end of the ship, and flames quickly spread across the vessel, consuming the masts, funnels, and bridge. Two minutes after hitting the mine, the great ship was gone, taking the admiral with it.[31]

The Russian fleet initially thought *Petropavlovsk* had been sunk by a sub-marine and began firing at phantom periscopes. After picking up the survi-vors from *Petropavlovsk,* the fleet resumed course for the harbor. Any misconceptions remaining about the presence of submarines were cleared up as the battleship *Pobieda* struck a mine, putting a 7-foot hole amid ship. *Pobieda* remained afloat, however, protected in part by her coal bunkers, and was brought back into port. The loss of the fleet's flag ship *Petropavlovsk* was a blow to the Russians. More crushing though was the loss of Admiral Makaroff in whom the men of the fleet had held complete confidence. Also lost were the fleet's chief of staff Rear Admiral Molas and four commanders. Of a crew of around 700, only 80 were rescued.[32]

The Japanese navy relied on a modified version of the Italian-designed Elia mine which, while it proved effective against *Petropavlovsk,* was prone to exploding from large swells or heavy currents and was difficult if not impossible to retrieve once it was laid. The cone-shaped mine was constructed of quarter-inch steel and held a charge of around 180 pounds of guncotton. It was attached to a reel on an anchor by a half-inch steel cable. During transport, the cable was wound tightly around the reel. Upon release in the water, anchor and mine sank to the bottom. As the anchor settled onto the sea floor, the mine released and floated toward the surface to a predetermined depth and was held in place by the cable. To help prevent damage to the minelayers, the mines were fitted with timers so that they would arm 15 minutes after being released. The depth settings could prove problematic as the mines often floated to a depth high enough to reach the larger cruisers and battleships, but not high enough to be effective against ships of a more shallow draft such as destroyers.[33]

The Japanese were not alone in their reliance on sea mines during the war. The Russian fleet began defensive mine-laying operations almost immediately after the initial attack on Port Arthur. While the minefields may have helped prevent the Japanese from entering the harbor again, they were not without cost. On February 11, only three days after the torpedo attack, the Russian mine ship *Yenisei* noticed a loose mine floating in the water. As the ship stopped to begin firing at the mine, the forward section of the ship drifted over another mine, which exploded. *Yenisei* sank within 15 minutes, taking almost half of her crew, including the captain, to the bottom. The cruiser *Boyarin,* sent to help *Yenisei,* also hit a mine. *Boyarin's* captain evacuated the ship. He scuttled it the next day. The loss of these two ships, coming on the heels of the Japanese attack, did nothing to help morale.[34]

The Russians used both contact and observation mines at Port Arthur. Of the two, the contact mines were by far the most common and were the only ones to inflict substantial casualties on the Japanese. The contact mines were generally of two varieties, a round mine that held 100 pounds of guncotton and a larger, buoy-shaped mine that held twice that amount. Both types were released in a manner similar to the Japanese mines and floated to a predetermined depth. The Russians deployed similar mines in their defenses at Vladivostok in Siberia. Here, too, they lost several ships from their own mines. Overall, however, the Russian mines proved successful in deterring Japanese incursions at Port Arthur. By the time the city surrendered in December 1904, the Japanese had lost no fewer than nine ships to Russian mines. Perhaps the most dramatic of these losses occurred on May 15, 1904, as the Japanese 2nd Battleship Division patrolled the harbor entrance, something they did on a regular basis. The Division had already safely passed over the Russian minefield twice that morning. At 10:10, however, the battleship *Yashima* struck a Russian mine. The resulting explosion could be seen by the Russian forces on shore. By 10:40, the crew of *Yashima* had gotten her back on an even keel, and the column began to reform. As the battleship *Hatsuse* moved to join the group, it was rocked by the explosion of yet another mine. A second explosion, possibly from her magazine, could be heard from shore. The ship lasted only a short time. A Russian sailor who witnessed the explosions was asked how quickly *Hatsuse* sank: "More quickly than *Petropavlovsk*," he replied. When pressed as to how he could tell, he responded simply, "I was on *Petropavlovsk*."[35]

In the end, the Russian mines saved neither the city nor the fleet. Japanese mines made it more difficult for Russian ships to escape before the end. The destroyer *Serditi,* one of a handful of smaller ships that made it out, hit a mine as it left the harbor but was able to escape. Most of the remaining Russian ships, including all of the fleet's cruisers and battleships, were scuttled as the Japanese land forces advanced on the harbor. The Russian navy had been convinced the city would not be surrendered and that the fleet could be raised once the city was relieved by the Russian fleet under Vice Admiral Zinovy Rozhestvensky. His fleet was nowhere near Port Arthur when the city fell on December 20, 1904.[36]

Rozhestvensky's fleet was destroyed by the Japanese five months later at the Battle of Tsushima. Here, too, the Japanese had planned to use mines, in this case, a floating offensive mine known as a linked mine. The linked mine was made up of four contact mines strung together by 100 meters of rope and then put out in front of an oncoming enemy fleet. Unanchored, these drift mines posed problems long after the war was over. The Japanese had used linked mines at the Battle of the Yellow Sea on August 10, 1904, when the Russian fleet tried to break out of Port Arthur, but the mines were spotted and the fleet managed to avoid them. In the eyes of the Japanese commander at Tsushima, Admiral Heihachiro Togo, the linked mines seemed an ideal weapon, they could be put out by small boats in advance of the Russian fleet at little or no risk, but with the potential to great damage if they were not discovered before the fleet reached them. Admiral Rozhestvensky was well aware of the potential danger and sent a warning out to his fleet. The warning proved to be for naught as heavy seas forced Togo to cancel the mine attack. The seas did not, however, save the Russian fleet, which was destroyed, forcing the tsar to sue for peace. Linked mines remained an integral part of Japanese battle tactics until 1930 when aircraft and high-speed battleships rendered them obsolete.[37]

The fighting at Port Arthur had demonstrated the power of mines at sea. Both sides suffered significant losses from mines and were forced to expend tremendous efforts on the daily task of clearing the mines laid the night before by the enemy. The Russians in particular also had to deal with the problems of mines—both their own and Japanese—that had broken their moorings and floated into the harbor or onto the beach itself. These mines posed a problem for civilians both during and after the war. Reports of merchant ships being sunk by mines from the war continued for several years. Not reaching the paper were the numerous deaths of Chinese civilians from these mines, both on the open seas and in Chinese waters. The Chinese delegation to the Second International Peace Conference at the Hague in 1907 addressed the issue in dire terms:

> In spite of every precaution being taken, a very considerable number of coasting trade boats, fishing boats, junks, and sampams have been sunk as a consequence of collisions with these automatic submarine contact mines, and their vessels have been utterly lost with their cargoes without details of the disasters reaching the western world. It is calculated that from five to six hundred of our country men in the pursuit of their peaceful occupations have met a cruel death through these dangerous engines.

Not surprisingly, the uproar caused by the errant mines left over from the Russo-Japanese War made the issue of regulating the use of sea mines one of the more controversial topics at the 1907 conference.[38]

The process for regulating war had begun in earnest in Geneva in 1863 and had moved in fits and starts through the remainder of the nineteenth century. In 1898, the Russian Tsar Nicholas II issued a call through the diplomatic corps for an international conference to regulate the use of weapons, in part motivated by a desire to stem the spending triggered by the ongoing European arms race. While the tsar had suggested that the conference be held in St. Petersburg, the Hague in the Netherlands was eventually selected as a more neutral location. The International Peace Conference of 1899—the First Hague Conference—met with mixed results. While the conference met with only limited success in addressing the arms race, it had addressed the rules of war, and, perhaps most importantly, it had taken the first steps toward the creation of an international court. Eight years later, representatives tried once again to codify the way war was fought.[39]

The Second International Peace Conference at the Hague in 1907 met with similar problems in halting the arms race but did succeed in its efforts to regulate the use of weapons. The use of sea mines was one of the more controversial items to be addressed at the conference. While it was clear to most of the delegates that there was a desperate need for regulating the use of sea mines, how the weapon should be regulated was not clear. The English representatives called for heavy regulation of submarine mines: unanchored contact mines should be prohibited, anchored contact mines should be designed so that they automatically disarmed if they broke loose from their moorings, mines should be used only inside the territorial waters of the nations involved in a conflict, and mines should not be used as part of a blockade. Perhaps most controversially, the British declared that any port which had sea mines in its waters should be considered a defended city and liable to bombardment, regardless of whether it had any other defenses. For the British, renouncing the use of sea mines offered few disadvantages: the Royal Navy, while having developed several types of mines, was decidedly more enamored of the torpedo and the submarine as defensive weapons. In addition, as the British had one of the largest commercial fleets, it had the most to lose as a neutral. In the case of war, the mine was still seen as a weapon of the underdog, meaning the British were unlikely to need the weapon and likely to encounter it.[40]

The other delegations disagreed with the British on a variety of points. The Japanese and Italians argued that an unanchored mine that disarmed itself within a short time should be allowed because it offered no real risk to civilian traffic if used correctly. The Dutch argued that neutral nations should be allowed to secure their ports, and a number of countries argued for the retention of defensive mines as a means to secure their coasts. The final agreement left the British feeling that the issue had not been completely dealt with and that there were significant gaps in rules. Unanchored mines were indeed forbidden, but an exception was made for mines that deactivated within an hour after being released. Anchored contact mines had to be built so that they automatically disarmed if they broke loose from their moorings. The agreement offered special protection for neutral and commerce ships. Contact mines were not to be used solely to target commercial shipping—neutral or otherwise. Once mines were abandoned, the belligerents were to notify ship owners where the mines were located and, upon the end of hostilities, the belligerents were required to remove any mines they had put out and to let their former opponents know where any mines in their waters were located. Neutrals were also allowed to use mines under the same rules, providing they notified ship owners of which areas to avoid. In the end, there was a consensus that, while the final agreement may not have proved the final answer to the problems posed by sea mines, it at least addressed the problems seen in the Russo-Japanese War.[41]

The 1907 Hague Convention provided guidance on a range of weapons systems including some whose use had just begun. When World War I came, however, many of the rules were bent if not outright ignored. These included prohibitions against the bombing or shelling of an undefended place, the dropping of explosives from balloons, and the use of poisonous gas. All of these were violated in spirit if not in fact.[42]

While landmines were not covered in the agreement, the question was already being addressed in some countries. The United States Army's 1909 publication, *The Engineer Field Manual,* provided readers with a discussion of how to construct mines in the field as well as appropriate tactics for using them. In addition, it set limits on the acceptable and legitimate uses of landmines:

> It is **not permissible** to plant such mines in any ground which is **not obviously** prepared for defense. Any person who ventures on such space does so at his own peril, but if there is a road or path open to passage through such ground[,] mines must not be placed therein, or in a place where the explosion would injure persons occupying the road. If any defensive works or recognized obstacles are thrown across the road, indicating that it is closed to traffic, the road may be mined to a reasonable distance in front of them. [emphasis is in original]

These rules set the tone for at least the American military's view of the landmine before World War I and appear almost verbatim in the Army Service School's 1909 manual *Military Demolitions,* written by First Lieutenant Douglas MacArthur. Furthermore, they are quoted in the Army's 1917 *Complete Infantry Guide.* Generals McClellan and Berry's Civil War–era ideas on the use of landmines had clearly prevailed in the United States Army. For at least the beginning of the next major war, however, the landmine remained on the sideline. It was the sea mines that once again drew the world's attention.[43]

5

The Great War

AS THE BRITISH FLEET prepared for gunnery practice off the coast of Ireland around 9:00 on the morning of October 28, 1914, the battleship *Audacious* was shaken by an explosion. The ship had struck a German mine. The Grand Fleet, responsible for guarding the British Isles, had unknowingly strayed into a freshly laid minefield. It was initially unclear what had happened to the battleship, and the ship's commander, Captain Cecil Dampier, thought that his ship might have been hit by a torpedo from an unseen submarine. Per orders from the admiralty, the rest of the fleet quickly steamed away lest they too be caught by the phantom submarine. *Audacious* was alone, save her escort, the light cruiser *Liverpool*.

When it became apparent that the ship was not going to immediately sink, Dampier decided to attempt to reach the coast 25 miles away, allowing him to beach the ship where it could be recovered and repaired rather than losing it to the sea. As the ship limped towards the fleet's harbor at Lough Swilly, it began to take on more water. Two hours later and still ten miles out, the dreadnaught ground to a halt, its engine rooms flooded. The captain began evacuating most of the crew but remained onboard with a volunteer skeleton crew to try to save the ship. The passenger liner *Olympic,* sister ship of the *Titanic,* responded to *Audacious*'s distress call at 1:30 P.M. and tried to take the battleship in tow. Heavy seas made the effort fruitless, though it must certainly have provided a startling view for the passengers onboard the liner. The battleship *Exmouth* arrived in the evening and also attempted to tow the doomed ship, but to no avail. The captain and the remaining crew soon left *Audacious* and waited for the inevitable.

Twelve hours after hitting the mine, the ship succumbed to its injuries, rolling over and then violently exploding. Its loss caused panic in both the admiralty and the British Cabinet. The admiralty worried that with the odds changed, the German High Seas Fleet might now take action. The Cabinet, in contrast, was concerned with the diplomatic ramifications of having lost one of its newest battleships as the Germans were about to bring the Ottoman Empire into the war. In the end, the British government decided that the loss of *Audacious* should be a state secret. While questioned many times about the ship, the government did not acknowledge its loss until two days after the war was over.[1]

Audacious was only one of many ships sunk by mines during the war, and sea mines were only one of the many mechanized weapons designed to take human life more effectively. The Civil War and the Russo-Japanese War proved to be only a preview of the horrors of mechanized warfare and the stalemate that could occur when tactics failed to keep pace with technology. Landmines, largely discredited by the Russo-Japanese War, saw a resurgence in the middle of the war as a counter to the newly introduced tank. The sea mine was an issue from the very beginning of the war until the very end, destroying both military and commercial shipping. Many of the nations involved in the war had signed the 1907 Hague Convention, which placed tight controls on the conduct of war. In addition to the laws regulating the use of sea mines, the convention prohibited the use of poisonous gas and established rules for the sinking of merchant ships. The rules proved futile. Poisonous gas appeared as early as the first month of the war when the French used tear gas on the Germans in August 1914. In the Second Battle of Ypres in April 1915, the Germans began using deadly chlorine gas. In 1917, the Germans undertook a policy of unrestricted submarine warfare, ultimately bringing the United States into the war. The rules governing sea mines fared little better. Despite the Hague Convention, both sides laid mines in commercial shipping lanes. By the war's end, the number of sea mines laid by both sides was in the hundreds of thousands. Over 70,000 mines were deployed in the Northern Barrage alone. Many of the mines laid during the war were in clear violation of the terms of the Hague Convention. The rules of war appeared to have been meant to be broken.[2]

SEA MINES

German mining efforts began on August 4, 1914, as the British government waited for an answer to its ultimatum to Germany over the invasion of neutral Belgium. That morning, *Königin Luise,* an excursion steamer, headed out to sea to mine the shipping lanes leading to the Thames River. The German steamer had been repainted to match the colors of the British Great Eastern Railway fleet and had a complement of 180 mines. The commander's orders were to mine the area around the entrance to the Thames River. When that proved unworkable due to the presence of British warships, the captain headed 100 miles north to Aldeburgh Napes, an area used by ships plying the waters between England and neutral Holland. The crew succeeded in putting out all of its mines by the end of the first morning. The steamer's work did not go unnoticed: a British fishing boat notified the navy that it had seen a ship "dropping things overboard, presumably mines." The destroyer *Lance* found the German ship, gave chase, and fired at it. The light cruiser *Amphion* soon joined the chase and within a few hours *Königin Luise* was no more. The British ships picked up the 53 surviving German sailors and headed off. The *Amphion* took on half of the prisoners. The ship's commander, Captain Cecil Fox, ordered them to be held in the forward part of the ship so that they would be the first to go should the *Amphion* strike one of the mines the men had put out.[3]

After disposing of the *Königin Luise,* the British ships headed back to port and attempted to steer clear of the freshly laid minefields. On their way they spotted another steamer painted in the same colors as *Königin Luise.* The ship was flying the German flag. When the British gave chase, the steamer *St. Petersburg,* which actually was a British Great Eastern Railway steamer, replaced the German flag with a British one. Upon inspection, the British discovered that *St. Petersburg* had the German ambassador onboard and was delivering him to the Netherlands—a neutral country. The ship had flown the German flag to ensure it would not be sunk by German submarines thought to be in the area. As the British returned to their homeward course, the *Amphion*'s bow struck a mine. The decision to berth the prisoners in the front of the ship proved prophetic: only one of the Germans survived. As Fox ordered an evacuation, the ship suffered a second explosion, possibly from hitting another mine. Fifteen minutes later, *Amphion* joined *Königin Luise* on the ocean floor, taking over 150 of its crew with it. The ships, quite literally, had sunk each other.[4]

The British government, upset that the mines that sank the *Amphion* were in a commercial shipping lane and unsure how many minefields the Germans had put out, quickly accused them of the wholesale mining of the North Sea, a clear violation of the Hague Convention. The British issued a diplomatic circular to this effect, adding that any ships entering the North Sea were at risk. In reality, the Germans had put out only the one minefield and, according to the author of a postwar official British history, were "strictly within their rights" as Germany had not signed the portion of the Hague Convention prohibiting the targeting of commercial shipping. The British also used German mining as one of their reasons to restrict the rights of neutrals in the North Sea and broaden the range of materials considered contraband. In

November, the German cruiser *Berlin* put out mines along the western coast of Ireland. The admiralty decided that the mines were the work of "a merchant vessel flying a neutral flag" and that the North Sea was now considered a war zone. All ships headed to Denmark, Holland, or Norway were to transit through the Straits of Dover where they found English guides to help them navigate—and English warships ready to search them in relatively safe waters.[5]

The Germans entered the war well-prepared for mining operations, having a tradition of using sea mines dating back to Karl Himly's use of observation mines in the harbor defenses of Kiel during the 1848 war between Denmark and Prussia. The German war plan was based in large part on their ground forces achieving a quick victory on the Western Front. Assuming the Royal Navy would act as it always had and would try to enforce a close blockade, the German command planned to keep its heavy forces in tightly defended ports, secured behind lines of mines covered by heavy guns. When the British fleet stormed in to destroy their enemy, it would be met with heavy fire and the constant threat of submarines. German ships would be able to fight close to home and to resupply and seek repairs relatively easily. In what the Germans viewed as a war of attrition, the British were expected to take heavy losses. In 1913, however, the Royal Navy abandoned its policy of close blockade. The threat of mines and submarines, as well as the problems posed by keeping the fleet supplied during long operations, led to what the admiralty described as "a steady and serious wastage of valuable ships." Simply put, the admiralty realized it did not have the resources to carry on war the way it had in the days of Nelson.[6]

Instead of a close blockade, when war came the admiralty chose to block traffic entering and exiting the North Sea. This left the two sides at an impasse. The German command, particularly the kaiser, was leery of sending its battleships out to be lost and fully expected the British to attack their anchorages. The British, in turn, were unwilling to attack the anchorages because they were concerned about losses to mines and submarines. British efforts to draw the Germans out met with only occasional success, though each battle resulted in a victory for the British.

Given the impasse, the Germans relied heavily on mines and submarines to thin out the British fleet. German mines were substantially more reliable than those of the British. Like most mines of the era, the standard German spherical mine was designed to separate from its anchor once it was dropped into the water and then float at a predetermined depth. One of the keys to the German success was their continued use of the Hertz Horn fuse developed shortly after the 1866 Prussian war with Denmark. By the beginning of World War I, the Germans had developed three variants of their spherical mines with charges ranging from 154 to 330 pounds and suitable for use at depths of up to 377 yards. During the war, the Germans continued to develop new mines, including an antisubmarine mine that used a 44-pound charge. The Germans used mines extensively around their naval bases, such as Heliogoland, and minefields close to shore were often covered by batteries. They also continued to develop their mine-sweeping and mine-laying technologies. At the beginning of the war, the Germans had 33 older torpedo boats available for mine-sweeping duty in the North Sea. By the end of the war, that number had increased dramatically. As of November 1918, the Germans had 227 vessels dedicated to mine sweeping including support ships.[7]

One of the Germans' major advances in mine warfare during the war was the 1915 use of submarines to lay minefields. Early versions of the submarines carried 18 modified Type IV mines. Later versions carried as many as 34 mines. The mines were launched from six dispenser tubes located in the bow of the submarine and were designed so that they would sink to the bottom and remain there for up to 20 minutes, allowing the submarine to clear the freshly laid field. This new type of minelayer had the advantage, of course, of being able to establish a minefield virtually undetected. It did not take long for other navies to adopt this tactic, and the British and Russians both had mine-laying submarines in service by the end of 1915. As the war progressed, the Germans continued to perfect their submarine-delivered mines, including a variant that could be fired like a torpedo. One of their more intriguing developments was a mine that waited days rather than minutes to rise from its anchor. With the development of this mine, the British could no longer be sure of their mine-sweeping efforts. An area could be swept and declared clear, precautions taken to block the entrance of submarines, and yet mines could still appear. Clearing these mines before they deployed proved almost impossible. As the war progressed, U-boat commanders varied their tactics, putting out progressively smaller minefields that, in turn, required more time to locate and sweep. Even if the fields they were able to put out were small, these submersible minelayers also allowed the Germans to mine in areas that might otherwise have been inaccessible. As an example, German U-boats were able to deploy minefields off the American coast almost immediately after the United States entered the war. These mines were responsible for sinking at least five ships and caused panic along the eastern seaboard.[8]

In contrast to the Germans, the British had largely dismissed sea mines as a weapon of the weak, and the admiralty had ended research on many types of sea mines by 1900. Despite this, there were still many officers in the Royal Navy interested in the weapon. One of the most prominent was the colorful admiral, Sir John A. Fisher, who guided the Royal Navy as First Sea Lord during part of World War I. In 1868, Fisher, then a lieutenant, had authored *A*

Short Treatise on Electricity and the Management of Electric Torpedoes, the first major British work on mine warfare. As with many of the works of this era, Fisher focused on the Confederate use of mines during the Civil War. He came down decidedly in favor of observation mines, which he felt offered better reliability and more control than contact mines. Fisher's advocacy of observation mines, particularly for harbor defenses, became a cornerstone for the Royal Navy's conception of mine warfare in the years before World War I. Fisher and others worked on both mine and torpedo warfare at HMS *Vernon* from 1872 onward. Although the group successfully promoted the Whitehead automobile torpedo, they made little progress in convincing the rest of the navy of the need for the widespread adoption of mines. This failure was due in large part to the prevailing view of most naval officers that mines were defensive weapons and, in view of the navy's emphasis on offensive operations, relatively useless. By the end of the nineteenth century, the admiralty had largely abandoned mine warfare. In 1895, they went so far as to end research on blockade mines—a weapon the Japanese used with great success ten years later.[9]

The tide of opinion appeared to change in 1903 when the British War Office decided to upgrade the country's harbor defenses by replacing the aging observation mine systems with newer contact mines. In addition, the destruction of *Petropavlovsk* and the appointment of John Fisher as First Sea Lord seemed to signal that the change might be permanent. Fisher, of course, was extremely supportive of the use of mines and recognized their importance in harbor defense. The continued loss of Russian and Japanese ships during the war in the Pacific highlighted the importance of both defensive and offensive mines, particularly those used in effecting a blockade. Despite this, many in the admiralty still sought to restrict the use of mines at sea. The Royal Navy was the most powerful in the world, and, in their view, it could only suffer from the widespread use of mines.[10]

The financial drain of the race to build larger and more powerful battleships also hampered efforts to promote mines. In a navy in which many officers questioned both the efficacy and the ethics of using mines, drawing money away from the development and construction of big ships seemed foolhardy. In addition, other new technologies vied with mines for the navy's attention and resources. Chief among these were submarines and torpedoes. By 1908, even Fisher had come to doubt the importance of mines, his opinion swayed not only by the development of the submarine and the torpedo, but by advances in mine clearance techniques. In June 1908, he argued that "channels obstructed by mines can be readily cleared, and thus in themselves present no serious obstacle to the movements of the Fleet." Not long afterwards, he urged a colleague not to worry about recent discussions on the use of offensive mines, as events over the last five years had shown that they were, simply put, "a damned folly."[11]

The Royal Navy's opinion of mines changed little over the next five years. In 1907, a 188-page report on navy war plans yielded only two paragraphs addressing mines. The main areas of mine warfare to develop during these years were those related to countermine operations: minesweepers and mine-sweeping techniques. In 1910, following the ouster of Fisher as First Sea Lord, the navy created a Trawler Reserve and an Inspecting Captain of Minesweepers to oversee it. In 1912, the navy finally rescinded its ban on the development of offensive mines, and discussions for using mines in blockading operations were reopened. In September 1912, Captain George Ballard proposed using mines as part of a commercial blockade of Germany should war come. The blockade included not only the German coast, but was to stretch from Belgium to Denmark. When objections were raised that this action was a violation of the Hague Convention, Ballard pointed out that the mines did not have to be construed as targeting only civilian traffic, but could also target Germany's navy, and thus the action was not technically illegal. In addition, as Britain had argued at the Hague Conference against this type of conduct, Germany was unlikely to expect it to now use mines as part of a blockade. He also pointed out that Germany, realizing the importance of offensive mines, had chosen not to ratify that portion of the Hague treaty. On a more cynical note, he suggested that if a few neutral vessels trading with Germany were "blown up…the traffic to German ports would almost certainly cease at once." The admiralty accepted Ballard's proposal.[12]

In 1913, the navy began providing money for developing and producing mines, as well as preparing ships for mine-laying operations. The navy had barely a year to put these plans into action before the theoretical war became real, not nearly enough time to ramp up production to meet the number of mines required. Even if they had met their production goals, Ballard's numbers did not take into account a four-year war, and thus the number of mines needed was grossly underestimated. To make matters worse, the admiralty failed to increase the number of ships equipped for mine-sweeping operations. When the war began, the Royal Navy was underprepared for the realties of mine warfare.[13]

The primary mine in the British inventory at the beginning of World War I was the Vickers-Elia mine—essentially a slightly modified version of the mine that had been used ten years earlier by the Japanese in their war with Russia. One of the modifications was a new mechanical firing arm designed to solve the problem the Japanese had of the mine detonating from waves or strong currents. This modification solved one problem only to replace it with another: the new firing mechanism did not always fire when tripped. British mines remained unreliable for the first two years of the war until the admiralty adopted a new mine, the H-2, equipped with a Hertz Horn firing mechanism. To make matters worse, the plans for the Vickers-Elia mine were passed on to the United States. When America entered the war in 1917, the United States Navy discovered to its horror that the mines they had been building were not to be trusted. Nor were there enough mines, faulty or otherwise, to carry out British war plans. Out of the 10,000 mines called for in 1905, only 4,000 were available. While seven ships were converted into minelayers in the years leading up to the war, Britain entered the war without any ships designed as minelayers.[14]

As of August 1914, many English ports, including naval bases, were largely unprotected. One of the Admiralty's first concerns was the defenses at Scapa Flow in Scotland, home port of the Grand Fleet. In the months that followed the outbreak of war, the harbor's defenses were strengthened by the addition of heavy guns and several older battleships. In addition, antisubmarine obstructions including nets were put in place, as were observation mines. By February 1915, rows of contact mines were in place. Upgrades continued throughout the war. The chief concern was the possibility of a submarine attack—something that was attempted only twice during the war. In November 1914, a trawler patrolling the area spotted and rammed *U-18* whose captain was ultimately forced to scuttle her. A second submarine, *UB-116,* tried to attack in October 1918. The noise of the submarine's entrance into Hoxa Sound leading into Scapa Flow was detected by British hydrophone operators. Once the submarine entered the sound, it passed over one of the many seabed cables designed to pick up a ship's magnetic field and relay its position to operators on shore. Knowing that no friendly ships were in the area, the operator detonated one of the sound's many observation mines, destroying the submarine instantly. Antisubmarine defenses had improved tremendously during the war.[15]

Scapa Flow, of course, was far from the only area the British defended with mines. In some cases, the British were known to use German mines against their owners. In the first months of the war, the Germans had put out two large minefields off the coast of Scarborough, each over 30 miles long and 10 miles deep. While the Germans had hoped to disrupt British naval traffic, the Royal Navy saw the mines as a way to protect the coast from raiders and adopted the minefield as their own, adding their own mines to strengthen the field. The British made only limited efforts at offensive mining for the first part of the war, though they did begin mining the North Sea in 1914. In addition to the navy's traditional animosity toward blockade mines, the supply of mines was limited, and most of the mines on hand were used to shore up the defense of the British coast. By 1915, John Fisher, who had returned from retirement in 1914 to resume the post of First Sea Lord, was pushing for the use of mines in the blockade of Germany. He was largely overruled by the very man who had brought him back to the service of the Empire, First Lord of the Admiralty Winston Churchill. The western Allies did not lay a major offensive minefield until America's entry into the war—two years after Fisher resigned as First Sea Lord.[16]

John Fisher and Winston Churchill locked horns a number of times in 1914 and 1915. Ironically, Churchill was largely responsible for Fisher being selected as First Sea Lord and had secured Fisher's appointment over the initial objections of King George V. The final blow in their relationship was Churchill's decision to take the Dardanelle Straits, culminating in the ill-fated Gallipoli campaign in 1915. The Ottoman Empire had closed the straits to traffic even before they formally entered the war, cutting off Russia's warm-water ports in the Black Sea. In Churchill's mind, the Dardanelles presented an ideal chance to turn the tide of the war. The Western Front had reached what seemed to be an unbreakable stalemate. Success was frequently measured in yards of territory taken rather than in miles. An attack on the Dardanelles offered a chance to take the war to the enemy in a new area. Success in the campaign opened the door to the Black Sea. It allowed Russian warships to come and go, allowed war material from the western Allied powers to reach their ally in the east, and, perhaps most important from the perspective of the British and French, allowed Russian grain to reach the west. The campaign also held the possibility of relieving some of the pressure on the Russian armies in the Caucasus by forcing the Ottoman Empire to divert its forces to deal with the British and French incursion. This was of particular import as Grand Duke Michael, commander-in-chief of the Russian army, had personally requested that the British and French find a way to distract the Ottomans. Perhaps most importantly, success might well trigger the collapse of the already unstable Ottoman Empire itself, removing one of Germany's allies from the war.[17]

In the beginning, Fisher and Churchill were in agreement on the importance of taking the Dardanelles. The initial plan, as proposed by Fisher, called for a joint land and sea assault on the straits including the deployment of 100,000 British and Indian troops to the southern end of the Dardanelles, a large contingent of Greek troops to the northern side of the straits, and a Bulgarian assault on the Ottoman capital, Constantinople, itself. The Royal Navy planned to support the effort with a fleet of older battleships that they would force through the straits. The plan, unfortunately, was unrealistic. Greece and Bulgaria had yet to enter the war and, having been at war with each other as recently as the Second Balkan War (1913), distrusted each other. Greece refused to act without Bulgaria. The latter was unwilling to take sides. When it did, in October 1915, Bulgaria entered the war on the side of the Central Powers. In addition, British Secretary of War, Field Marshall Horatio Kitchener, was unwilling to part with the 100,000 troops the plan called for because he felt they were desperately needed in France. Churchill and others in the admiralty seized on the one portion of Fisher's plan on which they could act. Based on intelligence that suggested Ottoman fortifications along the Dardanelles were outdated, Churchill decided that the navy could force its way into the straits and destroy the enemy fortifications by bombarding them from outside the range of the shore batteries. Once the fleet had silenced the Ottoman guns, they could deal with any minefields at their leisure. While Fisher had suggested the use of battleships to force the straits, he had not planned for them to act alone, and he ultimately opposed Churchill's efforts. The end result of the campaign was a military disaster that led to Fisher's resignation and almost ended Churchill's career.[18]

The British plans were in part influenced by the relatively light defenses encountered by *Inflexible* when it bombarded the Ottoman defenses in November 1914. Unfortunately for the British, the Ottomans took note of their deficiencies. When the combined British and French fleet under Vice Admiral Slackville Hamilton Carden arrived at the gateway to the Dardanelles in February 1915, the situation they confronted was very different from that portrayed in the initial intelligence reports. The Ottoman garrisons had been strengthened with German troops, and additional guns, including mobile howitzers, had been added. The minefields blocking the straits had also been increased and were now covered by searchlights and cannon fire. Because of these changes, as plans for the attack evolved, the number of ships involved had increased, ultimately including the *Queen Elizabeth,* one of Britain's newest battleships, the battle cruiser *Inflexible,* 16 older British and French battleships, four French cruisers, 19 destroyers, eight submarines, and 35 minesweepers (converted British and French trawlers).[19]

The main Turkish minefields were located at the entrance to the Dardanelle Narrows, an area that at spots is under a mile wide. The Ottomans and their German advisors had laid out ten lines of contact mines at 90-yard intervals, totaling 324 mines. While sweeping that many mines was a challenge in and of itself, as discussed above, the minefields were heavily protected. Ottoman fortresses armed with heavy guns overlooked the fields, and additional batteries supplemented by mobile howitzers had been set up to cover the minefields. The latter proved hard to locate, much less destroy. In addition, the Ottomans installed batteries of searchlights to cover the fields should Allied forces try to sweep the mines under cover of night. The combined effect was the creation of a tightly knit defensive position in which the minesweepers were unable to clear the mines because of heavy fire and the warships were unable to move close enough to neutralize the shore batteries because of the minefields. Further complicating the problem was the inability of the ships to deliver the plunging fire needed to reduce the fortress. Nor were the gunners able to reliably tell where their shells landed. Unlike artillery on the Western Front, the ship-based gunners generally lacked forward observers to direct their fire.[20]

Attempts to breach the minefields were decidedly unsuccessful. In large part, the failure was due to the decision to use trawlers as minesweepers. Not only were the trawler crews almost all civilians unused to working under fire, the ships themselves were unfit for the task assigned to them. First, they were not of a particularly shallow draft, which meant that their hulls were at

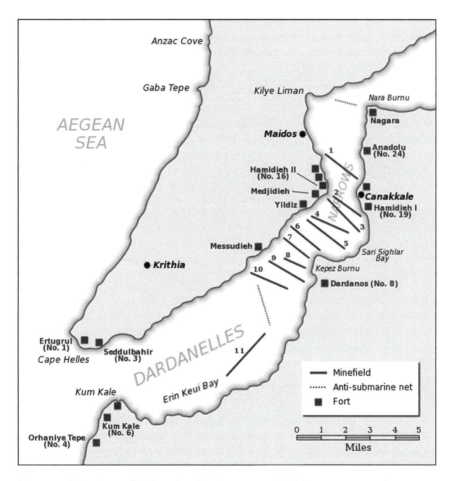

The minefields in the Dardanelles Straits in 1915. (Public domain map from Wikipedia, http://en.wikipedia.org/wiki/Image:Dardanelles_defences_1915.png.)

the same depth as the mines they were trying to clear—not a comforting thought for the men onboard. Perhaps more disconcerting for them, however, was that the ships were relatively slow, traveling at around 4 to 6 knots, and had to sweep into the current. This effectively reduced them to a speed of as little as 2 knots. If the warships proved unable to shut down the batteries covering the minefields, the sweepers would have to operate under heavy fire. This was exactly what happened. The minefields kept the large ships from coming in close enough to clear out difficult to locate mobile howitzers, and the fire of the howitzers kept the sweepers from clearing the mines.[21]

Early efforts to clear the minefields at night were met with the glare of spotlights and cannon fire. On March 1, 1915, a light cruiser and four destroyers escorted seven of the ersatz sweepers up the straits toward the minefields. At first all was fine. The sweepers began their work and, finding no mines, continued their advance. Shortly before they arrived at the first line of mines, though, night turned to day as the waters were lit by searchlights. Fire from multiple shore batteries began crashing down around the small ships, and they were forced to beat a hasty retreat. The larger ships exchanged fire with the batteries but had nothing to aim at. Similar efforts over the next week proved no more successful. Remarkably, there were no casualties. On March 10, the sweepers attempted to go into the minefield and then sweep coming down so that they could move more quickly. With shells splashing all around them, several of the crew forgot to lower their sweeps, and one of the ships was sunk by a mine. Efforts on March 13, the last attempt at night sweeping, met with even more problems. The light cruiser *Amethyst* was hit by fire from shore, damaging its steering gear and killing 24 of its crew.[22]

After trying for almost two weeks to breach the minefields at night, Admiral Carden decided the effort was futile and that clearing the mines would have to be done in daylight with more fire support from the large ships. Carden, however, was not to be the one to direct the attack. Six months at sea under stressful conditions had taken its toll on him. Beset by ulcers and according to his doctor about to have "a complete breakdown," Carden telegraphed the admiralty and requested to be relieved of his command. On March 17, he left the straits and was replaced by Acting Vice Admiral John de Robeck, who continued with his predecessor's plans for a daylight attack. On the morning of March 18, a fleet of 18 Allied battleships headed towards the narrows to engage the Ottoman batteries. The big ships were to silence the guns on shore, and then the sweepers were to move into the narrows and beginning clearing the lines of minefields. Much of the area in front of the mines had been swept the night before the attack, and a seaplane flyover failed to see any mines.[23]

As the battleships moved into the narrows they entered into a heated exchange with the shore batteries. While the Turks managed to disable the French battleships *Suffren* and *Galouis,* their guns were not strong enough to penetrate the armor on many of the battleships, and the gunners on shore were soon running low on ammunition. As de Robeck rotated out his ships, the French battleship *Bouvet* was shaken by an explosion. Barely a minute later the ship capsized and sank, taking its captain and over 600 men with it. The fleet was initially unsure what caused the explosion. It turned out to be a mine. On March 8, Turkish Lieutenant Colonel Gheel, having noticed the Allies's predilection for maneuvering ships off the Asiatic side of the straits where the waters were still, had ordered a field of 20 mines be placed to limit the enemy's ability to move. The line of mines was laid lengthwise rather than across the channel, which may well explain why it had not been swept. This layout put the mines directly in the path of the Allied fleet as it tried to turn around in the narrows. When the admiral called on the sweepers to check the area, they were once again driven back by cannon fire. The mine-field claimed three more victims that day—the battleships *Ocean* and *Irresis-tible* were lost, and the battle cruiser *Inflexible* was so severely damaged that it was in dry dock for six weeks. With heavy losses and little to show for them, the end result was a disaster.

On shore, Turkish forces had been preparing for the worst. Their supplies were running low, and news was sent to Constantinople that the Allied fleet might soon break through the minefields—the last major barrier protecting the Dardanelles and Constantinople (Istanbul). de Robeck was unaware of any of this. The losses suffered on March 18 ended Allied attempts to force the Dardanelles. Four days later, Admiral de Robeck and his army counter-part, General Sir Ian Hamilton, decided that the army would have to play a major role in taking the straits. On April 25, Allied troops, including a large contingent of Australians and New Zealanders, landed at Gallipoli. The fighting there became the stuff of legends. The lines quickly stagnated and took on the character of the Western Front, the very stalemate Churchill had hoped to break with the campaign. In short, the campaign was a disaster. As Churchill called for more ships, Fisher—worried about pulling desperately needed resources away from the North Sea—resigned in protest. Some 40 percent of the 500,000 men sent ashore were wounded. Another 10 percent died. Carden, Fisher, Churchill, and many others found their careers at a vir-tual end. Churchill was perhaps the only one to fight his way back into the public spotlight. The Turkish mine defenses, combined with withering cover-ing fire, had forced the British and French into a land campaign they were unable to win. The Dardanelle Straits did not reopen until the end of the war.[24]

The British had much more success in their efforts at stopping German submarines. German U-boats began taking a toll on Allied shipping early in the war. Finding an effective way to combat German submarines thus became a priority for the admiralty. While destroyers armed with depth charges and the convoy system were a tremendous help in this effort, antisubmarine mines also played a major role in thwarting German submarines. Mining efforts began in earnest in 1917 once the British had developed the H-2 mine discussed above. Some of the easiest targets for the U-boats were supply ships traveling between England and France. By mid-1917, some 30 U-boats a month were entering the Dover Straits, and channel shipping casualties to U-boats averaged 20 vessels a month. Vice Admiral Reginald Bacon, in command of the Dover Patrol, had been responsible for securing the straits since 1915. He had set up limited minefields as part of the area's defenses. The fields were usually a combination of deep minefields and nets sown with mines. The mine nets were an intriguing idea. Large wire mesh nets with mines attached to them were suspended from anchored buoys or strung between ships. When a submarine snagged the net, the mines were drawn alongside the submarine. The nets, however, proved difficult to maintain, and once the U-boats knew where the nets were, they were often able to go underneath them. Further complicating the matter, the early British mines frequently proved unreliable. The combined effect was that the mine nets had only limited success and, by 1917, it was apparent that these efforts were insufficient. In February, Bacon called for the establishment of a deep water mine barricade from Cape Gris Nez on the French coast to Varne Shoal (later extended to Folkstone) on the English coast. While the admiralty approved the project, implementation was delayed until October as the navy waited for the introduction of the H-2.[25]

While many people in the admiralty, including Director of Plans Admiral Roger Keyes, supported the plan for the Dover mine barrage, there was serious debate as to how parts of it should be implemented. Much of the debate centered on how many ships should be used for surface patrols and how the straits should be illuminated at night. Keyes's division argued for increased round-the-clock patrols as well as an extensive system of searchlights across the straits that would provide illumination throughout the night. All of these efforts were designed to force German submarines to submerge where they would be forced to navigate through the minefield. Bacon, however, was concerned that the night-into-day type of lighting the Planning Division called for would silhouette British patrol ships and make them easy targets for the U-boats. Further, he did not believe he had the resources to institute the level of patrolling the Planning Division called for, nor did he appreciate being told how to deploy his resources. Bacon and Keyes also disagreed on how the minefields themselves should be deployed. In addition to the deep water mines, Bacon called for two lines of mines just below the water line to target submarines traveling on the surface. Keyes objected to these shallow mines as he was concerned that they would put British surface ships, including those hunting the submarines, at risk.[26]

As instructed, Bacon abandoned his plans for shallow-water mines. Nevertheless, he initially refused to implement many of the Planning Division's modifications to his proposal, like the lighting. As a result, German submarines were able to travel on the surface and avoid the deep water mines. Attacks on Allied shipping in the English Channel continued unabated. On December 14, the admiralty tried to force Bacon's hand and required him to institute the level of patrolling requested by the Planning Division. When he failed to comply, he found himself in front of First Sea Lord John Jellicoe, and, on December 18, Jellicoe ordered Bacon to put Keyes's plan into action. The next day the searchlights and flares of one of the new night patrols forced *UB-59* to submerge, whereupon it hit one of the deep mines and sank. The combination of heavy patrolling and the deep minefield, which included over 5,000 mines, proved deadly for the U-boats, which soon began using the North Sea rather than the Dover Straits to transit to the Atlantic Ocean. Bacon's initial resistance to implementing heavy patrols in conjunction with the Dover Barrage ultimately factored into his dismissal as head of the Dover Patrol in 1918.[27]

Germany's February 1, 1917, declaration of unrestricted submarine warfare ultimately led to America's April 6 entry into World War I. Given the success of the Dover Barrage, the United States and Great Britain decided to collaborate on an even larger antisubmarine minefield in the North Sea known as the Northern Barrage. The goal of the Northern Barrage was to keep German submarines from leaving the North Sea and entering the Atlantic Ocean. The Americans brought with them a new weapon, the Mark 6 mine. The Mark 6 was a unique design. On the surface, it looked somewhat similar to other mines, a spherical mine attached to a mooring anchor. Like the German and British mines, the Mark 6 rose to a preset depth once it reached the ocean bottom. Unlike most other mines of the time, however, it did not rely on chemical horns. Instead, the Mark 6 was triggered by the electrical charge generated from steel touching copper in salt water. Attached to the mine was a copper wire that was suspended from a float. When a steel ship touched the wire, it created an electrical charge that detonated the mine, which contained 300 pounds of TNT. While the mine might not be directly against the ship, the ship was still likely to be close enough to the mine to be damaged, particularly in the case of a submerged submarine, where the depth of the water might amplify the blast's effect.[28]

While the mines were relatively untested, they seemed ideal for use in the barrage, and the United States Navy ordered 100,000 of the $400 mines for

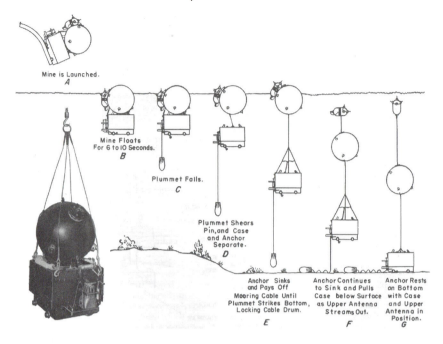

The American Mark 6 sea mine and its planting sequence. (Bureau of Naval Personnel, *Naval Ordnance and Gunnery,* vol. 1 [GPO: Washington, D.C., 1957], 319, and Bureau of Naval Personnel, *Mineman 1 & C,* vol. 1 [GPO: Washington, D.C., 1958], 206. Images modified by author.)

use in the North Sea. The main factory for producing the mines was ready for production in March 1918 and could load around 1,000 mines per day. The mines were then shipped to Scotland where they were assembled at almost the same rate they had been loaded. American minelayers, all converted cruisers or merchant ships, arrived in Scotland in June and began laying mines. Between June and October 1918, American and British minelayers laid almost 73,000 mines as part of the North Sea minefield, which stretched some 250 miles from the Orkney Islands north of Scotland to just off the Norwegian coast. Much of the area was mined with a combination of deep mines and shallow mines, restricting both surface and underwater traffic. The main exception to this rule was the waters immediately off the coast of Norway, which were not mined until late in the war. Here, the Allies chose to use only deep water antisubmarine mines so that surface traffic could continue unimpeded.[29]

Unlike the Dover Barrage, however, the Allied forces did not have enough ships to patrol the waters effectively, and the mining efforts in the North Sea never met with the same success as those in the English Channel. German sources reported that the Northern Barrage had no real effect on the U-boats

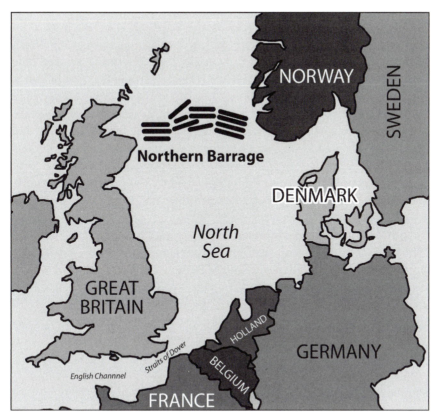

The Allied Northern Barrage. (Map provided courtesy of Joel West.)

because they were able to successfully avoid the minefields by following the Norwegian coast until that portion of the barrage was completed. Furthermore, they said that the U-boats could still navigate on the surface in that area as the Mark 6's wires were visible from the surface. The Americans and British faced similar problems with the Otranto Barrage in the southern waters of the Adriatic Sea where deep bottoms, in part, and enemy destroyers cut down on the effectiveness of Allied mines. As Gregory Hartmann observes in *Weapons that Wait*,

> It appears that mines would make the difference if properly designed, properly reliable, and properly supplemented by other forces. Either without the other, however, could be largely a waste of effort.[30]

Much like the North Sea, the Baltic Sea also was heavily mined. For the Russians, mining the Baltic meant keeping the Germans from closing in on the Russian coast, particularly the capital, St. Petersburg (renamed Petrograd during the war). For the Germans, it prevented western supplies from reaching Russia and kept the Russian fleet bottled up. The Baltic proved an ideal venue for mine warfare. Ships passing into the Baltic from the North Sea were forced to transit one of three narrow waterways: the 31-mile-wide Little Belt between the Jutland Peninsula (Denmark) and the island of Funen (Denmark), the 41-mile-wide Great Belt between the islands of Zealand (Denmark) and Funen, and the Sound between Zealand and the Swedish coast. Both Sweden and Denmark remained neutral throughout the war. Given the German and Russian backgrounds in mining, it is not surprising that both sides made effective use of their minefields. Furthermore, with many of the prime areas to put out offensive mines being in neutral territory, it is also not surprising that both sides came into frequent conflict with Sweden and Denmark over neutral rights.[31]

Both sides began laying mines immediately after the war began. As in the Crimean War, the Russians' first concern was protecting Petrograd, so they quickly blocked the mouth to the Gulf of Finland with 2,200 mines. A second line of mines was put out around Kronstadt. The Russians also began mining the Latvian coast, particularly the area around Riga. The Russians did not limit their efforts to defensive minefields. The metal ore trade between Sweden and Germany was vital to the Central Power war effort, particularly as the British blockade grew tighter; the Russians sought to capitalize on this weakness by setting up minefields along the trade route. They felt that putting mines along the route would not only hinder the Germans but also put Russia in a better position if Sweden, an old enemy, threw its hat in with the Central Powers. The Germans also were quick to act and began laying defensive minefields along their coast and offensive mines in the entrance to the Baltic Sea along the Belts and the Sound, including 243 mines laid in the Great Belt on August 4, 1914. Some of the mines in the Belts were placed in Danish waters, an action that unsurprisingly disturbed the Danish government. Swedish waters were not immune from German mines either, and the Germans placed mines in the Sound along the Swedish coast as well. Russian and German violations of Danish and Swedish neutrality ultimately forced the two countries to set up their own minefields in an effort to preserve their neutrality.[32]

The Russian mines proved relatively effective in keeping the Germans out of the Gulf of Finland for most of the war and tied up a large number of German ships in mine-sweeping operations. They also took a heavy toll on German warships. In November 1916 alone, mines cost the Germans seven of the eleven destroyers it sent to raid Russian traffic in the western Gulf of Finland. Mines also proved effective in slowing German efforts in October 1917 to take control of the Gulf of Riga during Operation Albion. While the Russian fleet eventually abandoned the gulf after a series of hard-fought engagements,

The locations of some of the main mining operations in the Baltic and White Seas. (Map provided courtesy of Joel West.)

Russian mines were responsible for damaging or sinking several destroyers, transports, and minesweepers as well as two dreadnaughts, including the *Markgraf*. As always, the success of the minefield was bolstered by shore batteries and the Russian fleet itself, which, despite the stress of the Russian Revolution, generally accorded itself rather well. German mining efforts were also rather successful: by 1916, German minefields in the Belts and the Sound effectively closed off the Baltic to English traffic including submarines.[33]

Sea mines were used with varying degrees of success in almost every theater of the war, frequently in ways that, in spirit if not in fact, violated the rules of war set out at the 1907 Hague Conference. If anyone in the world's navies had doubted the efficacy of sea mines before the war, little doubt remained after the war. In the Dardanelles, mines covered by fire from shore had proved capable of stopping an attacking fleet. In the English Channel, when combined with surface patrols, they prevented incursions by German submarines. In the Baltic, they helped prevent the Germans from taking the Gulf of Finland, but also helped the Germans keep British ships out of the Baltic Sea. They also forced a tremendous diversion of resources both into putting out mines and into clearing them. The latter proved a tremendous task both during and after the war. Sweeping the Northern Barrage after the war took a fleet of 100 ships well over ten months to complete.[34]

LANDMINES

Despite the efforts to rein in the problems posed by the mechanization of war, the European military was unprepared for the realities of World War I. All sides expected the war to be over quickly; none expected the stalemate that developed on the Western Front. During the Battle of the Somme in 1917, the British even turned to siege mining. On the morning of July 1, the British exploded a series of mines under the German lines. While the explosions killed a number of German soldiers, the British were unable to take advantage of the situation, in part because of German machine guns, and British casualties approached 58,000 men on the day of the attack. As line after line of men was cut down by machine gun fire, both sides began to look for new weapons to break the deadlock. In 1915, Major Ernest Swinton of the British army laid down the guidelines for a new tracked armored car that would carry two quick-firing Maxim machine guns, be able to reach speeds of four miles an hour, be invulnerable to small-arms fire, and be able to traverse a four-foot wide ditch and climb out of anything deeper. The new innovation, dubbed "the tank" because it resembled water carriers, made its combat debut in September 1916. Efforts to stop the new weapon led to the return of the landmine.[35]

The appearance of some 36 British tanks at the Battle of Flers on September 15, 1916, stunned German soldiers. Per Swinton's guidelines, the tanks were able to traverse No-Man's Land and helped lead British forces some two kilometers in three days. On November 20, 1917, the British massed their entire tank corps for the Battle of Cambrai. Some 324 were used just in the initial attack. Spanning a 12-mile front, the Tank Corps breached the German front, resulting in the capture of over 7,000 German soldiers in the first three days of the battle. While the British did not have sufficient forces in place to truly take advantage of their success, the future of the tank was assured. Over the course of the war other countries also began developing and using tanks including the Americans, French, and, to a limited extent, the Germans.[36]

While the early tanks were slow and prone to getting stuck, they were still very effective. Obstacles like barbed wire and *troups-de-loups* were easily over-run, and trenches could generally be breached with few problems. By their very design, the tanks were immune to small arms fire and some light artillery. Faced with a seemingly unstoppable opponent, the Germans looked to the landmine as a means to thwart the tank. Early attempts at antitank mines were based on modified artillery shells, hearkening back to Rains's experience at Yorktown in the American Civil War. In the illustrated examples, the Germans relied on the downward weight of the tank to set off the mine, often using fuses from hand grenades as detonators. In some instances, mines were combined with a barbed wire entanglement. When a tank entered the entanglement, it pulled a wire stay attached to the mine and set off a short delay fuse, allowing enough time for the tank to move over the mine before the mine detonated.[37]

By mid-1918, the Germans employed a mass-produced antitank mine. The mine was made from a sheet iron chest (E, EE, FF) measuring 25 centimeters long, 14 centimeters wide, and 7 centimeters high. The mine weighed 4.9 kilograms, including 1.6 kilograms of explosive. The charge was primed with two detonators (G). When a tank drove over the top of the mine (A, B), the downward pressure removed a pair of pins (H), releasing the firing pins (P) and activating a two- to three-second-delay fuse train, which, in turn, set off the main charge. A wire frame (C) underneath the top of the chest acted like a spring to make the mine less sensitive so foot traffic would not trigger it.[38]

Another version of the German antitank mine was built from a 2-inch deep, 8-inch by 12-inch wooden box with a tin cover. This mine was slightly more powerful than the mine discussed above, using a 7.5-pound charge, but operated on a similar principle: the downward pressure caused by the tank removed one or more of the four safety pins, releasing the firing pin and setting off the main charge. An added advantage of these mines was that each was fitted with a handle, allowing the Germans to throw them into the path of an oncoming tank when needed. According to an American Expeditionary Force Ordnance Bulletin, the mines could be handled without danger: the mines required a great deal of pressure to set them off and, according to the bulletin, "have been thrown about with impunity."[39]

German mines were generally buried so that the very top of the mine was just above ground level. In areas where the ground was soft, rocks or boards

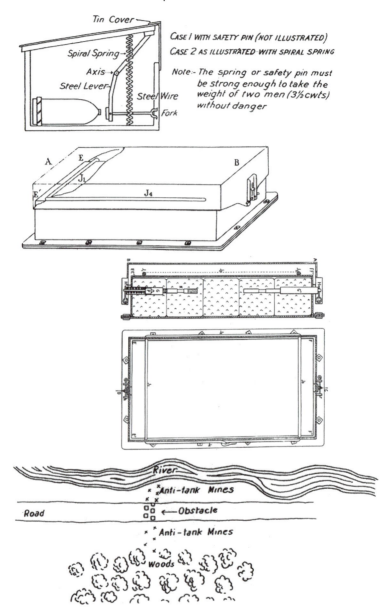

Examples of German landmines used in World War I and the layout of a field of German antitank mines in France. (German Traps and Mines, E.-in-C. Fieldwork Notes No. 59, September 29, 1918. Institute of Military History, Carlisle, PA, 227. Artillery Inspector, Ministry of War, French Army. "German Mine for Wrecking Tanks," Professional Memoirs, Corps of Engineers, vol. 11 [1919]: 305, 307. "The Barrier Type of Tank Defenses," Professional Memoirs, Corps of Engineers, vol. 11 [1919]: 304.)

were placed underneath the mine to keep the whole mine from being pushed down rather than just the pressure plate. Mines were frequently used in combination with other obstacles. The above illustration shows an example of this kind of defense encountered by American troops in the Argonne and at St. Mihiel, where German forces built antitank obstacles in the roadway to force tanks off of the road and into a minefield. The Germans used similar tactics in World War II. One German officer recommended using mines as part of a larger antitank defense including artillery, antitank guns, and heavy machine guns, stating that the mines

> complete the action of the other arms in anti-tank defense....When the tanks attack, all the arms suitable for the purpose must consider anti-tank combat their only mission until the last tank has been destroyed. If the tanks are destroyed by fire, the entire attack fails.

Concerned about the dangers of German antitank mines, in October 1918, the British began test fitting large rollers in front of the tanks in an effort to clear a path through minefields.[40]

The Germans were not alone in developing antitank mines during World War I. As the Germans began using tanks, the British were forced to consider how to stop their own creation. One design was based on an 8-inch tall, 18-inch by 14-inch wooden box filled with 14 pounds of explosives. Like its German counterparts, the British mine relied on the downward pressure of the tank to release a firing lever connected to the detonator. In other instances, the British relied on modified two-inch mortar shells. In some cases, the British mines proved counterproductive. One example of this was the Battle of St. Quentin Canal in September 1918 in which the American 301st Battalion ran into a field of British antitank mines (two-inch mortar shells) laid down in a previous battle, resulting in the loss of at least 5 out of 35 tanks. While there are indications that the minefield may have been marked, ironically by the Germans, the American mishap illustrates the problems encountered as mines began to be used without proper record keeping. The poorly recorded and unrecorded use of antipersonnel and antitank landmines became increasingly problematic as the use of landmines became widespread, particularly in the early years when tactical doctrine was still developing.[41]

By 1918, improvised antipersonnel mines and booby traps were fairly common on the Western Front. The British issued an advisory about German traps and mines in September 1918, warning soldiers to be careful when entering areas recently abandoned by the Germans. In particular, the advisory cautioned against entering "attractively furnished dug-outs....Single houses left standing when others have been destroyed" and against picking up war souvenirs and moving wire obstacles, ammunition boxes, and coal, as any of these might be booby-trapped. The booby traps fell into a range of types, including delay devices that might take days or months to detonate and disturbance-fused devices, relying on a triggering pressure plate, the removal of a pin, or the completion of an electrical circuit. In addition, the circular warned against antivehicular and antipersonnel mines. The design of both is similar to the German wooden box variety antitank mine.[42]

In 1916, *The Scientific American War Book* gave Americans a glimpse of the new weapons being used in the war in Europe. Among these weapons was the "mine grenade" developed by Norwegian engineer N. W. Aasen. The device consisted of an iron cylinder with a conical point filled with 12 ounces of explosives and 400 metal projectiles. The cylinder was buried in the ground and projected upward using a small explosive charge detonated from a distance by an electrical cable. A chain attached to the cylinder was also attached to the ground so that, when the mine was shot into the air, the chain would pull taut, setting off a detonator inside the mine and spraying metal pellets in a horizontal direction at a height of about three feet. The mines, designed to be used in groups about 20 to 25 yards apart, would have had a devastating effect on attacking troops. While the mine does not seem to have been employed during this war, it foreshadows the German S-mine, a bounding mine developed in the 1930s.[43]

By the end of the war, the foundations of modern landmine warfare were firmly in place. The use of the landmines, even booby traps of the type used by the Confederacy at Yorktown 50 years earlier, no longer seemed to raise any ethical questions. Over the course of the next 20 years, the British and Germans continued to work on antitank mines. Both had developed new antitank mines by 1929. When the Germans triggered World War II in Europe in 1939, they had two types of antitank mines, and one type of antipersonnel mine. The British also entered the war with several varieties of mines, though not in sufficient numbers to be of value. In the East, the Japanese built a variety of antipersonnel and antitank mines.

The American military, however, was relatively disinterested in landmines through the 1930s. American military manuals remained in many ways unchanged from their prewar counterparts. In the second edition of *Fortification,* published in 1928, Lieutenant Colonel William A. Mitchell's discussion of landmines differs from earlier works primarily in that it mentions the need for antitank mines, which he describes as "landmines with special charges which are placed where it is expected tanks will come." Unlike his late-nineteenth century and early-twentieth century predecessors, however, Mitchell gives no preconditions for the use of mines and states only that landmines "are planted in front of the ditch, in roads, or in some depression where the enemy might assemble."[44]

Mitchell's dropping of restrictions on the use of the landmine indicates a decided change in the American army's view of landmines following World War I, bringing it firmly in line with the attitudes of most other armies and the realities of the day. Despite this change, though, the American army did not have an antitank mine that could be issued to its troops until 1941—the Metallic Black type Anti-Tank mine or M-1. By 1942, the arsenal had increased to include only three types of mines: the M-1 and two antipersonnel mines. In part, the lack of American developments in landmines during the interwar years may have been due to the neglect of the War Department in America during these years triggered by the general spirit of isolationism and the financial problems caused by the Great Depression of the 1930s.[45]

If the landmine had emerged from adolescence by the end of the American Civil War, by the beginning of World War II it had matured into adulthood. While the failure of the Russian mines in the Russo-Japanese War seemed to dampen interest in the weapon, the introduction of the tank brought the landmine back into the forefront. Between the end of World War I and the beginning of World War II, the world struggled to maintain the uneasy peace struck at Paris and to address the problems posed by the increased mechanization of war. Among the agreements of the interwar years were treaties governing the use of poisonous gas and bacteriological weapons (1922 and 1925), the use of submarines (1922), the treatment of prisoners of war (1929), the plight of civilians (1934 and 1938), as well as a variety of attempts to limit and reduce naval armaments. Neither landmines nor sea mines were addressed in the treaties.[46]

6

World War II

BY THE END OF World War I, there was no question as to the importance of sea mines in a navy's arsenal. The sea mine had proven a successful tool for disrupting commerce, restricting the movements of a fleet, and blockading an enemy's port. In contrast, landmines had only come to the fore near the end of the war, and then primarily as a means to stop tanks. In the next great war, scientists on both sides worked to hone these weapons and to find ways to counter them. While the development of land and sea mines was not nearly as intertwined in these years as it had been in the first half of the nineteenth century, the weapons unsurprisingly often took similar paths. After all, both types of mines served the same purpose: automated killing machines.

Technical developments during the war generally occurred in three areas: fusing, sweepability, and delivery methods. Fusing, determining when a mine should fire, meant picking the correct target and detonating at the correct time. For sea mines, this translated to finding alternatives to physical contact, such as sound, magnetism, and water pressure, to set off the mine. For landmines during World War II, this could mean adjusting the pressure required to set off a mine so that it would be detonated only by its intended target or finding a way to increase a mine's surface area and make it easier to set off. The question of how to fuse a mine was closely tied to the problem of how to keep the enemy from sweeping one's minefield. At sea, changing the fusing often meant that one's opponent had to find a new way of clearing the minefield. On land, keeping an antitank mine from exploding when a person walked over it made it more difficult to locate and clear the field. Combining antipersonnel and antitank mines complicated the matter further. As landmine detectors were developed, the very materials used to construct mines had to change as well, to keep the field from being easily cleared. On both land and sea, fields of different types of mines would help prevent easy clearance. Both sides also looked for new and better ways to deliver mines. Perhaps the most important advance in this area was the use of aircraft to deploy both land and sea mines. Both types of mines emerged from the war with their reputations enhanced. This was particularly true of the landmine, a weapon that had begun to seem almost irrelevant following the Russo-Japanese War.

LANDMINES

Armies on both sides deployed millions of landmines during World War II, some of which remain active over 60 years later. While most major armies had developed factory-produced antitank mines by 1939, few were prepared to employ them effectively outside of fortified positions. Thus, during the lightening-like German campaign in the west in the spring of 1940, French and English forces made scant use of landmines in their withdrawal toward the coast. In contrast, the German military recognized the importance of landmines in such circumstances: German commanders like Major General Heinz Guderian extolled the benefits of antitank mines as part of a hasty (rapidly prepared) defense in the mid-1930s, precisely the situation the British and French faced in 1940. The Germans entered the war in 1939 much better prepared for mine warfare than their opponents—mobilization plans for the Western Wall, Germany's primary defense against the French, included the immediate deployment of both antipersonnel and antitank mines. As the war progressed, German use of landmines only increased: the Germans developed over 50 types of landmines, including the SD-2, an antipersonnel mine that could be dropped from an aircraft.[1]

Much like the Allied powers in the European Theater, most militaries in the Pacific failed to make heavy use of landmines early in the war. While the Japanese adopted a standard issue landmine, designed for use in both an antipersonnel and antitank capacity, in 1933, an American military report states that the Japanese did not learn to use mines effectively until 1944. The American military was even further behind the curve: it showed little interest in landmines until the late 1930s and did not produce its own landmines until late 1940. Experimental mines before 1937 were frequently metal boxes of TNT armed with a simple contact fuse. Introduced in October 1940 and deployed in 1941, the M1 antitank mine held 5.5 pounds of TNT and weighed around 10 pounds. While the M1 had enough power to stop a small light tank, rapid developments in armor during the war rapidly made it obsolete. The first American antipersonnel mine was not developed until two years later, and it was essentially a copy of the German S-mine discussed below. Copying a German mine design was by no means isolated to the M2. German mines served as the model for a wide variety of American land and sea mines during the war.[2]

The European Theater

The Germans entered World War II with three standard landmines—two antitank mines, the Tellermine-29 and Tellermine-35, and an antipersonnel mine, the Schützenmine-35 (S-mine). The Tellermine-29 was a rounded, flat mine with three fuses, usually set to detonate with 100 to 275 pounds of pressure. One advantage of the Tellermine series over previous mines was the addition of antihandling devices, igniters that would detonate the mine if it were lifted. This device subsequently became a standard feature on most German mines. In 1935, the Germans introduced the Tellermine-35, a slightly more powerful mine that used the entire top of the mine as a pressure plate rather than relying on single igniters like the Tellermine-29. The Tellermine-35 also had a wider range of pressure settings than its predecessor, ranging from 175 to 400 pounds. Later Tellermines retained many of the features of the Tellermine-35, particularly the use of the full-width pressure plate.[3]

In 1936, the Germans introduced the S-mine, what was to become one of the most feared mines of World War II. The S-mine functioned similarly to the Aasen mine developed during World War I in that it was usually configured as a bounding mine: when set off, the mine was propelled into the air, where it exploded. The cylindrical-shaped mine was five inches tall and contained some 360 small, irregularly shaped metal balls. When the mine was

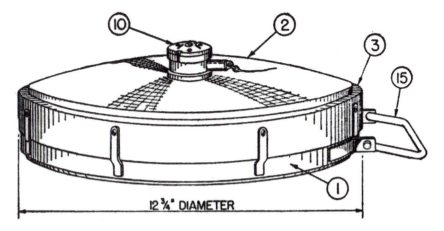

A German Tellermine-35 antitank mine. (U.S. War Department, "Enemy Landmines and Booby Traps," TM 5-325 [April 19, 1943], 44.)

detonated, either by a trip wire or by a pressure-sensitive fuse, a charge at the bottom of the mine shot the main charge into the air and set off a second delay fuse that detonated the mine about three to five feet in the air. The S-mine's effective range was between 150 and 200 yards. It could be deployed in a variety of ways, and the Germans developed a range of fuses for it, including pressure-sensitive fuses and a pull-type friction primer designed to be activated when a cord was pulled.[4]

The Germans were by far the leaders in the use of landmines both before and during World War II. In his influential 1937 work, *Achtung—Panzer!*, the German general Heinz Guderian talked at length about antitank mines and the problems they presented. He described antitank mines as a "valuable asset of anti-tank defense" because they could be deployed easily on short notice, particularly in areas of rough terrain. At the same time, however, Guderian recognized the limitations posed by landmines and pointed out that extensive minefields could cause problems due to the "precautionary measures" they required troops to take. He believed smaller, more erratically placed minefields would alleviate some of the problems, but he stated that even small minefields were a danger to friendly forces, particularly in mobile warfare, given that many soldiers might not be aware of the mines. Not surprisingly, Guderian described an opponent's mines as "an enemy of an extremely dangerous order" and added that "we must clear them at least in

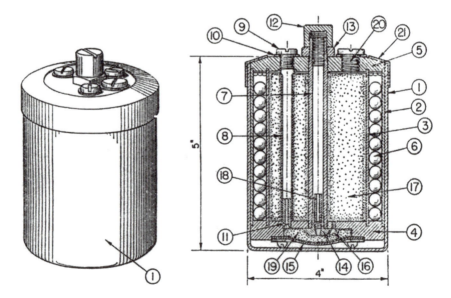

A German S-mine antipersonnel mine. (U.S. War Department, "Enemy Land-mines and Booby Traps," TM 5-325 [April 19, 1943], 68.)

part before the armoured assault proper can break into infantry combat zones." To counter an enemy minefield, he called for "panzer engineers" to precede the tanks and clear a path through the minefields.[5]

The German military's belief in the importance of landmines continued throughout the war. General of Panzer Troops Hermann Balck, who served on both the Eastern and Western Fronts, remained impressed with the utility of mines even after the war. In a postwar interview, Balck stressed the importance of keeping the control of landmines at the army group level rather than at the regimental level so that minefields were placed in a manner that benefited the entire front, rather than an individual regiment. He added that most commanders wrongly placed mines in front of their outposts in a narrow belt where the enemy could easily breach the minefield. Instead, Balck preferred using mines in groups inside his own lines where the enemy would be prevented from easily clearing them. His premise, which served him well on both fronts, was that once the attack began he could withdraw through the minefield. This maneuver left the enemy with the difficult task of navigating the mines in the middle of the battle and allowed him to concentrate his reserves on the main thrust of the attack, which by then was mired in the minefield.[6]

As the German army moved from the offensive to the defensive, it began to develop an ever-growing variety of mines. In part, the changes were caused by innovations in mine-detecting equipment. By 1942, both British and German forces were using metal detectors to locate landmines, a tremendous advance over the previous system, a wooden rod with a metal point that was used to prod the ground. To get around the new systems, the Germans developed a host of nonmetallic antitank and antipersonnel mines using wood, Bakelite (a plastic), and glass bodies. These alternative construction techniques, particularly the use of wood, became even more important later in the war as the Germans began to look for ways to save metal.

The earliest of the nonmetallic German mines, the Holzmine-42 (an antitank mine) and the Schü-mine-42 (an antipersonnel mine), were built from wood. These were basically boxes made of treated wood or pressed fibrous cardboard, filled with explosives, and fitted with standard antitank or antipersonnel fuses. The antitank mine, which had a firing pressure of 200 pounds, was in many ways reminiscent of the wooden antitank mines used by the Germans in World War I. The antipersonnel version, which was used as an alternative to the standard S-mine, required 75 pounds of pressure to detonate. As the mines were fitted with standard detonators, they could be detected with some Allied mine detectors. An American veteran recalled that, during the fighting in the Rhineland, Schü-mines caused a number of casualties, but not many fatalities as "it was not explosive enough to kill a man, but just enough to blow off a foot and put him out of action." He also related finding

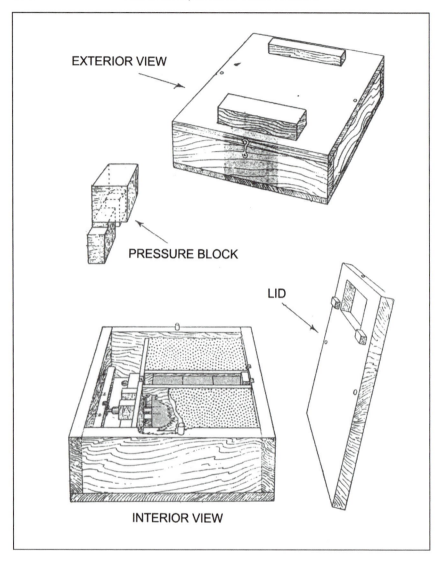

EXTERIOR VIEW

PRESSURE BLOCK

LID

INTERIOR VIEW

A German Schü-mine-42 antipersonnel mine. (U.S. War Department, Military Intelligence Division, "Antivehicle Wooden-Box Mines," Intelligence Bulletin, vol. 2, no. 12 [Washington, D.C.: Military Intelligence Division, August 1944], 60.)

an Army-issue boot with a foot still inside and lamented "there was virtually no defense against the shoe mine [sic]."[7]

In addition to wooden mines, the German and Italian militaries also built landmines with Bakelite bodies. The Italian Pignone antitank mines were made of Bakelite but relied on a metal detonator. While not detectable by some early Allied mine detectors, such as the British No. 2 mine detector, the metal fuse provided enough metal for newer mine detectors, including the British No. 3 and the American M-1, to locate the mine at depths of up to three feet.[8]

In order to avoid detection, the mines needed to be built without any metal. The German antitank Topfmine was one of the first mines to successfully address this problem. Like the Pignone, the Topfmine had a plastic body. Unlike the Pignone, however, the Topfmine had virtually no metal. Most parts were made of plastic, wood, or cardboard. Other parts, including screws, lids, and the fuse, were made of glass. When the pressure plate was depressed—requiring a force of over 300 pounds—it pushed down on a glass pressure head. The pressure head would then shear off the circular ridge that supported it and break a pair of chemical-filled glass vials, setting off the main charge. The Germans built an estimated 800,000 of these mines between 1944 and 1945.[9]

The Germans constructed a similar antipersonnel mine out of glass, the Glasmine-43. First used in combat in 1944, the Glasmine was generally fitted with a Buck chemical fuse, which contained a glass ampoule of acid surrounded by a flash powder. This fuse was almost identical in function to the fuses designed by Immanuel Nobel and Gabriel Rains over 75 years earlier. The one drawback to the Buck fuse was that it proved so fragile that the

A German Glasmine-43 antipersonnel mine with glass body. (U.S. War Department, "Mines in the Spotlight," Intelligence Bulletin, vol. III, no. 8 [April 1945], 31.)

standard German policy was to destroy the mines in place rather than to try to move them.[10]

Other variants of nonmetallic mines, including antipersonnel and antitank mines, were made of clay. Both types used a standard antipersonnel fuse, making them vulnerable to mine detectors. They differed from each other primarily in the size of the explosive charge each carried. The spherical concrete mine was another nonmetallic variant. It was formed by pouring concrete around an explosive charge or charges in a spherical mold and then arming the mine with a standard antipersonnel fuse. Because the clay mines and concrete mines both relied on standard fuses, they had enough metal in them to be found with a standard mine detector.[11]

No matter which mines the Germans used, their orders were to keep a record of where the mines had been deployed, how many mines were used, and what types of mines had been placed. This was done largely for their own protection as well as to allow for the recovery of mines for reuse. The Germans typically laid out deliberate (planned) minefields using 24-meter measuring wires with wooden markers every meter to mark the location of the mines. One end of each wire also had a series of four rings. By changing which ring they started from, the Germans were able to easily offset each row of mines. When possible, minefields were based around a nondestructible landmark, such as a road crossing. In instances where this option was not available, the Germans placed a series of three-foot stakes or beams, often made of metal, as navigation points. Many other items were used to ensure that identifying points could be found even if the minefield had been shelled. While the Germans were exceptionally careful in laying out deliberate minefields, hasty minefields were often poorly recorded.

In most cases, the engineers marked the minefield edges near their own lines with stakes or warning signs to alert German troops to the presence of the minefield and safe paths through the field. Most minefields generally included both antipersonnel mines and antitank mines. In the case of antipersonnel minefields, the edges of the field were sown with antitank mines to prevent tanks from being used to clear the minefield; similarly, antitank minefields had antipersonnel mines on the edges and the interior to prevent the troops with mine detectors from clearing the minefield. Minefields were generally established in areas that could be covered with fire so that Allied troops or vehicles that became mired in the minefield were easy targets. An American armor officer remembered that, during the fighting around the Siegfried Line in Germany, American units lost 48 of 64 tanks in less than 30 minutes while trying to traverse a muddy minefield. The accompanying infantry forces also took heavy casualties, both from the antipersonnel mines mixed in with the antitank mines and from the "extremely heavy small-arms, mortar, and artillery fire." Roadways were also frequent targets for mining, particularly the areas where vehicles were forced to leave the road due to obstructions and the areas surrounding major road signs.[12]

Other German tactics tied up troops, complicated Allied sweeping efforts, and increased damage. German engineers often included dummy mines in their minefields and sometimes sowed minefields with scrap metal: clearing these took as much time as it did to clear real mines. Lest the approaching enemy decide the area was safe to pass through, however, in most cases, engineers usually included a few live mines in dummy minefields. Furthermore, they frequently booby-trapped minefields, in some cases using the antihandling devices discussed earlier, in other instances burying mines on top of each other or otherwise attaching them to another mine. Early on in the war, Germans began using long wooden boards to increase the surface area of the Teller antitank mines and to connect groups of mines together so that they would explode in unison. This technique could also shorten the time it took engineers to lay a minefield: instead of digging a separate hole for each mine, engineers could plant a group of mines in one trench.[13]

By mid-war, the Germans and Italians had found a more efficient way to spread out the surface area of their antitank mines: the bar mine. The Italian B2 and N5, and the German Riegel-43, were made from narrow 2.5- to 3.5-foot-long sheet metal cases and could be detonated by pressure anywhere along the top surface. By increasing the surface area, each mine became more efficient, increasing the chances of its being set off and lessening the amount of time it took to lay a minefield. The bar mine design proved successful enough that it is still in use, and British and other military forces have developed mechanical trenching systems to help automate the construction of minefields using bar mines.[14]

In 1943, the Germans added yet another device to increase the effectiveness of antitank mines: the tilt rod. Roughly two feet tall, the tilt rod was attached to the mine's igniter. The rod stuck out of the ground and, when caught on the bottom of a tank hull, detonated the mine to which it was attached. This considerably increased the area of the tank that could set off the mine and, like the bar mine, increased the overall effectiveness of a minefield.[15]

The Second Battle of El Alamein (October 23 to November 4, 1942) and the Battle of Kursk (July 4 to August 23, 1943) are two of the best examples of the use of landmines, particularly antitank mines, during World War II. In both cases, the defending forces relied on landmines to create a defensive barrier and to help determine the path the attacking forces would take. The principal difference lay in the ability of the defensive forces to hold their positions once the attacker had cleared the minefields.

At the Second Battle of El Alamein, German forces under Field Marshal Erwin Rommel needed to hold off a much larger British force. In an effort to stop the British advance, Rommel ordered his engineers to put out 451,372 landmines. While the initial plan called for 30 percent of the mines to be antipersonnel mines, available supplies limited the number of antipersonnel mines to only 6 percent of the mines used. Surprisingly, 180,000 of the mines were British antitank mines from a series of abandoned British minefields. While the Germans recovered some of the English mines for use in new minefields, two of the British minefields were incorporated directly into the Axis defenses. In all, the Axis spent over three months preparing the minefields at El Alamein. Most, if not all, of the minefields were covered by artillery fire.[16]

In September 1942, the British Eighth Army established a School of Minefield Clearance in Egypt to help address the problems posed by the extensive minefields. The British had almost a full month to prepare for the assault on the German minefields at El Alamein. In preparation, the school trained several detachments of engineers. Each detachment had a command group, a reconnaissance group, and four gapping groups, with the latter responsible for the actual clearance work. The ten-man gapping groups each used a concrete roller mounted on a boom in the bed of a truck to find the edge of the minefield. Once they found the edge of the minefield, they began clearing it using mine detectors and probes to locate the mines.[17]

The school also developed new tools for clearing minefields. One of the new tools, the Scorpion, was ready for use in time for El Alamein. Based on a Matilda-model tank chassis, the Scorpion had a large wheel, mounted on a metal framework in front of the tank, with chains attached to it. As the tank moved forward, the spinning wheel served as a flail, beating the soil and, when successful, detonating any mines. In practice, the flail did not function as well as the British had hoped and was subject to damage when mines went off, sometimes kicking up mines and leaving them sitting, undetonated, on the machine's deck. In addition, the chassis on which the Scorpions were built were old, and a number of them had mechanical problems before they ever saw action.[18]

While the British were able to breach the minefields with a minimum of casualties, clearing the minefields took much longer than anticipated. The German minefields were much denser than the British had expected, and the paths through the minefields were not as numerous or as wide as had been planned. This density meant the 250-foot-deep fields were equivalent, in terms of mine removal, to 1600-foot-deep fields. The British took about four hours to clear each of the mine belts, though the rate of clearance varied tremendously depending upon the strength of the enemy defense. Once the

British broke through the Axis defenses, the Germans and Italians did not have the reserve forces they needed to stop the British advance.[19]

Less than eight months after their defeat at El Alamein, the Germans found themselves on the other side of minefields at the Battle of Kursk on the Eastern Front. Earlier in the year, Soviet forces had pushed westward following the Battle of Stalingrad and formed a salient around the city of Kursk. The Germans planned a pincer-like attack on the northern and southern sides of the salient, hoping to trap the Soviet forces and regain the momentum they had lost during the winter. Much like the Germans at El Alamein, Soviet forces under Marshall Georgi Zhukov had three months to prepare their defenses and put out two large belts of minefields. Unlike the Germans, however, the Soviets used antitank and antipersonnel mines in roughly equal numbers, totaling 241,497 antitank mines and 237,502 antipersonnel mines.[20]

Marshall Zhukov's plan was to let the Germans begin their attack and then bring his reserves to bear, halting the attack and beginning a fresh Soviet offensive. His ability to successfully execute this plan underscores one of the greatest differences between El Alamein and Kursk: the number of troops available to the defenders. While Rommel's available forces were limited to 107,000, Zhukov had over 500,000 troops at his disposal.[21]

Crossing the Soviet minefields added at least a full day to the German advance, and mines accounted for at least 42 percent of German tank losses during the first two days of the battle. In addition to losing tanks directly to mines, the Germans also lost tanks as a side effect of the mines because the Soviets had created weak spots in the minefields designed to lead the Germans into areas covered by antitank guns. In an effort to further slow the Germans, the Soviets positioned snipers to kill mine clearance crews and created a mobile obstacle corps to replace cleared mines and to put out mines behind the Germans in anticipation of the German retreat.[22]

Soviet landmines were generally very similar to those used elsewhere in Europe. Among the more common were the YaM-5, a large wooden box-type antitank mine, and the PMD-6, a wooden box-type antipersonnel mine. In addition to the PMD-6, Soviet forces also made extensive use of the POMZ antipersonnel mine—a stake mine that resembled a standard American hand grenade attached to a stake. Like their German counterparts, the Soviet wooden mines could be difficult to detect, although later mine detectors could find them from the metal nails used in building the mines. The TMB-2 was another nonmetallic antitank variant used by the Soviets. Eleven inches in diameter and five inches tall, the TMB-2's case was constructed of impregnated cardboard and carried an 11-pound charge. The Soviets also used sheet metal antitank mines, including the ten-inch diameter TM-41. Most, if not all, of the above Soviet designs are still in use.[23]

Mines also played a major role in Germany's coastal defenses, particularly the line of fortifications along the western coast of Europe known as the "Atlantic Wall." By mid-1942, it was apparent to the Germans that they needed to be prepared to defend the western coast of their empire from a possible cross channel invasion. Construction on the Atlantic Wall began in earnest in May 1942 and included massive concrete-reinforced gun emplacements as well as multilevel bunkers and fortified firing positions. In late 1943, Field Marshall Erwin Rommel was assigned to inspect the progress of the construction of the fortifications. He was not happy with what he found; the Atlantic Wall fortifications were far from complete, and the construction effort was disorganized. The completion of the Atlantic Wall was of paramount importance to Rommel. In his mind, the best chance the Germans had for stopping the Allied invasion of Europe was to stop it where it had to start, on the beaches. The field marshall played an active role in the preparations for repelling an invasion, including developing his own beach obstacles. His experiences in North Africa played a major role in his plans. He had seen the power of the heavily defended mines first hand when he attacked the British Gazala Line in 1942 and with his own minefields at the Battle of El Alamein. To stop the invading Allied forces on the European coast, Rommel planned to establish a 1000-meter deep minefield along the coast with ten mines planted every meter. The area behind the fortifications would be protected by an equally deep minefield. In all, Rommel's plan called for around 50 million mines. Fortunately for the Allied forces in June 1944, the Germans did not have nearly that many mines available and planted less than 20 percent of what Rommel wanted. Regardless, that still left the Allies around 8.5 million mines to contend with, and German land and sea mines took a heavy toll on D-Day.[24]

Perhaps the most significant innovation in landmine warfare to come out of World War II was the development of air-delivered landmines. One of the earliest of these mines was the Italian 4AR antipersonnel bomb, nicknamed the "thermos bomb." First used by the Italians in the 1941 North African campaign, the bomb was designed to arm after it hit the ground and to explode when moved. Delivered by low-flying aircraft, the bomb was lethal to 100 feet and considered "very dangerous." Painted tan and slightly over 12 inches in length, the thermos bomb easily blended into the sandy North African terrain. The metal cup (4) on top of the mine had three projections (5) that caused the cup to come off while the bomb was in flight, releasing the primary safety on the main fuse. The secondary safety devices were released on impact, arming the mine after a delay of a few seconds, allowing the mine to fully come to rest before it was armed. Once armed, the mine was both waterproof and dustproof, allowing it to remain active for quite some time after being dropped.[25]

The Germans developed a similar weapon, the SD-2 or butterfly bomb, which they first used during the early stages of the air war against the Soviet Union. The SD-2 consisted of a three-inch pod attached to a set of vanes that opened in flight, causing the device to spiral downward much like a sycamore seed. The SD-2 could be fused for airburst, detonation on impact, or arming on impact. In the latter case, its detonation was set either for time delay or for disturbance. SD-2s were originally dropped in groups as individual bombs but were later used as submunitions, clustered in a large canister that opened once it had been dropped by an airplane. The Germans developed a variety of canisters for the SD-2 for use on most of their combat aircraft. One of the advantages of the canister deployment system was that it lessened the pilot's exposure to antiaircraft fire as he no longer had to make a steep dive in order to drop his payload. Despite its diminutive size, the SD-2 caused casualties in a 50-foot radius. The Germans usually used a mix of fuses when they dropped the SD-2s, setting a third of the bombs to explode in the air, a third to explode when they hit the ground, and the remaining third to explode when disturbed. The SD-2 was particularly successful when used as an airfield denial weapon and against troops in the open. The American military ultimately copied the SD-2 and used it during the Korean War.[26]

The Pacific Theater

While the focus of landmine warfare in the European Theater in World War II was on antitank mines, much of the fighting in the Pacific Theater took place in the jungle, limiting the use of tanks and placing the focus of landmine warfare on antipersonnel devices. The Japanese had ample time to develop their skills in using landmines during the war as the Allied war effort in the Pacific focused largely on gradually working their way across a series of island chains. Each island generally meant an amphibious assault, in effect, a miniature Normandy invasion.[27]

The Japanese were well ahead of the United States in developing landmines. Their first modern landmine was the Type 93, a disc-shaped mine with a single detonator. The fuse assembly relied on a brass cap that, when crushed, pushed down on the firing pin, which was supported by a wire called a shear wire. When the wire broke, it released the firing pin, setting off the mine. The mine could be set as an antipersonnel mine or antitank mine, depending on the strength of the shear wire used. The Japanese developed a second, heavier mine in 1939, the Type 96. Where the Type 93 required additional explosives to be planted underneath it to make it effective against later

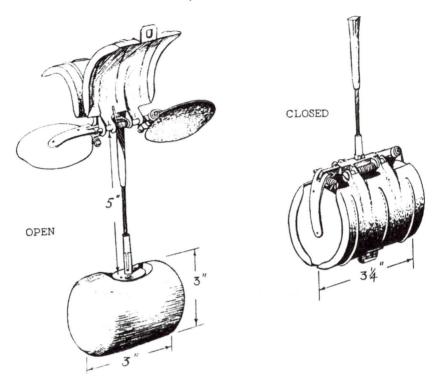

A German SD-2 or "butterfly bomb," an air-delivered antipersonnel mine. (U.S. War Department, Amendments no. 1, 13. Military Intelligence Division, Tactical and Technical Trends no. 34 [Washington, D.C.: War Department, September 23, 1943], 23.)

tanks, the Type 96 carried a stout 46-pound charge. The heavy charge was not without its penalties. While the Type 93 weighed a scant 3 pounds, the Type 96 weighed over 100 pounds. The Type 96 relied on two iron alloy horns similar to Hertz Horns as detonators. The horns each held a glass vial filled with an electrolytic fluid. When the horns were broken, the fluid was released and reacted with a chemical electric fuse to set off the mine. The mine could be used as a standard landmine or in shallow water against landing craft. Both the Type 93 and Type 96 remained in service throughout World War II.[28]

In 1944, the Japanese developed their own version of the bar mine, dubbed the "yardstick mine" by American soldiers. Roughly three feet long, the mine had a steel case and four evenly spaced firing devices attached to about 6 pounds of explosives, almost three times as much as held in the Type 93. In addition to being used as standard antivehicular mines, the Japanese also used yardstick mines to keep Allied planes from using abandoned Japanese airstrips.[29]

A Japanese Type-96 antivehicular mine. The Type-96 mine was also used in shallow water. (U.S. War Department, "Minefield Patterns in the Defense of Iwo Jima," Intelligence Bulletin, vol. 3, no. 10 [Washington, D.C.: Military Intelligence Division, June 1945], 20.)

Like the Germans and Italians, the Japanese developed a series of nonmetallic mines, the Type 3 series. The Japanese produced two variations of the mine, the Model A, featuring an earthenware case, and the Model B, featuring a wooden case. First seen on Leyte Island in 1944, the Model A relied on Bakelite for most of its internal parts, including the fuse body cover, plunger, and striker. The only metal components the mine contained were the springs, pins, and striker. The Japanese built two versions of the Model A, a 10.5-inch version with 6.5 pounds of explosives and an 8.5-inch version with 4.5 pounds of explosives. One of the unique features of this mine was that its fuse could be set off either by being pressed or by being pulled, which meant that it could also be used with a trip wire without changing the fuse. According to Japanese sources during the war, either version of the Model A was powerful enough to blow the tracks off of a heavy tank. The Model B had the same internal workings and fuse as the Model A.[30]

The Japanese also used a variety of improvised landmines, usually based around a hand grenade, a mortar shell, or an artillery shell. The "coconut mine" was perhaps the most inventive of the Japanese improvised landmines. Described as a "simple but not particularly effective device," the mine consisted of a hollowed-out coconut filled with black powder and fitted with a Model 91 hand grenade with only the grenade's five-second pressure detonator protruding from the coconut. A similar endeavor used a wooden box instead of the coconut. Like Type 3, U.S. forces first encountered these mines on Leyte Island.[31]

Another, more successful, improvised mine was the Mark I landmine. The Mark I was functionally identical to the Aasen landmine developed during World War I. The mine was built around a 155 mm mortar shell with the fins removed and fitted with a pull-type fuse. The shell was placed in the top portion of a container resembling an artillery shell case. Underneath the shell was a bag of black powder that served as the propelling charge. The shell's pull fuse was attached to the container with a five-foot chain. When the propelling charge was set off, either by command or a trip wire, the shell was shot into the air, and the chain activated the pull fuse, setting off the mine about five feet in the air. American sources considered the mine effective for a radius of about 70 yards.[32]

The Japanese made extensive use of landmines and other obstacles in areas where they expected Allied landings. In general, they seem to have preferred placing the mines (typically Type 96s) as a second layer of defense behind large concrete pyramids, designed to block the progress of landing craft and tanks, and in front of a line of barbed wire. In addition, they frequently used antitank mines on the flanks of their antitank ditches.[33]

Once Allied forces made it past the beach defenses, they faced the problem of clearing the Japanese from entrenched positions in the island's interior, a problem made more difficult by the use of booby traps. In addition to improvised versions of the Russian and German stake mines and the standard explosive booby traps, the Japanese also used old-style area denial weapons, including the *panji* pit (a variant of the Roman *lilia*), essentially a large, camouflaged pit filled with pointed stakes. Allied forces were also known to use *panji* pits in the jungle as part of their defenses and to hinder Japanese retreats.[34]

In contrast to the Germans, who had a clear landmine warfare doctrine before the outbreak of World War II, the Japanese until mid-1944 were typically haphazard in setting out their minefields and frequently did a poor job of concealing them. Consequently, American troops found the minefields fairly easy to clear. As the war progressed, however, the Japanese became more adept in establishing defensive positions and in disguising their mines. In 1944, the Japanese issued a directive to their troops that provided guidelines for using landmines.[35]

The 1944 instructions called for minefields to be placed such that they were covered by fire and difficult to find. In addition, the instructions included four recommended minefield patterns. Previous to this, there seems to have been no standardized pattern, even in minefields put out by the same unit. Other than telling troops to avoid putting out mines in such a way that they would hinder friendly troops, the instructions surprisingly offered no provisions for mapping the area being mined or for marking it so that friendly troops did not stumble into it. These instructions were a stark contrast to German instructions, which provided not only standardized patterns, but also standardized ways of recording and marking minefields.[36]

The Japanese landmine defenses at Iwo Jima were among the most effective in the war. The Japanese followed many of the guidelines in the 1944 instructions discussed above. While the landmine patterns used on Iwo Jima did not necessarily conform to the instructions, the landmines were generally laid out in an organized fashion and in many cases were marked on the Japanese side. The minefields were typically covered with protective fire, making it difficult to clear an area of mines. Added to this, the island's metallic soil rendered mine detectors useless and forced the Americans to clear paths through the minefields using hand probing tools. Iwo Jima was also the first time the Americans encountered significant organized fields of Japanese antipersonnel mines. An American Marine recalled that the beaches at Iwo Jima were "littered" with yardstick mines and remembered having woken up to discover that the solid wall of his foxhole near the beach was in fact a 500-pound bomb with a landmine strapped to it.[37]

At the close of World War I, few nations had factory-produced landmines. Most, if not all, of these mines were antitank mines. By the end of World War II, the German military alone had used some 40 types of antitank mines and at least a dozen types of antipersonnel mines. At battles like Kursk and the Second El Alamein, mines proved to be an effective barrier in slowing the advance of attacking forces, particularly when the minefields were covered by fields of fire. In addition, minefield effectiveness was frequently augmented by combining mines with other obstacles.

Over the course of the war, the construction of landmines and the way they were used changed tremendously. Among the more important changes were the spread of bounding munitions, the introduction of nonmetallic mines to defeat mine detectors, and the development of air-deployed landmines. Many of the landmine designs from World War II are still in use, particularly German and Soviet designs.

By war's end, landmines had been used in every theater of operations. With 500,000 mines used by just the Soviets at the Battle of Kursk alone, the nations involved in the war faced a tremendous cleanup problem. While most countries were successfully cleared of World War II-era landmines within a decade, parts of Egypt and the former Soviet Union still have areas that have not been fully cleared of landmines, a problem that foreshadowed the current landmine crisis. As the tentative peace that followed the end of World War II degenerated into the Cold War, the armies of the world were firmly committed to the use of landmines on a large scale, and mines were to play a major role in the many proxy wars that followed.

Teddy Bottinelli, a second lieutenant in the American army during the invasion of Italy, probably spoke for many veterans on both sides when he recalled the following after the war:

> The thing I hated most were the minefields.... That was the thing that put the fear of God in you. It's an eerie feeling because it's something unseen. It's there and it's not there, you know?[38]

As the use of landmines continued to grow after the end of the World War II, his statement began to apply to civilians as well.

SEA MINES

Given the success of both offensive and defensive mines in World War I, it should not be surprising that naval mines played a major role in every theater of operations during World War II. The technology behind the mines, however, had undergone a fundamental change. While most sea mines in World War I had been contact fused, many of the mines used in World War II could be fired by a ship simply passing over them. Known as influence mines, this new generation munitions responded to a variety of a passing ship's characteristics, including its magnetic field, sound, and even the pressure change it generated in the water. Almost overnight, the development of these mines rendered existing sweeping technologies obsolete. In some instances, minefields were put out without a known way to clear them. A new method for laying minefields, the airplane, was introduced as well, allowing the mining of not only distant harbors, but rivers too. In the European Theater, many of the battlegrounds were familiar: the English Channel, the North Sea, and the Mediterranean. In the Pacific Theater, mine warfare centered on the waters of the Japanese Empire. Allied mining efforts against Japan, particularly air-delivered mines, put a stranglehold on the island nation.

The European Theater

The mining of sea lanes began almost immediately in World War II. As in World War I, British shipping made an easy target for the Germans, and the Germans quickly began putting out minefields around the British Isles in an effort to affect a blockade. The British in turn tried to replicate many of their mining efforts of the last war, reestablishing the Dover Channel minefields to provide a safe line of communication with the continent and eyeing the possibility of rebuilding the Northern Barrage. While the British entered the war much better prepared for mining operations than they had been at the onset of World War I, they were unaware that the Germans had developed magnetic-based influence mines and were consequently surprised and distressed when English ships began setting off mines in freshly swept areas. As influence mines did not have to come into contact with a ship, the Germans designed many of their influence mines as ground mines, which sat on the sea floor, safe from traditional mine-sweeping technologies designed to snag the lines of moored mines. Having disposed of the need for an anchor, the bulk of a ground mine's mass could be dedicated to explosives, making them both more powerful and easier to put out.

The problem the British faced with the new German mine was not so much the design of the mine, but rather the fact that they did not initially know what type of mine they were dealing with and hence had no way to develop sweeping techniques or countermeasures. The British had begun experimenting with magnetic influence mines in World War I and had continued research on these mines, including sweeping technologies, through 1939. British designs were based on the rate of change in the magnetic field generated by a ship, i.e., a change measured by speed of horizontal movement. The German magnetic mines worked on a slightly different principle and looked for a vertical change in the magnetic field caused by a ship passing over the mine. One of the drawbacks to the German system was that it required the ship's northern magnetic pole to be oriented downward, a trait possessed only by ships built in the Northern Hemisphere. While this, of course, was the case for most ships the Germans targeted, once the British understood how the mines were designed, the design made it easier to construct a viable countermeasure. During the first two months of the war, the Germans relied on submarines and surface ships to plant mines in Allied trade routes and in British and French ports. The former laid exclusively magnetic ground mines, and the latter laid both magnetic and contact mines. However, the number of submarines available for mine-laying operations was limited, and the rebuilding of the Dover Barrage in September and October began to restrict submarine operations. The navy began pressing for the German air force to begin mine-laying operations, which they finally consented to in November. This decision proved to be the undoing of the edge magnetic mines had given the Germans.[39]

The Germans had experimented with aerial mining in the 1930s, and it was an integral part of their mining strategy. Aerial mining offered a myriad of advantages over surface and subsurface mining efforts. Not only could the planes reach their targets more quickly than submarines or ships, but the aircraft did not have to worry about being caught in their own minefields. German aerial mines were substantial, each carrying a 1000-pound charge. To make sure the mine was not damaged when it hit the water, designers added a parachute to break its fall. Deploying the mines, though, proved to be politically complicated. In January 1939, Herman Göring, the head of the German air force, consolidated his control of German air power, including the use of aircraft in naval attacks and mine-laying operations. As with other air leaders, Göring saw mining operations as being of only limited value. When the demand came from Admiral Erich Raeder, the navy commander in chief, to supplement the navy's mining efforts in English waters, the air force initially resisted. Not only would the mining effort tie up planes and limit bombing missions, the air force was concerned that there were not enough air-delivered mines available yet. Despite these concerns, the air force flew several mining missions over English harbors in November 1939. The mines were successful, sinking five merchant ships on November 19 and the minesweeper *Mastiff* the following day. Adolph Hitler placed a great deal of faith in the new weapon. On November 23, 1939, he announced that there would be no need to invade Great Britain; all that was needed was a blockade to keep imports from reaching England, and this could be accomplished with mines, particularly those laid by the German air force. In the end, according to Hitler, England "could be forced to her knees by the u-boat and the mine."[40]

Unfortunately for Germany, Hitler was unaware of what had transpired the day before on the tidal flats of the Thames River. On November 22, a bomber dropped one of its aerial mines off target, and it landed in tidal flats of the Thames. Although the mine was designed with a safety device to explode it if it did not land in the water, the safety on this mine failed. Once the British recovered the mine and examined it, they understood why their mine-sweeping efforts had failed and quickly began designing new sweeping tools and other countermeasures. The German navy had assumed their magnetic mine would take the British completely by surprise. This was not to be the case; the British had already begun researching magnetic mine sweeps concurrent with the development of their own magnetic mines and quickly developed a magnetic sweep. They also built degaussing equipment to change the polarity of the metal in the ship, a process that prevented the ships from detonating the German mines. As the German air force had worried, deploying the new mines too quickly and in too few numbers had given the British a chance to develop countermeasures quickly. The British also began copying the mine and sent a sample to the United States, which served as the model for one of the first American air-delivered sea mines.[41]

As the war progressed, the German air force became an active participant in mine-laying efforts. Many of the mining missions were carried out using HE-111 bombers flying at low altitude, no more than 1200 feet. Each bomber carried two mines strapped to the fuselage. When a plane approached its target, it often had to enter a steep dive to reach the proper altitude, many times in the face of antiaircraft fire. Between April and June 1940, the German air force laid over 1000 mines in British waters. The air force played an active role in mining Russian waters as well. Once the British introduced degaussing, however, Allied ships in the Atlantic were relatively immune to German magnetic mines. The Germans learned a valuable lesson from their experience with the magnetic mine. In 1940, when they developed a pressure influence mine that was set off by the pressure change caused by a passing ship, they chose to not use it until they had sufficient numbers to deploy and a means to sweep it, lest the British copy it and use it against them as they had the magnetic mine. In the end, this mine, nicknamed the Oyster Mine, was held in reserve until the Allies' June 1944 invasion of Normandy. Ironically, the British had developed a similar mine and also initially delayed using it because they were concerned the Germans might copy it.[42]

British mining efforts in the first part of the war were largely defensive in nature. As mentioned above, one of the Royal Navy's first actions was to rebuild the Dover Barrage, and Royal Naval mine layers laid over 3,000 mines in the English Channel on September 11 alone. In October, they established a second line of deep-water mines across the Channel. As in World War I, the naval base at Scapa Flow was equipped with submarine detection equipment and command-detonated mines. The British also tried to rebuild the Northern Barrage. This effort proved impractical following the German invasion and subsequent occupation of Norway in April and June 1940. As an alternative, in 1941, the British established a deep-water antisubmarine field from the Orkney Islands to Iceland and Greenland. It proved relatively ineffective. British aerial mining efforts began on April 13–14, 1940, with mine attacks on the Elbe River, the German naval base at Kiel, and the port city of Lübeck using Hampden bombers. Thirty-eight mines were laid at each location. Between April and May, British forces using Hampden, Beaufort, and Swordfish aircraft laid 263 magnetic mines in German waters, sinking 24 ships. In June and March, British aerial mining efforts in the Baltic and Northern Seas sank another 75 ships. Between April 1940 and December 1941, British air-delivered mines were responsible for sinking or damaging 164 Axis ships at a cost of 94 aircraft. Direct air attacks on Axis shipping (bombing, strafing, etc.) destroyed or damaged another 105 at a cost of 373 aircraft. Statistics for the next six months are similar, with air-delivered mines sinking or damaging 318 ships at a loss of 283 aircraft versus direct attacks sinking or damaging 92 ships at a loss of 369 aircraft. If there had been doubt as to the efficacy of aerial mining, it was now largely gone. While damages to Axis shipping caused by direct attack caught up to those from mining in the second half of 1943, aerial mining as an offensive weapon had taken root in the Royal Navy. Over the course of the war, British aircraft laid some 48,148 mines in the European Theater.[43]

British submarines also conducted numerous mining operations during the war, including the Mediterranean Sea where they were responsible for mining the Italian-controlled ports in North Africa, such as Tripoli. The Mediterranean was also the site of one of the first joint American-British aerial mining campaigns in August 1942. The operation relied on the new American Mk 13, a lightweight, magnetic ground mine designed to be used by either submarines or aircraft. The Mk 13, the first new mine designed by the United States during the war, proved useless in the Mediterranean. Designed to be used without a parachute, the mine could not be dropped from an altitude of over 200 feet. In addition, in the process of making the device difficult to sweep by decreasing its sensitivity, it could be used reliably only in shallow waters. The combination of an ineffective and dangerous-to-lay mine meant that Allied airmen were loath to use it. The Americans shipped around 500 of the mines to the Mediterranean. Of the 41 mines used, 27 of them were dropped as bombs rather than mines. The remainder of the original shipment was sent back and redeployed in the Pacific where, as discussed later, they were put to good use.[44]

The British and Americans were not alone in their use of mines in the Mediterranean. The Italian navy had begun plans to use mines to block enemy access through the Sicilian Channel between Sicily and Tunisia as early as 1936, using a combination of air, sub-surface, and surface delivered mines. When the time came to put the plan into action in June 1940, though, the Italians were critically short of supplies. Their mine reserves totaled only 25,000. In addition to facing a shortage of planes, they also had to contend with a severe fuel shortage for their ships, a problem that only got worse as the war progressed as an increasing number of ships were needed to escort convoys bound for North Africa. Further complicating matters, their sub-delivered mine (the T.200) proved dangerous to handle; its use had to be largely abandoned by 1941. Despite these setbacks, the Italian navy succeeded in putting out some 17,000 of its mines by January 1941, including 4,500 in the Sicilian Channel. One of the areas they were not able to mine initially was the waters around the Italian port of Tripoli in Libya. Consequently, when British naval forces arrived off the Libyan shore in April 1941, they were able to shell the port at will. Following the attack, the Italian navy was able to draft a fleet of 5 cruisers and 15 destroyers to complete the field using a combination of magnetic and contact mines.[45]

One of the biggest challenges the British faced in the Mediterranean was the isolation of their naval base on the island of Malta. The base served as the focal point of British air and naval operations in the area, particularly those aimed at stopping the flow of supplies to German and Italian forces in North Africa. In October 1941, a British battle group designated Force K arrived at Malta and began to attack Axis convoys. The battle group was relatively successful in its endeavors and was responsible for sinking ten ships in November alone. In December, Force K headed toward the previously unmined waters off of Tripoli. The Italian mining efforts of the spring and summer paid off: Force K took heavy casualties when they entered the minefield. Of the three destroyers and three light cruisers that entered the minefield, one of the cruisers and one of the destroyers were sunk. Both of the remaining cruisers were damaged. The loss of the ships was a tremendous blow to British convoy interdiction efforts, and it was nearly a year before Allied surface ships again threatened Axis shipping in the area.[46]

Malta itself also suffered because of Italian mining efforts. While the Italian and German air forces tried to bomb Malta into submission, their efforts never fully succeeded, in part because the Axis was never able to mount a full-scale invasion of the island. Axis air and surface attacks did, however, help prevent supplies from reaching the island on a regular basis. One of Italy's other means of isolating Malta was the Sicilian Channel minefield. Between September 1941 and January 1942, no major British convoys were able to reach the island. When they finally did, it was largely due to the efforts of British code breakers. Having broken the main Axis codes, British intelligence learned of two paths through the Sicilian Channel minefield, allowing them to snake a convoy carrying 21,000 tons of supplies through the channel and into Malta. The gaps in the minefield were short-lived, though, and were closed by February; the island did not begin receiving regular supplies until late 1942. Maintaining the Sicilian Channel minefield was a daunting task for the Italians. At best, a mine could be expected to last for a year, assuming it was not damaged or swept. Anchored mines were particularly problematic because, when their cables broke, they became floating mines and a danger to any ship in the area. Despite receiving supplements of German mines, the Italians suffered throughout the war from an inadequate supply of mines. More importantly, they were plagued by a lack of fuel, and by early 1943, mining efforts were curtailed to make sure fuel was available for convoy escort ships. In September 1943, the issue became a moot point: Italy surrendered to the Allies.[47]

Sea mines played a major role in the naval war between the Soviet Union and Germany as well. Both sides began laying extensive minefields following Germany's June 22, 1941, attack on the USSR. The Germans and Finns were by far the dominant force in the Northern Theater, which included the North Sea, the Baltic Sea, the Barents Sea, the White Sea, and the Arctic Ocean. The Gulf of Finland was one of the German navy's first targets, and German ships disguised as commercial vessels began mining operations ten days before the German attack. In late June, Finnish ships and submarines also began laying mines in the Gulf. Axis minefields soon blocked the exit to the Gulf of Finland, effectively bottling up the Soviet's Red Banner Baltic Fleet for much of the war with the exception of the occasional submarine that braved the barrier. The German mining effort in the Baltic Sea was also very effective, though the minefields cost the Germans at least ten of their own merchant ships just in the first six months of fighting.[48]

The Germans also mined the waters of the Barents Sea to block Allied shipping bound for the port of Archangel. While most of the Axis mines were ship laid, the Germans also laid a limited number of air-delivered mines in both the Northern Theater and in the waters off the city of Odessa in the Black Sea. As in the European Theater, the German use of air-delivered mines was hampered by a lack of available aircraft. German submarine mines in the North totaled only 550. Despite this, the mines were well-placed and posed a problem for Soviet ships. Had the Germany navy not seen the British as their primary adversary, German mining would undoubtedly have taken a higher toll on Soviet shipping. Regardless of the area or the delivery system the Axis used, the Soviets were beset by a decided lack of minesweepers and minesweeping gear through much of the war.[49]

Not surprisingly, Soviet mining efforts for the first few years of the war were largely limited to defensive fields. The Gulf of Finland and the entrance to the White Sea leading into Archangel were among the first areas to be defended by minefields. Soviet mining efforts were hampered in part by the Soviets having fallen behind in mining technology—when the war with Germany began, the Soviets had yet to develop influence mines or ways to sweep them, nor did they have an efficient way to lay mines using submarines, one of the few vessels capable of easily breaking the Axis blockade in the Baltic. Still, Soviet forces laid over 8,000 mines in 1941. As the tide of the war began to change, however, the Soviets were able to begin offensive mining operations. In 1942, the Soviets began using submarines to lay a few minefields in the Baltic to harass Axis shipping, a move that, coupled with torpedo attacks on Axis shipping, prompted the Germans to begin putting out extensive antisubmarine minefields. The next year, Soviet torpedo bombers dropped mines in the Danube and Dnepr rivers to disrupt German river traffic. By 1944, mining efforts in the Baltic had widened to include air-delivered mines. Soviet planes laid 244 mines in the Baltic during the first half of 1944 and another 694 by the end of the war in May 1945. British planes laid another 1,563 mines in the Baltic Sea near the end of the war to block traffic between Germany and Sweden, an effort that Soviet sources argue caused more trouble for them than it did for the Germans.[50]

The Pacific Theater

Influence mines, submarine minelayers, and air-delivered mines all played major roles in the Pacific war, much as they did in the war in Europe. The war in the Pacific, however, brought with it a unique twist. The home waters of the two main players were some 5,000 miles apart. In addition, one of the players, Japan, was an island nation trying to control a large and unwieldy, not to mention recently acquired, empire. Japan relied heavily on its colonies for both food and raw materials, making it an easy target for blockade. To make matters worse, its transportation infrastructure was substandard, and shipping items by sea was frequently easier than shipping over land. Not surprisingly, the American Navy recognized this weakness and sent its submarines after Japanese shipping immediately after the United States entered the war. Armed with mines and torpedoes, the submarines took a heavy toll on Japanese merchant shipping. Japanese mining efforts during the war were largely defensive, geared toward either stopping the depredations of American submarines or guarding the approaches to the many islands the Japanese held in the Pacific. By mid-war, the Americans began supplementing the submarine-laid minefields with air-delivered mines, culminating in Operation Starvation, a largely successful effort to stop the flow of supplies into Japan itself.

During the interwar years, the American Navy had continued to develop mining technology, most notably the submarine *Argonaut,* which was specifically designed as a minelayer. By and large, though, the navy tended to rely on the mines they had developed during World War I. With the outbreak of World War II in 1939, the navy began preparing for the possibility of American involvement in the war. These preparations included increasing the number of both minesweepers and mine-sweeping gear and stepping up efforts to expand the number and types of mines the navy had available. In addition to the degaussing techniques the navy had learned from England in 1940 to counter magnetic mines, the Americans also developed high-speed sweeping gear so that minesweepers would not slow down the rest of the fleet during sweeping operations. By mid-1941, the navy had over 23,000 Mk 6 moored mines available, and another 35,000 were on order. They also had a number of Hertz horned Mk 4s, left over from the buildup during World War I.

Like many navies, the Americans had traditionally viewed sea mines primarily as defensive rather than offensive weapons. The success of German and British offensive mining, particularly air-delivered mines, however, caused the Americans to rethink this view, and the Naval Ordnance Laboratory was soon working on a series of these mines. The first of these, the Mk 12, was in production by mid-1941, and used a magnetic-based firing mechanism copied from the German mines used in the Atlantic. An initial run of 3,000 units was planned. Two thousand of these were intended for use as submarine-delivered mines, and the balance (Mk 12 mod. 1) were fitted with parachutes to be air delivered. Production of the first truly new mine, the Mk 13, was delayed until early 1942 due to manufacturing problems. Like the Mk 12, it was designed to be used by either submarines or by aircraft. Unlike the Mk 12, it did not require a parachute when dropped by air, and could also be used as a bomb. The Mk 13's first deployment proved less than ideal. In 1943, it was redesigned and introduced as the Mk 26 mod. 1, a 1000-pound parachute mine with the ability to self-sterilize. Over the course of the war, the Americans, like the British and the Germans, developed a range of naval mines, including magnetic, acoustic, and pressure influence mines.[51]

The American Navy recognized Japan's vulnerability to mines before Japan's December 7, 1941, attack on Pearl Harbor. One of the more logical ways to mine Japanese waters was by using submarines, a plan first discussed in July 1941, if not earlier. While the navy initially resisted arming its submarines with mines rather than torpedoes to attack Japanese shipping, by late 1942, a shortage of torpedoes helped convince the submarine commanders to supplement their torpedoes with mines. Ironically, *Argonaut*, the only American submarine designed as a minelayer, was never used during the war for its intended purpose and served instead as a supply submarine. In October and November, six submarines—*Gar, Grenadier, Tambor, Tautog, Thresher,* and *Whale*—set out to plant mines throughout the waters of the Japanese Empire. The first five of these submarines operated in the South Pacific, mining the Gulf of Siam, the Gulf of Tonkin, and Cape Padaran off the coast of what is now Vietnam, with Mk 12 mines; these submarines laid one minefield apiece. The five minefields, each composed of 32 mines, sank at least six ships and damaged another six. Determining the exact number of casualties the minefields inflicted is dicey because the Japanese were initially unaware of the minefields and tended to credit most of the lost ships to torpedo attacks. *Whale* had another objective, Kii Suido, a passage separating the islands of Honshu and Shikoku of the Japanese homeland. The *Whale's* fields of Mk 10 mod. 1 contact mines accounted for the sinking of at least one Japanese cargo ship and possibly several others. Over the next few months, the submarines *Sunfish, Drum,* and *Trigger* followed *Whale's* path, laying Mk 12 and Mk 10 mod. 1 mines off Nagoya, Bungo Suido, and Inubo Saki. *Trigger* had the unique opportunity to witness the effects of its mines off Inubo Saki north of Tokyo. After laying its second line of mines, *Trigger's* crew was surprised by a freighter and its escort. The submarine quickly finished laying the last of its mines, pulled away, and went to periscope depth. As they watched, the freighter struck one of the freshly laid mines. If there any had been any doubt in the minds of the crew about the usefulness of the mines, it was probably gone.[52]

American submarines continued to mine the waters of the Japanese Empire throughout the war, eventually laying some 658 mines in 33 separate minefields. The minefields proved effective. Submarine-laid mines sank or damaged 54 Japanese ships during the war. The Japanese were no strangers to this type of warfare and conducted limited mining operations off the coast of Australia early in the war. Nevertheless, they had not counted on the American Navy being as successful as it was in disrupting Japanese freight traffic with mines or, for that matter, torpedoes. In the fall of 1942, the Japanese began establishing antisubmarine minefields to protect their shipping lanes. By the end of the war, the Japanese had set up minefields in the East China Sea, the Philippines, the Dutch East Indies, and the waters of the Japanese homeland, including La Perouse, Tsushima, and Tsugaru Straits. The minefields in the East China Sea were the work of Vice Admiral Oikawa Koshiro. Worried about the heavy toll American submarines were taking on Japanese freighters, Oikawa proposed a large mine barrage to protect shipping along the coast to compensate for the paucity of available escort ships. His original plan, which called for a line of mines reaching from the shores of the Japan islands to Borneo, initially met with resistance from the Naval General Staff, who were concerned that the large number of mines the barrage required would cut into the reserves being stored in case the Soviet Union decided to declare war on Japan. Yet, by late 1943, the General Staff began to relent, and the Japanese navy began planting extensive minefields. When the American Navy became aware that the Japanese were out establishing antisubmarine minefields, they ordered their submarines to stay below 108 meters. As it turned out, Japanese mines were much more effective in deep water than American intelligence had expected, and the mines actually were placed as deep as 450 meters—50 meters or more below the maximum operating depth of many of the American submarines. This practice kept the mines largely out of the path of surface ships. While Japanese mines are officially credited with destroying only two submarines, they are considered as a possible cause for a number of submarines being listed simply as "lost."[53]

The Japanese relied principally on two types of naval mines during the war, the Type-92 and the Type-93. The Type-93 was a Hertz Horn fused moored contact mine. It could be planted in waters as deep as 1000 meters, though in waters deeper than 180 meters, the mines tended to pull towards the bottom, keeping them out of the strike zone for a submarine. In addition, the longer the anchor wire, the shorter the time it tended to last, meaning that deep minefields needed to be reseeded frequently. To protect shipping in the area, the mines were set to deactivate if they broke free of their moorings. Mines in a field were usually laid at a range of depths to keep submarines from finding an easy path through them. These mines were also used in the water defenses surrounding many of the Japanese-held islands, though close to shore they were supplemented by Type-96 landmines, which were designed to be used both on land and in shallow waters. The Type-92 was also a moored mine but was command detonated, much like the antisubmarine mines employed by the British at Scapa Flow during World War I. These mines were planted in groups of six and were largely used to block harbor entrances. Each mine held 1,100 pounds of explosives and had a hydrophone detector attached to it that was monitored on shore. To minimize the chance for false positives, the hydrophone operators also had equipment that looked for the magnetic signal of an approaching submarine. There is no evidence that the Type-92 was successful in sinking any submarines.[54]

While the command-detonated antisubmarine mines may have served as deterrents rather than actually inflicting casualties, the contact-fused mine-fields of the East China Sea and elsewhere in the Pacific Theater presented a clear danger to American submarines, particularly when combined with surface patrols as they were at the entrance to the Sea of Japan. Countering this Japanese edge, a series of American victories in the Pacific in late 1943 and early 1944 brought with them a treasure trove of captured Japanese military documents. Among them were "Notice to Mariners" maps intended for Japanese freighters, which showed the minefield boundaries outlined in red. Translating these maps became a priority for the Joint Intelligence Command in the Pacific, and the information gleaned from them allowed American submarines to safely transit the minefields. In late 1944, the submarines gained an added advantage, FM Sonar, a technology originally developed for mine-sweepers, which allowed them to identify mines using sonic waves. While the new technology allowed the submarines to breech the minefields around the Japanese homeland in 1945, it did not make the process easy, and navigating a minefield was a tedious process. Part of the problem was that sonar registered any object it encountered, including schools of fish, rather than just picking up mines. A well-trained sonar operator, however, could tell the difference between the sounds generated by fish and other objects and those of mines, which became known as "Hell's Bells." Between sonar and captured charts, by mid-1945, American submarines could hunt and mine wherever they wanted.[55]

Submarines were not the only the way American forces laid mines in Japanese waters. By mid-war, the navy began using airplanes to lay distant minefields. While early air-delivered mining efforts relied on smaller aircraft that could not carry as many mines as a submarine, planes could reach their destinations much faster than submarines and could usually lay minefields at a lower cost in both men and machines. Air-delivered mines ultimately played a major role in the war in the Pacific, though this role was not readily apparent early on. Despite Naval Ordnance Laboratory's efforts at developing air-delivered mines, many in the navy, including the commander in chief of the Pacific Fleet, initially resisted the idea, arguing that what the navy needed were bombs and depth charges. America's first aerial mining efforts were in conjunction with the British in the Mediterranean (discussed above) rather than in the Pacific and unfortunately did little to inspire confidence in air-delivered mines. It would take a concerted education effort on the part of the navy's Mine Warfare Section to convince army and navy aviators of the importance of air-delivered mines. While the Mk 13 proved relatively useless in the Mediterranean Theater, it worked well in the shallow waters of Southeast Asia and China where antiaircraft defenses were light. American aerial mining in the East began with a raid by ten B-24s to block the entrance to Rangoon (now Yangon) in Burma (now Myanmar) on February 23, 1943. The 40 mines dropped by the American Army Air Force virtually shut down the port. Over the next few months, the Japanese lost six ships to the mines. Rangoon went from being a major port to being almost unused.[56]

The success of the attack on Rangoon led Allied air forces to expand their mining efforts throughout the India-Burma Theater, which included Burma, Southeast Asia, Malaysia, and Singapore. In all, American and British planes mined 37 targets in the theater with a total of 4,580 mines at a cost of nine aircraft. These operations included almost every major port in the region and effectively shut down Japanese sea traffic in the area. The Allied air mining effort spread to China in late 1944, where American Army Air Force planes dropped another 1,239 mines at a cost of only four planes. The 1944 mining effort is credited with so damaging Japanese supply lines that they had to halt their offensive in China. The successes in China and Southeast Asia were duplicated in the southwest Pacific. Rather than being the work of Army Air Force bombers, however, all but four raids in this area were carried out by Royal Australian Air Force PBY-5 Catalina aircraft. This is one of the few times that this plane, which was designed as a patrol craft, was used as an offensive weapon. Australian PBYs were even used for long range attacks. Given that they were amphibious, they were able to refuel at sea from aircraft tenders. Between 1944 and 1945, Australian PBYs and American B-24s dropped 2,522 mines over 49 targets in the southwest Pacific. Eleven aircraft were lost in the effort. As in other areas, the end result was that Japanese shipping was paralyzed. By 1945, there remained little doubt that air-delivered sea mines were an invaluable strategic tool in stopping enemy shipping.[57]

While most American air-delivered mining campaigns attempted to achieve strategic objectives such as stopping Japanese merchant traffic, the United States also used these mines to accomplish tactical goals. One of the best examples of this is the navy's use of air-delivered mines during the air raids on Japanese shipping in the Palau Islands. The Palau Islands were a key part of the Japanese military's inner defensive line, and Peleliu (Beliliou) was a major port in the island group for Japanese shipping. As such, it was a prime target for the Americans. On March 30, planes from the carriers *Lexington, Bunker Hill,* and *Hornet* attacked the harbor at Peleliu. While most of the planes on the mission carried bombs, several squadrons of the carrier-based Avenger bombers carried mines to keep the Japanese ships from escaping once the attack had begun. The pilots responsible for laying the mines faced a difficult task: fly in low under heavy antiaircraft fire and drop their ordnance in a precise location. Fred Foisy, who flew in one of the Avengers, recounted that, "First, [we] had to avoid getting hit by anti-aircraft and machine gun fire. Believe me, there were plenty of guns located on many ships and almost every available foot of shore. After we place the mines, we must get clear of the ships and shore batteries, then avoid Jap fighters that were sure to come from a nearby island." Fortunately, most of the Japanese planes in the area were quickly neutralized. The raid was a tremendous success. Ships attempting to flee their anchorage during the attack soon realized the way out of the harbor had been mined. In all, over 30 Japanese ships, including two destroyers, were destroyed, a total of almost 130,000 tons. The Japanese also lost 150 planes. Japanese losses from the attack did not end after the raid was over. The 78 mines dropped during the raid closed the harbor and many of the channels in the islands for up to 20 days as the Japanese desperately tried to sweep the mines. This effort was complicated by the American Navy's decision to set delayed-arming switches on some of the mines and also by the lack of minesweepers inside the harbor when the attack began. The minesweepers would have to sweep their way in. In the end, the Japanese, who had moved their base of operations to Palau after devastating air attacks on their base at Truk in February, decided that Palau, too, was not a good choice. The raid cost the Americans only two aircraft; both crews were recovered.[58]

The largest American mining effort came at the end of the war: Operation Starvation, the strategic aerial mining of the waters of the Japanese home islands (March–August 1945). Operation Starvation differed from many of the previous American aerial mining efforts. Where many of the previous operations were carried out at low altitude with smaller aircraft, Operation Starvation was carried out at high altitude using B-29 Superfortress long-range bombers, which could carry a 20,000 pound payload, over twice that of the B-24s used early on in the India-Burma Theater. Over the five month campaign, B-29s laid over 12,000 mines, a third more than Allied planes had laid in the Pacific over the previous two years. The types of mines used in each operation varied and included magnetic, acoustic, and pressure mines. The latter two of these were considered unsweepable. The mammoth effort effectively ended Japanese freighter traffic, not only with China and its other remaining possessions, but even between the islands of Japan itself. Combined with the strategic bombing of Japanese rail lines, it became almost impossible for the Japanese to import or move vital food supplies, much less war material. The United States Strategic Bombing Survey estimated that between March 28 and August 15, 1945, mines dropped during Operation Starvation sank or damaged 293 Japanese merchant ships. In part, the high casualty rates were a result of the combined use of acoustic and magnetic mines. This combination made sweeping extremely difficult. In addition, many of the mines were modified to be triggered only by larger ships. When it became apparent that the mined waters were not going to be cleared quickly, the Japanese, desperate for supplies, began running the minefields. After the war, Japan's Prince Konoye reported that Operation Starvation was "equally as effective as the B-29 attacks on Japanese industry at the closing stages of the war when all food supplies and critical material were prevented from reaching the Japanese home islands."[59]

Once the war was over, the Allies and the defeated nations faced the Herculean task of clearing the sea mines put out during the war. To put the job into perspective, the British had laid over 260,000 mines just in the European Theater. The United States had dropped another 12,000 mines in Operation Starvation. In all, somewhere between 600,000 and 1,000,000 mines were laid during World War II. Many of the mines used after 1943 were acoustic or pressure mines. In some cases, mines combined multiple types of influences. Sweeping World War I–style contact mines was not particularly difficult; sweeping the influence mines was another matter. Many of these were never recovered. Demining efforts on the Thames River, one of Britain's main waterways, did not end until 1948. Clearing the Mediterranean took another two years. In spite of this, declaring an area free of mines did not necessarily mean anything. In 1949, a Belgian steamer detonated a ground mine outside the port city of Dunkirk. Not only had the waters been swept repeatedly, but they had been in active use. The magnetic mine had apparently been buried in the sand and uncovered by a shift in the currents. In the Pacific, the American Navy had been clearing Japanese minefields as it went, but there were still many mines remaining, not to mention the mines that had been air dropped by the United States. Not surprisingly, the number of mines cleared came nowhere near the total of mines dropped. In fields of influence mines, fewer

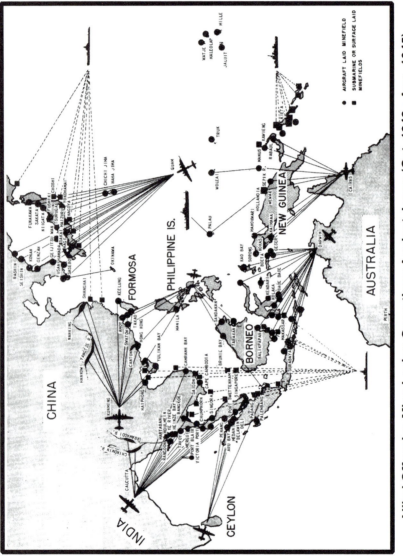

Allied Offensive Mine Laying Operations Against Japan (Oct. 1942 - Aug. 1945)

The Allied offensive mine-laying operations against Japan from October 1942 to August 1945. (Ellis A. Johnson and David A. Katcher, *Mines Against Japan* [White Oak, MD: Naval Ordnance Laboratory, 1973], 24.)

than half of the mines dropped were recovered. Furthermore, although many of the mines used in Operation Starvation were self-sterilizing, the sterilizing devices did not always work. Clearing the mines in the Pacific took years. Ultimately, the task was handed over to the Japanese Maritime Self Defense Force.[60]

7

Mine Warfare Since 1945

BY THE END OF World War II, mine warfare had become firmly entrenched in the militaries of the world. Since then, the development of sea mines has continued on the paths set during the war, and arms manufacturers have developed increasingly sophisticated influence mines. The use of aircraft to deliver sea mines has carried on as well, perhaps most notably during America's efforts to close the port of Haiphong during the Vietnam War. During undeclared wars, sea mines have also been used as political weapons, as in the mining of the harbor in Managua during the Sandinista years in Nicaragua. Like their sea-borne brethren, air-deployed landmines have also remained popular, particularly as a means to block land-based supply lines. Fusing technology has improved as well, and advanced landmines now employ influence-based fuses similar to those used in sea mines. Many of these mines can also disarm themselves or be turned off from a distance. Unfortunately, the use of self-sterilizing mines has been limited by cost. Many of the landmines still in use are markedly similar to those designed during World War II and rely on a simple pressure fuse. Cheap and plentiful, these mines, which are frequently nonmetallic, have been widely available and heavily used, particularly in the many wars of national liberation and civil wars that have been fought since World War II. Many, if not most, of these mines have been laid in hastily prepared minefields with little or no record keeping. In addition, although mines in World War II were generally used to control the movement of enemy troops, many of the mines put out during these civil wars have been used to control the civilian population, particularly in Cambodia where roads and farmland were mined in the 1970s and 1980s. The result has been a tremendous growth in the number of civilian casualties, with numbers rising even after a war has ended. In 1992, international concern over the use of antipersonnel mines led to the formation of the International Campaign to Ban Landmines (ICBL), culminating in a 1997 treaty to ban the use of antipersonnel landmines.

In the 1970s and 1980s, the world also reexamined the use of naval mines, supplementing the work done at the 1907 Second Hague Convention. As with landmines, there were also tremendous advances in sea mine technology as the Soviets, Americans, and others designed smarter mines that would target enemy ships but not friendly ships. Many of the mines in active use, however, are based on designs that have barely changed since World War I: the American Navy continued to use a modified version of the Mk 6 through the 1980s, and a number of navies still rely on Hertz Horn contact mines as their primary sea mine. North Korea has been one of the chief suppliers of these contact mines, essentially copies of the M-08, a World War II–era Soviet mine that North Korea received as part of Soviet aid during the Korean War (1950–1953).

THE KOREAN WAR

The Korean War was the site of one of the first large-scale naval mining efforts after World War II: Wonsan in North Korea. On June 25, 1950, North Korean forces invaded South Korea. Within five days, the United States had fully committed its military forces to defending the southern republic. The United Nations voted to join the effort two days later. On September 15, United Nations (UN) forces under the command of American General Douglas MacArthur landed at the port of Inchon and began the process of retaking South Korea and taking the war to the North. As UN troops closed in on the port city of Wonsan on North Korea's east coast, UN naval forces prepared to land thousands of American Marines to take the city. Mine defenses at Inchon had been limited, and the navy had no reason to think Wonsan would be different. As minesweepers began their approach to the port, they realized that the North Koreans had learned their lesson: the approaches to Wonsan were heavily mined. As part of the aid to North Korea, which had little to no navy, the Soviet Union had provided its ally with over 4,000 mines. The North Koreans and their Soviet advisors laid 3,000 of these mines at Wonsan. Clearing them took 16 days. By the time the harbor was cleared, UN land forces had already taken the city.[1]

One of the reasons that the clearance effort took so long was that the navy had allotted only ten minesweepers for the mission, an effort that should have taken 30. The American Navy had once again relegated countermine measures to the back burner. UN forces also lacked proper military intelligence, including accurate charts of the region. The North Koreans mined the approaches to the harbor with contact mines. These were relatively easy to clear, and the sweeper crews made reasonably quick progress, aided by the spotting efforts of a helicopter and sonar. Clearing a path to the harbor was a two-step process. The large American sweepers cleared a channel 15 feet deep. This channel then was reswept by smaller South Korean vessels, which continued into the harbor.

As the South Korean minesweepers moved through the swept channel, a number of mines began detonating, sinking one of the ships. The men on the sweepers were stunned. Lieutenant Commander D'Arcy Shouldice, one of the American mine clearance officers at Wonsan, recalled, "[e]verything went into a tailspin—all our plans—we didn't know what type of mine we had triggered—we didn't know where—we didn't know how many—we were back where we started." In the morning, they realized the North Koreans had sown the interior of the minefield with magnetic mines. The contact mines in the approaches had been meant to make them complacent. The tactic had worked. The UN minesweepers, who until that moment had thought their work was almost done, would need another six days to finish clearing a path through the mines. Clearing Wonsan proved costly as well as time consuming. The UN fleet lost four minesweepers, a tug, and several South Korean vessels. Four destroyers were also damaged. UN forces encountered similar, albeit smaller, minefields at Hajeu, Kunsan, and Chiannampo. Having lost control of the sea to a country with no navy, the United States Navy decided to move minesweeping and mine countermeasures off the back burner and established the Mine Countermeasures Station in Florida.[2]

The sea was not the only place the North Koreans used mines: the North Korean army made frequent use of tactical fields of landmines during the war, including "bouncing betty" bounding mines and Soviet-style wooden box mines. The latter, being made of wood, were hard to detect and were often planted with grenades underneath them as antihandling devices. UN forces also made extensive use of landmines during the Korean War. The American military had a range of mines available to them during the war, including antitank, antipersonnel, and bounding mines. The army had strict guidelines governing the use of standard landmines. These included minefields being covered by fire, being well-recorded, having lanes allowing friendly troops to pass through the field, and being coordinated with natural obstacles to make bypassing the minefield difficult. The exception to these rules was during retreats when "the situation requires drastic action" and mines needed to be put out to "harass and slow the enemy, destroy his morale, and inflict as many casualties as possible." According to the guidelines, this action was allowed only on orders from the corps or army commanders. In a final break with the pre-World War I landmine doctrine, post-World War II army manuals even provided detailed instructions on the construction and use of explosive-based booby traps.[3]

In his 1909 work, *Military Demolitions,* First Lieutenant Douglas MacArthur wrote of mines, "It is not permissible to plant them in any ground not obviously prepared for defense." Forty years later, as commander of United Nations forces in Korea, MacArthur approved United Nations' forces scattering M-83 butterfly bombs on North Korean supply routes as part of Operation Strangle. These attacks proved moderately successful in disrupting Communist movements. Later in the war, the United States Air Force used a combination of M-83s and 4,000 pound air-bursting bombs against supply lines. The pair proved a powerful combination as troops seeking shelter from the air-bursting bombs were forced to run through areas sewn with disturbance-fused butterfly bombs. The M-83s proved demoralizing to ground troops, particularly when encountered at night. Fifteen years later, the American military used similar tactics along Viet Cong (VC) supply routes during the Vietnam War. Unfortunately, the bombs did not discriminate between Allied and Communist forces. When Allied forces occupied former Communist positions, they sometimes found unexploded M-83s. American Army manuals from the Korean War warned against the dangers of trying to disarm the mines.[4]

The M-83, essentially a copy of the German SD-2, was one of the American military's first air-deployed landmines. In 1951, the military established Operation Doan Brook, an eight-year study of the feasibility of air-delivered landmines. One of the major problems the Doan Brook team faced was the development of a device that would bury itself rather than remain above ground like the butterfly bomb. The team originally hoped to modify standard bombs with new fuses. Unfortunately, this approach necessitated delivering munitions in such a way that the bomb would bury itself three to four feet under the ground. In order to do this, pilots were forced to enter a steep dive to drop the bombs from low altitudes. With airplanes flying faster and antiaircraft accuracy improving, this tactic was dangerous. This issue was of great concern to test pilots who cautioned the designers, "For God's sake don't come up with some gimmick which requires a kamikaze pilot to deliver it." Over the next eight years, Operation Doan Brook continued to develop new technology and tactics. In addition, the team explored the question of which intelligence channels were better able to aid in selecting appropriate targets.[5]

The effectiveness of American conventional landmines during the Korean War was mixed. One veteran credits four fields of landmines at the Pusan Perimeter as having killed or wounded over 100 North Korean soldiers in a single night. At the same time, despite the use of landmines, North Korean and Chinese "wave tactics"—throwing wave after wave of soldiers at a position—often proved overwhelming for UN forces.[6] Norman MacLeod, a former American military scientist, was particularly disturbed by the success of wave tactics against American forces at the Chosin Reservoir in 1950. In an effort to combat the problem, MacLeod developed the Claymore—a command-detonated, above ground mine that used a shaped charge to blow 700 small steel cubes off of the face of the mine toward an intended target up to 40 feet away. The American military was impressed with MacLeod's design but wanted a more efficient weapon—with the range increased to 160 feet and the weight dropped from 5 to 3.5 pounds. The military formally adopted a revised version of the mine in 1956. Variations on the Claymore were used by both sides in America's next major conflict, the Vietnam War. American production of the mine during Vietnam reached 80,000 per month.[7]

THE VIETNAM WAR

Indochina was the site of one of the longest running proxy wars of the Cold War. In an effort to maintain French support against the Soviet Union

A Claymore Mine. (Photograph VA008902, No Date, James Padgett Collection, The Vietnam Archive, Texas Tech University.)

in Europe, the United States gradually began underwriting French efforts to maintain control of its colonies in Indochina. American involvement continued following the French withdrawal from the region after the French defeat at Dien Bien Phu and the subsequent breakup of French Indochina into Cambodia, Laos, and North and South Vietnam. Vietnam proved particularly troubling for the United States because it was divided into two regions, the Democratic Republic of Vietnam in the north (backed by China and the Soviet Union), controlled by the communist Viet Minh, and the Republic of Vietnam in the south controlled by a nominal democracy (backed by the United States). Both China and the United States provided substantial aid to their client states. By the late 1950s, the United States not only provided financial support to the south, but had also deployed American military advisors. The first American combat units deployed to Vietnam arrived in 1965, and by 1968 American forces in Vietnam totaled over 540,000. Soviet and Chinese support for the north included large numbers of weapons and as many as 170,000 Chinese soldiers.[8]

The American experience in Vietnam not only provides an excellent example of the conduct of landmine warfare during wars of insurgency, but also highlights some of the technological advances spawned by World War II, particularly the use of air-deployed landmines. In addition, it illustrates how the use of landmines by guerrilla forces can cause reprisals against civilian populations, and the public relations dangers associated with the use of air-deployed landmines.

In 1969, General William Westmoreland described the American Army as "having undergone in Vietnam a quiet revolution in ground warfare tactics, techniques, and technology." The Electronic Battlefield, developed by the Department of Defense's JASON Committee, which was established to study the problems of air interdiction, was part of this revolution. In its August 1966 report to Secretary of Defense Robert McNamara, the committee stated that American bombing operations in North Vietnam had been a failure. As an alternative, it recommended the establishment of an anti-infiltration line around South Vietnam using electronic sensors and photoreconnaissance to listen and watch for potential targets. Known as the "McNamara Line" after its sponsor, Secretary of Defense McNamara, the plan required virtually no ground forces: it was executed predominantly from the air.[9]

Once targets were identified, they were subject to air strikes using air-burst munitions. Alternative routes were blocked with air-delivered minefields. In addition, mines were dropped directly over supply lines. Even if the Viet Cong succeeded in clearing the road of mines, vehicles forced off the road during an air attack likely encountered mines along the road's edge. The latter mines were self-sterilizing in order to allow Allied personnel to conduct road-watching and mine-laying operations. The committee estimated the system's cost at $800 million per year, with air-delivered mines taking up a large portion of the budget. By December 1967, the military had anti-infiltration systems in place in Southeast Asia. While the JASON Committee plan was never fully implemented, variations of it were used to deny the Viet Cong (VC) and North Vietnamese access to many areas, particularly along the Ho Chi Minh Trail.[10]

The Ho Chi Minh Trail was one of the principal routes of infiltration into the South, running from North Vietnam, through Laos and Cambodia, to South Vietnam. Before 1964, the trail had consisted of poor quality roads that were unusable during the rainy season. That year, however, the VC began a road construction program along the trail that threatened to make the trail usable all year. Although the United States Air Force and Navy began round-the-clock bombing operations in the area in April 1965, infiltration rates from the North tripled in 1966 to 90,000. In an effort to staunch the flow of supplies and personnel, in November 1967, the United States military launched Operation IGLOO WHITE along parts of the Ho Chi Minh Trail in Laos. Based largely on elements of the JASON Committee Plan, Operation IGLOO WHITE used a wide range of electronic sensors and area-denial weapons to thwart Viet Cong activity. Seismic and acoustic sensors were air dropped along suspected supply routes and then monitored by tracking stations. When a tracking station detected activity, it called in air strikes. As in Korea, the military combined air-burst munitions with air-delivered mines. In addition, per the JASON Committee plan, antivehicular and antipersonnel mines were dropped along alternate routes to disrupt traffic and slow down construction crews trying to repair bomb-damaged roads.[11]

The U.S. Air Force used three basic types of air-delivered landmines during the Vietnam War: the Wide Area Antipersonnel Mine (WAAPM), the Dragontooth mine, and the Gravel mine. Much like the Korean War–era butterfly bombs, these mines were deployed as cluster munitions, allowing pilots to mine large areas in a matter of minutes. Generally, the mines were deployed by tactical fighters rather than strategic bombers. WAAPMs, also know as "spider mines," were small spherical mines that shot out eight trip wires after hitting the ground. The mines were designed to spin during their fall and armed when their rotation speed reached 2,300 rpm. When the wires on a mine were disturbed, the mine went off, spraying metal pellets up to 60 meters. A single dispenser carried 540 mines. Thus, a fighter carrying two canisters could lay a 1,080-piece minefield in a matter of seconds. The air force used two versions of the mine in Southeast Asia, the BLU-42 (Bomb, Live Unit) and the BLU-54. The principal difference between the two was that the BLU-54 was a bounding mine and the BLU-42 was not. Both variants were equipped with timers that sterilized the mine after a preset interval, usually 25–35 days. Bounding mines were used extensively by all sides in Southeast Asia and proved effective weapons. As in World War II, the mines were generally set to explode near waist height, maximizing casualties without necessarily killing people. This strategy had the advantage of tying up valuable support personnel in caring for the wounded.[12]

Like WAAPM, Gravel (XM-41) maximized wounds without necessarily causing death. It consisted of a small explosive charge and pressure detonator enclosed in a canvas cover. When deployed, the device fell like a leaf from a tree, hence its Vietnamese name, "the leaf mine." Rather than causing damage from flying metal fragments like many mines, Gravel relied purely on the blast from the explosive. While the military had initially hoped the blast would be enough to blow out a truck tire, it was more likely to take off a person's foot. Like many of the air-dropped munitions, Gravel could be set to self-sterilize. As an alternative to airdrops, the military developed a dispenser that could be mounted on a trailer. The Air Force also used a Gravel derivative, called Micro-Gravel or button bomblets, to aid in setting off audio sensors signaling activity on the trail.

Gravel was not the only antivehicular mine the military had problems with. At 0.7 ounce, the Dragontooth mine fit easily in the palm of the hand and was difficult to locate. Each mine dispenser carried 4,800 mines, and the mine's triangular shape formed vanes that caused it to drift on its way down, creating a wide dispersal area. Unfortunately, the Dragontooth did function well in its intended role. Air Force Major R. D. Anderson testified at a Senate hearing on the Electronic Battlefield project that the Dragontooth was "purely antipersonnel" and "if a truck rolls over it, it won't even blow the tire."[13]

A new controversy over landmines was brewing. The military had arrived at the decision that air-delivered mines were often ineffective somewhat earlier: in July 1968, they had begun to switch the emphasis of IGLOO WHITE away from deploying landmines in favor of electronic sensors. The image of untold numbers of landmines raining down on parts of Laos and North Vietnam was unsettling for some Americans, including members of Congress. In addition, the Electronic Battlefield proved extremely expensive. In 1968, research costs alone totaled $82.8 million. By 1969, less than three years after the program began, expenditures on new technology topped $2 billion. In 1970, members of the Senate began speaking out against the high costs of the new technology and questioned the morality of some of its weapons systems, particularly air-delivered landmines.[14]

William Proxmire was one of the most vocal skeptics of the Electronic Battlefield during Senate discussions. In addition to questioning the funding of the Electronic Battlefield program, he also called into question the use of air-delivered mines. In particular, he noted the inability of both mines and sensors to tell the difference between civilians and soldiers, stating:

> in such underdeveloped parts of the world as Vietnam, whole villages may be wiped out by seeding wide areas with air dropped explosive devices designed to kill anyone who ventures into their neighborhood.

In addition, the senator worried that the Soviets might feel compelled to engage in building similar weapons, triggering a new type of arms race.[15]

The VC made particularly effective use of landmines during the war. Their use of landmines had a major impact on both American tactics and troop effectiveness during the war. Furthermore, the liberal use of landmines sometimes triggered a violent response in American soldiers, who lashed out against a faceless enemy—best illustrated by the massacre at My Lai in which American soldiers executed over 300 unarmed Vietnamese civilians, including the elderly, women, and children. This, in turn, hurt support for the Americans in the countryside and fueled antiwar protests in the United States and elsewhere.

One of the main problems American forces faced was the unconventional nature of VC landmine warfare. In World War II, mines had usually been used to secure a specific area, even if they were occasionally used as booby traps. The VC, though, generally avoided fighting set-piece battles and tended to use mines individually or in small groups, either to set up an ambush or for harassment value. Many of the mines the VC used were improvised from salvaged material, including dud bombs, artillery rounds, and spent artillery casings. The VC also used a wide variety of ready-made mines, including bounding mines, modified hand grenades, and directional mines. Directional mines were perhaps the most versatile mines available to the VC. These mines were usually placed above ground and were used in large numbers by both Allied and Communist forces. The VC employed directional mines in a variety of roles: the mines were used against vehicles, ground personnel, and heliborne forces. Ironically, the VC acquired many of the ready-made mines directly or indirectly from Allied forces. In some instances, the VC bought mines from corrupt officials; in other instances, the VC dug up entire minefields. Other mines were imported by the VC from China or produced in VC factories.[16]

Throughout the Vietnam War, American and Allied forces constantly struggled against VC mining of supply routes. While the American military had certainly dealt with this type of mine warfare before, the Vietnamese developed mining to a virtual art form. Much of the VC's knowledge came from the experience of their predecessors, the Viet Minh, during the French-Indochina War. The key to VC tactics was to create a false sense of security among the soldiers assigned to countermine operations. On dirt roads, the VC dug numerous holes but planted few if any mines or planted metal objects that set off mine detectors. After the American engineers swept the road, the VC repeated the process. Eventually the engineers, weary of fruitless searches, became lax in their efforts. Once the engineers relaxed, the VC mined the road. On asphalt roads, the VC smeared mud on the road to hide mining efforts. Again, they planted few if any mines until the Americans grew complacent. Another technique used by the VC was to dig a tunnel underneath the road and place a command-detonated charge in the tunnel. Dirt shoulders made locating these tunnels extremely difficult once the openings had been filled in. Alternately, the VC placed firing wires alongside Allied communication wires that also ran underneath the road. One American effort to counter this activity involved requiring a strict accounting of wires and prohibiting running multiple wires next to each other.[17]

The VC frequently employed landmines in ambushes. Command-detonated mines were particular favorites of the VC in these endeavors. These mines allowed the VC to select both the time to begin the ambush and their targets. While truly disastrous road attacks were not frequent, they did occur. One of the worst instances occurred in December 1967, when two platoons of the 5th Cavalry were caught in a devastating ambush. Hit with a grenade and mortar attack accompanied by command-detonated landmines, the unit was taken completely by surprise and was unable to offer any organized resistance, suffering 42 casualties and effectively losing the majority of their 11 armored vehicles. Four Armored Cavalry Assault Vehicles (ACAV) and one tank were destroyed and another three ACAVs and one tank severely damaged. To combat this problem, crew members frequently improvised additional armor by adding flack jackets, ammunition cases, and sandbags to the vehicle flooring. The military eventually developed supplementary armor kits as well as new mine clearance devices, including tank-mounted rollers and jeep-mounted mine detectors.[18]

Procedural solutions, however, were as important, if not more important, than technological solutions. To allow more flexibility, armor units adopted a herringbone pattern to their driving instead of following single file, thus allowing them to easily bypass disabled vehicles. Also, unit commanders were advised to avoid setting patterns in their movements as the VC tended to wait until the second or third time Allied forces used a route before mining it. Engineers and other troops assigned mine detection duties were encouraged to remain vigilant in their search for mines. American commanders also began using night ambush patrols to thwart VC mine-laying details. Nonetheless, the success of these patrols in armor units was hampered by the limited number of troops available for patrol.[19]

Paying bounties to Vietnamese civilians was another technique that had measured success. Villagers often knew the signs the VC used to mark mines. In many instances, the VC informed the villagers of mine locations and indicators to prevent civilian casualties, helping maintain a support base within the villages. The willingness of villagers to cooperate with Allied forces was limited by their fear of VC reprisal. The South Vietnamese Army worked around this problem by rounding up as many people as possible for questioning, thus making it difficult for the VC to identify from whom information had been obtained. American forces found it difficult to replicate this technique due to the large number of interpreters it required. Not surprisingly, a Marine Corps manual advocated watching civilian traffic, pointing out that a lack of civilian traffic in a usually well-traveled area might indicate the presence of landmines.[20]

As in other wars, educating soldiers about the dangers of mines was an important step in reducing casualties. The Combined Intelligence Center in Vietnam and other groups published numerous booklets detailing VC mine-marking techniques. While these manuals were helpful, common sense and careful observation played the most important role in mine detection. A postwar analysis of methods of detection of enemy mines and booby traps revealed that 66.4 percent of detection was done by sight. This compares to 29.2 percent by detonation, 1.7 percent by mine detectors, 0.5 percent by VC mine markers, 0.5 percent by scout dogs, and 0.4 percent by informers.[21]

Fatigue was one of the main reasons soldiers failed to see mines. An analysis of mine casualties during the war found that casualty rates increased rapidly as the day wore on. Simply put, "When a soldier plodded through a rice paddy up to his waist in water for several hours in the hot humid atmosphere he became terribly fatigued, his ability to concentrate was low and he was an easy mark for a Viet Cong booby trap." To counter the problems of troop stress and fatigue, commanders alternated lead units and personnel over the course of the day. Rotation kept fresh troops at the front of the formation and significantly helped reduce casualties from mines and booby traps. Commanders were also told not to allow their troops to move in single file. Instead, the troops were to spread out, thus avoiding multiple casualties from a single mine detonation.[22]

Some units, like the 9th Infantry Division, attempted to analyze VC mine operations by using computers. The unit collected, analyzed, and published data in their "Monthly Mine and Booby Trap Report." One of the key points the command stressed was to avoid areas likely to be mined, particularly rice paddy dikes and obvious trails. Other areas included gates to houses, stream crossings, and shady areas that provided relief from the scorching Southeast Asian sun. In order to get information to the troops, the 9th Division frequently briefed their men on how to avoid mines. As part of the briefing, the lecturer gave the men a detailed account of an actual mine incident. At the end of the briefing, the troops were given a summary of how to avoid becoming a mine-related casualty.[23]

Not all soldiers needed to be warned of the dangers of landmines. For some, the fear of mines was almost debilitating; for others, landmines incited violence against civilians. General Norman Schwarzkopf recounted one American battalion in Vietnam being "so demoralized by landmines and booby traps that they'd lost their will to fight." He also linked the atrocities at My Lai to the faceless nature of the landmine:

> the troops are walking along and suddenly somebody is dead or has lost a limb; a helicopter swoops in and takes him away, and there is nothing the men can do to even the score.

If the incident is near a village, like My Lai, it was easy to assume that the villagers knew about the mines. He added that, if he had told his men that the villagers knew and to "Go clear the place out, they'd have killed everyone in sight." The House Committee on Armed Services investigating the My Lai massacre agreed with Schwarzkopf's analysis, though they stated that what happened at My Lai was clearly wrong and questioned the legal sanity of those involved.[24]

Accounts by line soldiers also concur with Schwarzkopf. After the story of the My Lai massacre broke, a veteran reported a similar incident to a newspaper in Wisconsin. He stated that after several soldiers in his company were wounded by a booby trap, the unit responded by killing 60 civilians.[25] Lieutenant William Calley, the platoon leader at the My Lai massacre, spent a great deal of time in his memoirs discussing the problems of VC mine warfare and its impact on the troops. In describing the problem of identifying the enemy, he pointed to instances of children and farmers planting mines. Later in the book, he wrote about the tension this situation created:

> if you're in Vietnam you've got to blow a little steam off. If you're a GI who has lost eighteen friends in a minefield with a Vietnamese village a few hundred meters away—well. You think, *Why didn't they tell us, "Hey there's a minefield over there." Or Christ! Or simply say afterwards, "We're sorry about it."*…And so a bad feeling sets in.[26]

American forces also encountered mines during heliborne operations. The role of the helicopter was perhaps one of the most striking technological features of the Vietnam War. General Westmoreland compared fighting the Vietnam War without helicopters to General George Patton trying to fight without tanks. Helicopters provided supplies to remote bases, removed casualties from the battlefield, and, most importantly, allowed the Allies to bring to bear superior forces against the Viet Cong almost at will. Heliborne forces repeatedly inflicted heavy casualties in assaults on VC strongholds. Lacking air support of their own, the Viet Cong and the North Vietnamese Army (NVA) sought other means to combat American attacks. The most vulnerable point of a heliborne assault is while the troops are disembarking. Hence, the Viet Cong made landing zone denial a priority in creating base defenses. A second VC priority was creating defenses that kept their own losses as low as possible and still yielded a high kill rate. Landmines provided an efficient solution. Besides using the mines as a standard perimeter defense, the VC also modified pressure-fused and command-fired mines for use directly against helicopters.

Perhaps one of the most ingenious antihelicopter mines was constructed by planting a group of pressure-sensitive mines in a potential landing zone and then covering the mines with a sheet of metal. When the helicopter attempted to land, the downward pressure of the rotors (prop wash) forced the metal sheet down onto the mine underneath. In another instance, live grenades wrapped in paper were scatted throughout the landing zone (LZ) and set off when the prop wash blew the paper off. Prop wash was also used to detonate directional mines. A line was stretched from the mine to a tree. When the tree bent from the prop wash, it pulled the line, detonating the mine. More frequently, the antihelicopter mines were command detonated. A frequent ruse was to fashion dummies from logs and place them near trees. When a helicopter came down to check on the dummy, the VC would set off a mine hidden in a nearby tree. In other instances, Claymores were placed on top of 30- to 40-foot poles and set off when a helicopter came within range.[27]

These tactics proved very effective. In one instance during the Battle of Suoi Tre on March 19, 1967, an American assault force took heavy casualties due to VC antihelicopter mines; these mines destroyed three helicopters, damaged six, killed 25 soldiers, and wounded 28. Three days later, the 38th South Vietnamese Ranger unit discovered a group of command-fired mines in a planned landing zone. The mines consisted of a large central hole filled with "eight 75-mm., seven 81-mm., fourteen 60-mm., [rounds] and 105 pounds of TNT" connected to three smaller holes, each filled with various ordnance and 35 pounds of TNT. Following this discovery, many of the assault groups began subjecting LZs to heavy preparatory fire immediately preceding air assaults in order to destroy any mines or booby traps that might have been set up. To avoid cratering the ground and creating excessive debris that might damage the helicopters, the Americans used instantaneous fused bombs. While the use of preparatory fire to soften up LZs proved highly successful, it also told the VC that a landing was to be expected and removed the element of surprise essential to many heliborne operations.[28]

VC landmine warfare remained a constant problem throughout the Vietnam War, despite American mine countermeasures. In a May 1971 report, the Military Assistance Command Vietnam (MACV) listed mine and booby trap detection as a top priority problem area, affecting "both tactical and logistical operations." Furthermore, MACV felt that current clearing techniques were "hazardous and require[d] excessive time and resources." A postwar study on the strategic lessons of the war revealed that VC and North Vietnamese Army landmines accounted for 70 percent of American vehicle losses and 11 percent of combat deaths in the American Army. In contrast, landmines were responsible for only 1.65 percent of American combat deaths during the Korean War.[29]

While landmines played a major role in the Vietnam War, both sides also used water mines. Viet Cong water mines were largely restricted to the country's rivers and were often improvised mines or landmines adapted for use in the water. In several instances, the Viet Cong floated contact mines, some of which were from the Soviet Union, down the Saigon River, though with little if any success, in large part due to navy minesweeping efforts. As on land, a command-detonated mine was a favorite way for the VC to begin an ambush. An example of this occurred on the Vam Sat River during Operation JACK-STAY in late March 1966. As the convoy of 18 American and Vietnamese boats came up to the first bend in the river, VC forces on shore detonated an improvised electrically fired mine and began firing at the boats from both sides of the river. Had American planes not bombed and strafed the Viet Cong positions, the VC's next step would have been to attack with heavier weapons. In rare instances, the Viet Cong were even able to acquire a few Soviet influence mines. Whether or not the VC succeeded in sinking ships was in some ways immaterial: the United States Navy was still forced to divert personnel, materials, and research efforts to counter the mines.[30]

Not surprisingly, American water mining efforts were substantially more sophisticated than those of the Viet Cong. Vietnamese rivers, a crucial supply line for the Viet Cong, were obvious targets. In 1967, the navy mined five of Vietnam's rivers, the Cua Sot, Kien Giang, Song Ca, Song Ma, and South Giang. The American efforts were remarkably successful. Before the mining operation, half of all supplies from North Vietnam reached the rebels in the South via the river system. By the end of 1967, the North Vietnamese were looking for other routes. Coincidently, many of those routes involved the Ho Chi Minh Trail, which was also being mined. One of the major advancements in the American sea mine program to come out of Vietnam was the development of Destructor and later Quickstrike munitions. Both of these

A Viet Cong River mine. (Photograph VA003008, no date, Douglas Pike Photograph Collection, The Vietnam Archive, Texas Tech University.)

relied on a relatively simple idea. Rather than building mines that could become obsolete, the military built kits to modify existing bombs to be used as mines. The Mk 75 was one of the first Destructor variants and worked by replacing the standard fuse on a bomb with a magnetic influence fuse. These mines saw extensive use during the Vietnam War, particularly during the mining of Haiphong Harbor, North Vietnam's main port.[31]

Haiphong was the point of entry for around 85 percent of supplies coming into North Vietnam. Mining the harbor was discussed as early as 1969, though President Nixon rejected the idea because Soviet and Chinese freighters were frequent visitors to the port, and he and his advisors were concerned that the sinking of one of their ships might prove problematic. They were also concerned that the Chinese would merely switch to overland routes. As the United States searched for an exit strategy from Vietnam and peace talks with the North broke down, the Nixon administration decided that mining the harbor was worth the risk to force a peace settlement. As the end goal of the mine blockade was to bring the North Vietnamese back to the peace table, the navy recognized that it would likely be tasked with clearing the fields once the fighting was over. With this in mind, they were very careful that all the mines they used were sweepable. They also set most of the mines to self-sterilize or self-destruct after a preset time. In the words of Rear Admiral Brian McCauley, who commanded the mine clearance operations after the cease fire in 1973, "even as the mines were dropped, the process of mine removal had been started." Mining operations began on May 8, 1972, with the dropping of 36 Mk 52 mod. 2 magnetic mines. The laying of this initial minefield took about two minutes. With the mines set to arm in 72 hours, the United States announced that they had mined Haiphong and suggested that any ships that wanted to leave do so immediately. Of the 36 foreign merchant ships in port on May 8, only nine decided to leave before the mines activated; it appears that North Vietnamese officials refused to provide pilots to any of the ships. Most of the mines planted after the first day were magnetic Mk 36 Destructor mines. Haiphong was only one of seven major North Vietnamese ports mined during the operation, which continued until January 14, 1973.[32]

As expected, one of the protocols signed as part of the Paris Peace Accords included a provision that the United States would clear the sea mines put out at Haiphong and elsewhere. Operation END SWEEP, the clearing of Haiphong Harbor, began on February 6, 1973, and ended on June 20 the same year. The sweeping operations were extremely successful. In large part, the success was due to careful planning on the part of the navy. As mentioned above, many of the mines had already been neutralized by the time sweeping operations began. In addition, the navy had started training for END SWEEP in July 1972 and had already assembled all the sweeping equipment they needed to clear the minefields. In addition to fulfilling treaty obligations, the United States was also observing the 1907 Hague Convention requiring a country to clear its minefields once the war was over.[33]

In 1974, American forces relied on their experience in END SWEEP when the Egyptian government asked for help reopening the Suez Canal. The canal, a vital international waterway, had been subjected to almost 30 years of bombing and mining dating back to World War II. Although the canal had been cleaned and reopened following World War II and the 1956 Suez War, a combination of mines and sunken ships closed the canal once again during the 1967 Arab-Israeli War, also known as the Six-Day War. The canal remained closed for the next eight years and was even mined by the Egyptians again during the 1973 Arab-Israeli War, also called the Yom Kippur War. Clearing operations for Operation NIMBUS STAR began in April 1974. It took less than two months for an international force under the command of Admiral McCauley, who had commanded END SWEEP, to reopen the

The towed mine clearance device used in clearing the mines in Haiphong Harbor during Operation "END SWEEP." (Photograph VA030525, No Date, Glenn Helm Collection, The Vietnam Archive, Texas Tech University.)

canal. It took another six months to finish the sweeping effort, which ultimately cleared some 8,500 explosive devices, including grenades, mines, shells, and bombs. Some of the ordnance had been in the canal since World War II.[34]

While the fighting in Vietnam ended in 1975 with the fall of South Vietnam, unrest in Cambodia and Laos lasted into the 1990s. Armies and irregulars on all sides in these wars and civil wars planted millions of mines, and few of the minefields were recorded. Once the fighting ended in these countries, the people were faced with the unenviable task of trying to clear millions of landmines and tons of unexploded ordnance, including bombs dropped by the United States during the war against North Vietnam. In many cases, landmine clearance was hampered by ongoing fighting.

The Viet Cong and North Vietnamese use of landmines as part of a guerilla war provided insurgent forces worldwide with a successful model of how to use landmines to offset the odds when faced with more numerous,

A Soviet-style POMZ antipersonnel mine in place in Cambodia. (Picture taken by author.)

and often better equipped, forces. At the same time, the American use of air-deployed mines suggested that the weapon could be a public relations nightmare when used against guerilla forces, an experience echoed by the Soviet use of the weapon in Afghanistan. In the civil wars that followed the Vietnam War, various factions looked to landmines to fulfill yet another purpose: controlling civilian populations.

THE POST-VIETNAM LANDMINE PROBLEM

At the beginning of the twentieth century, only 10 percent of wartime casualties were civilians. In World War II, the casualty rate rose to over 60 percent. By the 1980s, the figure increased to 90 percent. This increase reflects the changing nature of war during the twentieth century. In part, this was due to the mechanization of war, which provided militaries with more destructive power than they had before—fleets of bombers, atomic weapons, and, on a smaller scale, landmines. More importantly, the basic understanding of how war should be fought had changed with the development of concepts of absolute war: the involvement of the entire society in supporting the war effort; and total war: war without restraint.[35]

In the aftermath of World War II, which was often fought as a total war, representatives of the nations of the world attempted once again to examine how war should be fought. Of particular concern was the treatment of civilians. The Convention Relative to the Protection of Civilian Persons in Time of War (August 12, 1949) was one of the first postwar treaties and provided guidelines for the treatment of civilians in occupied territories as well as the treatment of enemy aliens during wartime. Other postwar treaties dealt with the treatment of both prisoners of war and injured members of the armed forces and the protection of cultural property during war.[36]

In October 1980, the United Nations Conference on the Prohibitions or Restrictions on the Use of Certain Conventional Weapons Deemed to be Excessively Injurious or to Have Indiscriminate Effect adopted a series of protocols that addressed some of the problems posed by the mechanization of war. The protocols provided guidelines for the use of a range of weapons including incendiary weapons, weapons designed to leave fragments in the body that could not be detected by X-rays, and landmines. Protocol II, the Protocol on Prohibitions or Restrictions on the Use of Mines, Booby-Traps and Other Devices, banned the use of mines "either in offence, defense, or by way of reprisals, against the civilian population." It also confined the use of remotely delivered mines to areas that contained a military objective or military forces; furthermore, it required that the use of mines be accurately recorded so that the mines could be recovered or that mines be self-sterilizing. The treaty also forbade the use of booby traps in most settings, save those in military locations. Perhaps most importantly, it prohibited in all circumstances the use of booby traps "designed to cause superfluous injury or unnecessary suffering." By 1982, 38 countries, including the United States and the Soviet Union, had signed Protocol II.[37] This did not, however, prevent the Soviet use of air-deployed mines during their war in Afghanistan. Nor did it prevent nonsignatory nations from using mines to control their civilian population.

Cambodia's landmine problem largely predates Protocol II, though by less than a decade. Although both American and Vietnamese forces used mines in Cambodia during the American phase of the Vietnam War, mines from this era make up only a small portion of Cambodia's mine problem. During the 1970s, the Khmer Rouge established numerous minefields along the country's borders with Vietnam and Thailand. While the minefields on the Vietnamese border were intended to protect the country from an invasion, Khmer minefields were also used to control the Cambodian people, increasing the danger for people fleeing the Khmer oppression, and as a way to secure control of agricultural land.[38]

The landmine problem in Cambodia did not improve when Vietnam invaded the country in December 1978 to oust the Khmer Rouge. Even though Cambodia's capital, Phnom Penh, fell to Vietnamese forces in January 1979, the Khmer Rouge continued to fight a guerilla war into the 1990s. All sides in the war relied heavily on landmines to secure their defensive positions and territory. In 1985, the Vietnamese began work on the K5 barrier belt, a 600-kilometer-long mine belt running along the Cambodian-Thai border, designed to prevent incursions by Khmer forces based in Thailand. The K5 belt contained as many as three million landmines and was built by forced labor. The belt effectively closed off the Cambodian border with Thailand, making it as difficult for Cambodians to leave the country as it was for Khmer forces to enter the country. The Vietnamese kept few if any records of the location of individual mines, and their allies and enemies were no better.[39]

The erratic and unrecorded use of landmines in Cambodia has made mine clearance a complicated and tedious process. The American State Department estimated that, as of 1998, there were still four to six million active landmines in Cambodia. Mine clearance teams recovered some 8,080 mines the following year. While demining groups cleared around 155 square kilometers of mines between 1993 and 1999, the Cambodian Mine Action Center reported that as of 1998, 664 square kilometers were still known to be mined, and an estimated 1400 square kilometers was suspected to be mined, roughly 1.2 percent of the country. The effect has been devastating. Many of the minefields are scattered in agricultural areas, making it dangerous to use the land until it can be cleared of mines. Landmine awareness programs and mine-clearance and unexploded ordnance (UXO)–clearance operations have had a degree of success. As of mid-2000, landmines and other UXO injured, on average, 83 people a month. In 1996, the monthly average for UXO and landmine casualties was 254.[40]

In Africa, Angola, too, has wrestled with UXO issues, having suffered through revolution and civil war since 1961. The country gained its independence from Portugal in 1974 after over a decade of guerrilla war. Since independence, three separate groups have vied for control of the country. Like many of the colonial and civil wars following World War II, the civil war in Angola was intertwined with the Cold War. The Soviet Union, the United States, and their surrogates provided money and material, including landmines, to the various factions. In addition, South Africa and Zaire invaded

Angola in the mid-1970s in support of opposing factions. South Africa invaded Angola several more times in the 1980s, usually to attack guerrillas conducting operations in South African-occupied Namibia. During these civil wars, landmines became a common weapon not only to set up defensive perimeters but also as an offensive weapon to deny the opposition the use of large areas of land, including farmland and diamond mines.[41]

The U.S. State Department estimates that there are some six million landmines buried in Angola, a country roughly twice the size of Texas. One in every 416 Angolans has a landmine-related injury. While a number of international groups are working in Angola to help clear landmines, both government and rebel forces are reported to have laid fresh minefields, in some instances in areas that had recently been cleared.[42]

Latin America has faced similar problems. Years of civil war and border wars in the region have left active minefields in many areas. Many of the mines in these countries were deployed during insurgency wars. As in Angola, these wars were usually caught up in the international politics of the Cold War, with both the United States and Soviet Union supplying weapons to the various factions. Columbia is one of the more heavily mined countries in the region. The Columbia Campaign to Ban Landmines reports that there are active landmines in 135 of the country's 1,050 municipalities, roughly 13 percent of the country.[43]

Conversely, Latin America has also been the site of some successful demining programs. One of the best examples is El Salvador, where former soldiers from both sides of the 1980s civil war played an active role in locating and removing minefields. These efforts were so successful that no landmine-related accidents have been reported in El Salvador since 1994.[44]

Europe has not been immune to the landmine problem either. The most well-known examples are the mines left from the wars fought in the Balkans during the 1990s following the breakup of Yugoslavia. The two countries that suffered most from landmines during these wars were Bosnia and Croatia, which were both invaded by Serbia after they left the Yugoslav federation. During the war in Croatia (1990–1995), Serb and Croatian forces put out as many as 1.5 million landmines. As of 2000, some 7.9 percent of the country was still mined. The war in Bosnia (1992–1995) left similar results. As of 1998, three years after the end of the war, there were an estimated 30,000 minefields in Bosnia, containing 750,000 landmines. By March 2000, only 18,223 of these fields had been recorded.[45]

Perhaps the most grievous example of the problems posed by modern landmines, however, is Afghanistan, which suffered not only civil war but also a Soviet invasion and occupation from 1979 to 1989. Like the Americans in Vietnam, the Soviet Union originally entered Afghanistan to support a friendly government and was then faced with a long, drawn-out war, fighting guerrilla forces backed by another nation, the United States. The Soviets used many of the same weapons and tactics that the United States had used a decade earlier in Vietnam. Among these tactics was the use of air-delivered landmines to deny guerrilla groups access to roads. The Soviet PFM-1, essentially a copy of the American Dragontooth mine, was particularly dangerous to children, who tended to think the mine was a toy.[46]

Following the Soviet withdrawal in 1989, an international effort began to try to clear the many landmines scattered in the country. The effort, sponsored in part by the United Nations, included training refugees in mine-clearing operations. In part, the mine-clearing effort was designed to encourage Afghan refugees, particularly in Pakistan, to return home. While the initial program was not as successful as the United Nations had hoped it would be, it was a major step in the development of international involvement in landmine clearance projects. Between 1990 and April 2000, some 465 square kilometers were cleared of landmines, including 205,842 antipersonnel mines and 9,199 antitank mines. Roughly 717 square kilometers still remained to be cleared at the end of this time period. The Soviet withdrawal did not bring peace. Fighting has continued in Afghanistan, including years of civil war and, most recently, the American intervention to remove the Taliban following the 2001 bombing of the World Trade Center.[47]

The use of landmines in the years since World War II has by no means been restricted to wars of insurgency. Most, if not all, of the conventional wars fought since World War II have made extensive use of landmines. Both Arab and Israeli forces used defensive mines during their various wars, including the Israeli War of Independence (1948–1949), the Sinai War (1956), the Six-Day War (1967), and the Yom Kippur War (1973). Indian and Pakistani forces also used defensive mines during their many wars (1947, 1965, and 1971), as did the British and Argentines in the 1982 Falkland Islands War. In Europe, many of the frontiers along the border of the Iron Curtain were mined. In the case of East Germany, the mining of its borders with West Germany was more to prevent their own population from leaving than to keep people from the west out.

The Persian Gulf War (1991) was one of the better examples of both the effective and the ineffective uses of landmines. Following their occupation of Kuwait, Iraqi forces established deep defensive positions along the Saudi Arabian–Kuwaiti border. These positions generally consisted of a line of barbed wire, oil-filled antitank trenches that could be set on fire, and a 100- to 200-meter-deep belt of landmines. The defenses were particularly troubling to the American soldiers scheduled to liberate Kuwait. An American

Marine remembered that "Iraqi minefields terrified most Marines, myself included" and compared the planned attack to the bloody assault on Tarawa Island in World War II. By the time the attack came, though, Iraqi positions had been subjected to fierce preparatory fire and bombing, and the minefields were no longer effectively covered by fire. Having suppressed Iraqi covering fire, American forces were able to breech the minefields quickly with a minimum of casualties. Perhaps the most unique mine-clearing method the American military forces used during the war was flying B-52 strikes against Iraqi minefields.[48]

While the Iraqi military relied on landmines as defensive weapons, the American military tended to concentrate on the use of air-deployed landmines as offensive weapons. One of the first tasks Coalition forces faced during the war was the destruction of Iraqi air power. A component of this effort included neutralizing Iraqi airfields. This was done in part by using bombs designed to create large craters in the runways and then seeding the runway with air-deployed mines to prevent construction crews from repairing the runway. Coalition forces also used air-deployed mines in attacks against Iraqi armor units. One of most successful of these was the Gator mine (CBU-92/B), a cluster munition that puts out a mixed field of 72 antitank mines and 22 antipersonnel mines. These mines not only were used to limit the movement of Iraqi forces in battle, but were also successfully used to slow the retreat of Iraqi forces.[49]

In the last 50 years, many militaries have developed automated mine dispersal systems. Air-deployed antipersonnel mines such as the butterfly bomb and WAAPM have been supplemented with air-deployed antitank mines like the American Gator mine. Many militaries have developed automated dispersal systems for ground-based vehicles. The British Ranger system can be mounted on a variety of vehicles and can put out a 100-meter-deep antipersonnel minefield in a single minute. The United States has developed a similar system, Artillery Deployed Antipersonnel Mines (ADAM), using 155 mm howitzers that can scatter a field of bounding antipersonnel mines at a range of up to 17 kilometers. The British and others have developed automated systems for laying bar mines as well. Under good conditions, a crew of two soldiers can put out around 400 antitank mines per hour.[50]

One of the common elements of modern scatterable munitions is that they are designed to self-sterilize after a preset period of time. This feature is an imperative for scatterable mines for several reasons. On a public relations level, it helps prevent civilian casualties. More importantly from a military standpoint, self-sterilization allows one to put out a minefield to harass or block the enemy and still be able to move over the mined area a short time later. While early versions of self-sterilizing mines, like those used by the

United States, were set to deactivate within a month or so, more recent mines, such as ADAM, are frequently set to deactivate in a much shorter time span, sometimes as little as four hours.[51]

Regardless of the many innovations in landmine warfare since 1945, the majority of the mines being used today are not very different from those in use at the end of World War II. Most mines, particularly the antipersonnel mines used in the Third World, use basic pressure fuses, are not equipped to self-sterilize, and are relatively inexpensive, costing less than $5 each. Many of the mines are nonmetallic, making them very difficult to locate with normal mine detectors. While landmines are not entirely responsible for the rise in civilian casualties from war, these devices have certainly played a role in the increase, particularly in deaths that occur after the war has actually ended. The problems caused by the indiscriminate use of landmines led several nongovernmental organizations (NGOs) in the early 1990s to call for an end to the use of landmines.[52]

THE ICBL

In October 1992, six NGOs met in New York City to formally launch the International Committee to Ban Landmines (ICBL). Three of the six organizations were American—the Vietnam Veterans of America Foundation, Physicians for Human Rights, and Human Rights Watch. Of the other three, one was British, Mines Advisory Group; one was French, Handicap International; and one was German, Medico International. Jody Williams of the Vietnam Veterans of America Foundation took on the role of ICBL coordinator. The ICBL's mission was twofold. First, it sought to promote and secure an international ban on the production, stockpiling, and use of antipersonnel mines, and, second, it aimed to obtain resources for civilian demining operations and for helping the victims of landmines.[53]

The ICBL has been surprisingly successful in its mission and has brought together a variety of international organizations to work toward a common goal. Over 1,200 NGOs from around 60 countries have joined the ICBL since 1992. Part of its success has been its use of new communication technology, including faxes, the World Wide Web, and email. The ICBL held its first international conference to promote the antipersonnel landmine ban in London in 1993. Some 40 NGOs were represented. Attendance doubled the following year at the conference held in Geneva.[54]

Governmental support for limiting the use of antipersonnel mines began quickly. The American government announced a unilateral one-year ban on the export of antipersonnel mines in 1992. After extending the ban several times, the Clinton administration announced a permanent ban on the export of antipersonnel mines in 1997. A number of nations followed the American example. In 1993, France announced it would no longer export antipersonnel mines. In 1994, Sweden, a major weapons producer, and Italy, one of the top three producers of antipersonnel mines worldwide, both announced they would no longer export antipersonnel mines. The Italian government went so far as to completely stop the production of antipersonnel mines by Italian companies and promised to support demining operations. In 1995, Belgium became the first government to completely ban the use, stockpiling, and production of antipersonnel mines; Belgium was followed shortly by Norway.[55]

In early 1996, the ICBL attempted unsuccessfully to have a review commission amend the 1980 Convention on Certain Conventional Weapons so that it completely banned the use of antipersonnel mines. Following the deadlock in the debates at the Review Conference, the Canadian government informed the ICBL that it was interested in hosting an international conference to further discuss the ban. Titled "Towards a Global Ban on Anti-Personnel Landmines," the October 1996 conference brought together representatives from over 70 governments and dozens of NGOs. Fifty of the countries represented at the conference signed a declaration recognizing the need for a total ban on antipersonnel mines, and the Canadian government called for a treaty-signing conference to be held in December the following year in Ottawa. Over the next year, the ICBL and involved governments, including Canada and Austria's, labored to hash out a workable treaty to ban antipersonnel mines.[56]

The ICBL attended the 1997 Ottawa negotiations as an official observer. This status gave the ICBL the same rights as observer governments, including the right to sit in on all conference sessions. While unable to make formal suggestions for the wording of the treaty, the ICBL was able to make informal suggestions to participating governments. The three week negotiations came to a head when the United States, a last minute attendee at the conference, called for a 24-hour delay during the final day of the negotiations. The American attempt at delay was part of its effort to gain exemptions to the ban on antipersonnel mines based on American needs. The desired exemptions included American minefields in Korea, certain smart mines capable of self-sterilization, and a delay of when the treaty would come into effect.

The American effort failed. On December 3–4, 1997, over 120 countries signed the Convention on the Prohibition of the Use, Stockpiling, Production and Transfer of Anti-Personnel mines and on Their Destruction, agreeing that

1. Each State undertakes never under any circumstances:

   – To use anti-personnel mines;

- To develop, produce, otherwise acquire, stockpile, retain or transfer to any-one, directly or indirectly, anti-personnel mines;

- To assist, encourage or induce, in any way, anyone to engage in any activity prohibited to a State Party in this Convention.

2. Each State Party undertakes to destroy or ensure the destruction of all anti-personnel mines in accordance with the provisions of this Convention.

By the end of April 1998, four additional countries had signed the treaty. In 1997, the Nobel Committee awarded the Nobel Peace Prize to the ICBL and its coordinator, Jody Williams.[57]

While 149 countries have ratified the treaty as of the writing of this book, 40 countries have yet to sign it, and five have signed it, but not ratified it. The omissions are significant, including Russia and many of the other successor states to the Soviet Union, the United States, China, India, Pakistan, Israel, North and South Korea, and many of the Arab states. In short, the list includes the major producers and, in the case of China, exporters of land-mines, and countries likely to be involved in a large-scale conventional war. Many of the countries have refused to sign the treaty because they have not been able to identify a viable alternative to landmines, particularly for secur-ing borders. In addition, there are likely to be insurgent groups that do not feel bound by their government's signing of the treaty. While the treaty may lower the number of landmines used, it is unlikely that the problem will go away.[58]

SEA MINES

Like landmines, sea mines have also undergone tremendous changes since World War II. In addition to the proliferation of air-delivered sea mines dis-cussed above, a number of navies have also developed mines based around submarine torpedoes. The American version, the Mk 60 Captor mine, was introduced in 1979 and uses sonar to track its prey. When Captor (encapsu-lated torpedo) detects the signature of a submarine, it launches a Mk 46 mod. 4 torpedo, which uses sonar to track the submarine. The Mk 46 is an extremely fast torpedo and was designed specifically to use against nuclear submarines. The British Hammerhead and the Russian Cluster Bay/Cluster Gulf mines work in a similar fashion. Captor and Hammerhead are both designed to be laid by ship, submarine, or aircraft. A number of countries have also developed shallow-water anti-invasion mines using both contact and influence fuses. Perhaps the most disturbing mines to come out of the Cold War era was the Soviet antisubmarine nuclear mine. With a destructive yield of 5–20 kilotons, the mine was designed to destroy nearby submarines at any depth, making it an effective solution for true deep water mining operations. Mine clearance techniques have also changed, in large part to deal with the proliferation of "unsweepable" influence mines. Many of the new sweeping devices are towed sonar arrays designed to look for ground mines, which are by far the mines most difficult to sweep for. Other detectors, such as the French PAP 104 and Honeywell Mine Neutralization System vehicle are sonar equipped remote controlled submersibles.[59]

Despite the many technological advances in naval mines, including options such as self-sterilizer, many of the mines that have actually been used in combat since 1975 bear a closer resemblance to the mines of World War I and World War II than they do to mines like Captor or Destructor. This includes two of the more controversial uses of sea mines in recent years, the Iranian mining of the Persian Gulf during the 1980–1988 Iran-Iraq War and the rebel mining of Managua, Nicaragua, in 1984.

In 1979, Marxist revolutionaries known as the Sandinistas overthrew the dictatorial government of Anastasio Somoza in Nicaragua. While the American government attempted to work with the new government, by 1981 it was apparent that the Sandinistas were supporting guerrilla forces in neighboring countries and President Jimmy Carter formally ended aid to Nicaragua. Carter's successor, Ronald Reagan, took an even stronger stand against the Nicaraguan government and began blocking Nicaraguan efforts at obtaining commercial credit and foreign aid. In addition, the Reagan administration began providing aid to several anti-Sandinista groups collectively called the Contras. In 1983, the American Central Intelligence Agency (CIA) began using contract agents to carry out acts of sabotage in Nicaragua disguised as Contra actions, including the destruction of several oil storage facilities. In January 1984, Contra rebels and CIA agents began mining several of the country's major ports including the west coast ports of Corinto and Puerto Sandino, the east coast port of El Bluff, the waters of Lake Nicaragua. By April, when American involvement in mining became common knowledge, around 75 mines had been planted in the various harbors. Most of the mines were either acoustic or magnetic influence mines. CIA agents were responsible for 30 to 40 of the mines. These held about 300 pounds of explosives, and were responsible for most of the significant damage. While the CIA mines were well constructed, other mines, probably those laid by the Contras themselves, were rather crude and appeared to be "home made." The goal of the mining operation seems to have been more to create a sense of panic rather than actually to sink ships as the latter might cause an international incident, especially if it belonged to another country. The detonation of a few mines, however, might well cause international shipping underwriters to quit writing insurance policies on ships bound for the country, further damaging the Nicaraguan economy. While the Nicaraguans were able to clear the minefields within a few weeks after the end of the mining operations, the mines were responsible for killing two fishermen and injuring 15 sailors. As planned, the mining extracted a toll of on the Nicaraguan economy as well, an estimated $10 million.[60]

American actions in Nicaragua caused an international outcry, and in 1985 Congress ordered the end to funding for the Contras. In April 1984, Nicaragua filed suit against the United States in the International Court of Justice at the Hague. In the Case Concerning Military and Paramilitary Activities in and Against Nicaragua (*Nicaragua v. U.S.*), the Nicaraguans alleged that the American actions in Nicaragua were a violation of the charters of the United Nations and the Organization of American States as well as international law and requested that the court order the United States to end their actions and to compensate Nicaragua for damages. The mining of Nicaraguan waters was only part of their case. The American defense was that it was acting "for the purpose of collective defense" and, in effect, combating Sandinista backed insurgency efforts in Latin America. In January 1985, the Reagan administration announced that it would end its participation in the case. The court handed down its decision on June 26, 1987. It found for Nicaragua and ordered the United States to pay restitution in the sum of $370 million. The court was decidedly critical of the American mine-laying effort and referred to it as a violation of international law and custom. In addition, as the United States had not issued a warning about the presence of the mines, the court also ruled that the United States had violated the 1907 Hague Convention. The American government ignored the ruling.[61]

Sea mines became an international issue again in 1987 near the end of the Iran-Iraq War. During the course of the eight year war, both sides had declared exclusion zones in the Persian Gulf in which traffic was not permitted. The Kuwaiti government, which had supported Iraq, was particularly concerned about Iranian threats against shipping and in April 1987 began leasing foreigner tankers to carry oil shipments. In May, a Soviet tanker licensed by Kuwait hit a mine. In June, a small field of Iranian contact mines was found in one of the gulf channels. On July 22, the United States began reflagging Kuwaiti tankers as American and providing escort ships. Two days later, one of the tankers struck an Iranian mine. As mine casualties began to mount, Britain, France, and Saudi Arabia sent minesweepers to assist in the Gulf. On August 10, an American tanker hit a mine in the Gulf of Oman. The Iranians quickly blamed the United States as having put out the mines, though they later admitted that they had put out the mines themselves as a defensive measure against a possible American attack. In September, an American military helicopter destroyed the Iranian ship *Iran Ajr* while the latter was in the process of putting out a minefield near Bahrain. Ships from the American Navy retrieved both the ship's crew and nine of the mines they were in the process of deploying. The mines were M-08 type sea mines—a Russian designed mine that had come to Iran through North Korea. While the mine may have been of recent production, the design itself dates from before World War I. On April 13, 1988, the American frigate *Samuel B. Roberts* suffered extensive damage after striking an Iranian mine. Four days later, the American Navy attacked offshore oil platforms that had been used by the Iranian military and destroyed almost half of the small Iranian navy. In more recent years, Iran has begun trying to purchase more sophisticated mines. Given the history of Iranian mining efforts, this could pose a tremendous threat to oil shipments coming through the Persian Gulf.[62]

While the 1907 Hague Convention is still the dominant treaty regulating the use of sea mines, the weapons have come up in several international arms control treaties including the 1971 Treaty on the Prohibition of the Emplacement of Nuclear Weapons and Other Weapons of Mass Destruction on the Sea-Bed and the Ocean Floor and in the Subsoil Thereof and Protocol II to the 1980 Conventional Weapons Treaty. In the former, the primary concern was with the use of nuclear antisubmarine weapons such as the Soviet one discussed above. While the treaty spoke generally about the problems posed by the use of nuclear weapons, particularly in an environment as fragile as the ocean, it only banned the use of nuclear weapons more than 12 miles from a country's coast. The second of the treaties, as discussed above, was originally geared towards the use of landmines. In 1981, it was modified so that the section restricting the use of landmines and the requirements for minefield recording and clearance were also applied to naval mines.[63]

CONCLUSIONS

In the early nineteenth century, many military professionals denounced the use of both land and sea mines. During the War of 1812, a British admiral referred to the American use of naval mines as "a Diabolical and Cowardly contrivance." Union General George McClellan had similar words for Confederate mining efforts during the American Civil War, and described those responsible as "guilty of the most murderous & barbarous conduct." In the years that followed, both weapons gained grudging acceptance. For landmines, the issue was a question of the weapon proving its worth, something that did not happen until World War I. The sea mine suffered from a different stigma: it was viewed as a weapon of the weak. In the years before World War I, many members of the British and American navies were reluctant to promote mine warfare lest the use of mines come into common practice, a possibility that could only harm their status as one of the world's premiere navies. Doubts about the efficacy of sea mines were largely dispelled by the success of mining efforts by both sides during World War I. World War II brought about an even more effective way to plant land and sea mines, using aircraft. Not only could the mines be delivered at great distances with limited risks, in the case of landmines, hundreds of mines could be put out in a short amount of time.[64]

That the two types of mines should develop along similar paths is not surprising. Many of those involved with the development of mines in the first half of the nineteenth century, including Immanuel Nobel and Gabriel Rains, worked on both land and sea mines. Even though this largely changed by the 1870s, the two types of mines served similar purposes, denying one's enemy the use of an area, and faced similar challenges including how to lay minefields more effectively, how to increase a mine's efficiency, and how to minimize friendly casualties. Thus, air delivery became a standard way of putting out both types of minefields, influences became a common means for distinguishing targets, and self-sterilizers developed to allow mines to be put down and not need to be cleared when the area was occupied by friendly forces. The devices also raised similar ethical issues, particularly the problem of civilian casualties and what to do with the mines once a war was over.

As sea mines came into widespread use earlier than landmines, they were the first to be addressed in international law. Deaths and shipping losses caused by mines left over from the Russo-Japanese War caused international concern and were directly responsible for the restrictions placed on the use of mines by the 1907 Hague Convention. The widespread use of landmines presented similar problems in the years following World War II and came to a head with the intentional targeting of civilians in areas such as Cambodia and Angola in the 1970s, 1980s, and 1990s. Where the Hague Convention had been concerned with the problem of drifting mines, the Ottawa Convention was concerned with antipersonnel mines. Despite the concerns raised by land and sea mines, both weapons are still widely used.

The Ottawa Convention's effort to ban an entire class of mines has proved particularly difficult for some nations to sign off on. In particular, the United States has maintained that it needs to be able to continue using mixed fields of mines in Korea until a better weapon can be found. The American military bases its demand for an exception on the way it uses mines in Korea: carefully defined, marked, and recorded fields. American mines in South Korea are used largely as a barrier device to slow a potential North Korean invasion like the one that occurred in 1950. The American military considers antipersonnel mines necessary in these fields to prevent North Korea from using the human-wave tactics they relied on in the 1950s and to prevent the North Koreans from easily clearing the antitank mines.

The American military also has argued that it should be allowed to continue using its scatterable mines, such as Gator, which allow them to automatically put out large mixed minefields, and has pointed out that these mine systems are designed to self-sterilize, preventing them from causing casualties after the mines are no longer needed. As in Korea, there is a perceived need to include antipersonnel mines to prevent easy breaching of the minefields.[65] In part, the American military's preference for this system is probably based on its success with it against Iraqi forces in the Persian Gulf War.

American Army officers have added yet another reason why the United States should not sign the Ottawa Convention and forswear the use of antipersonnel mines. Given America's commitment to take an active role on the international stage, particularly in the defense of South Korea and in the Persian Gulf, the United States should not give up an effective weapon. Indeed, this was President Bill Clinton's position when he refused to have the United States sign the Ottawa Convention. While he said the American military would work to develop an alternative to antipersonnel mines he stated,

> I will not send our soldiers to defend the freedom of our people and the freedom of others without doing everything that we can to make them as secure as possible.

His concerns seem justified. A 2000 Dupuy Institute study found that if the United States observed the antipersonnel landmine ban and its opponents did not, the United States could expect a 3 percent increase in casualties. This study is particularly sobering given the anti-insurgency wars the United States is now fighting and current tensions with North Korea.[66]

Appendix A

HAGUE CONVENTION 1907: CONVENTION VIII RELATIVE TO THE LAYING OF AUTOMATIC SUBMARINE CONTACT MINES

Inspired by the principle of the freedom of sea routes, the common highway of all nations;

Seeing that, although the existing position of affairs makes it impossible to forbid the employment of automatic submarine contact mines, it is nevertheless desirable to restrict and regulate their employment in order to mitigate the severity of war and to ensure, as far as possible, to peaceful navigation the security to which it is entitled, despite the existence of war;

Until such time as it is found possible to formulate rules on the subject which shall ensure to the interests involved all the guarantees desirable;

Have resolved to conclude a Convention for this purpose, and have appointed the following as their Plenipotentiaries:

(List of Plenipotentiaries)

Who, after having deposited their full powers, found in good and due form, have agreed upon the following provisions:

Article 1
It is forbidden - 1. To lay unanchored automatic contact mines, except when they are so constructed as to become harmless one hour at most after the person who laid them ceases to control them; 2. To lay anchored automatic contact mines which do not become harmless as soon as they have broken loose

from their moorings; 3. To use torpedoes which do not become harmless when they have missed their mark.

Article 2
It is forbidden to lay automatic contact mines off the coast and ports of the enemy, with the sole object of intercepting commercial shipping.

Article 3
When anchored automatic contact mines are employed, every possible precaution must be taken for the security of peaceful shipping.

The belligerents undertake to do their utmost to render these mines harmless within a limited time, and, should they cease to be under surveillance, to notify the danger zones as soon as military exigencies permit, by a notice addressed to ship owners, which must also be communicated to the Governments through the diplomatic channel.

Article 4
Neutral Powers which lay automatic contact mines off their coasts must observe the same rules and take the same precautions as are imposed on belligerents.

The neutral Power must inform ship owners, by a notice issued in advance, where automatic contact mines have been laid. This notice must be communicated at once to the Governments through the diplomatic channel.

Article 5
At the close of the war, the Contracting Powers undertake to do their utmost to remove the mines which they have laid, each Power removing its own mines.

As regards anchored automatic contact mines laid by one of the belligerents off the coast of the other, their position must be notified to the other party by the Power which laid them, and each Power must proceed with the least possible delay to remove the mines in its own waters.

Article 6
The Contracting Powers which do not at present own perfected mines of the pattern contemplated in the present Convention, and which, consequently, could not at present carry out the rules laid down in Articles 1 and 3, undertake to convert the materiel of their mines as soon as possible, so as to bring it into conformity with the foregoing requirements.

Article 7
The provisions of the present Convention do not apply except between Contracting Powers, and then only if all the belligerents are parties to the Convention.

Article 8
The present Convention shall be ratified as soon as possible.

The ratifications shall be deposited at The Hague.

The first deposit of ratifications shall be recorded in a procès-verbal signed by the representatives of the Powers which take part therein and by the Netherlands Minister for Foreign Affairs.

The subsequent deposits of ratifications shall be made by means of a written notification addressed to the Netherlands Government and accompanied by the instrument of ratification.

A duly certified copy of the procès-verbal relative to the first deposit of ratifications, of the notifications mentioned in the preceding paragraph, as well as of the instruments of ratification, shall be at once sent, by the Netherlands Government, through the diplomatic channel, to the Powers invited to the Second Peace Conference, as well as to the other Powers which have adhered to the Convention. In the cases contemplated in the preceding paragraph, the said Government shall inform them at the same time of the date on which it has received the notification.

Article 9
Non-Signatory Powers may adhere to the present Convention.

The Power which desires to adhere notifies in writing its intention to the Netherlands Government, transmitting to it the act of adhesion, which shall be deposited in the archives of the said Government.

This Government shall at once transmit to all the other Powers a duly certified copy of the notification as well as of the act of adhesion, stating the date on which it received the notification.

Article 10
   The present Convention shall come into force, in the case of the Powers which were a party to the first deposit of ratifications, sixty days after the date

of the procès-verbal of this deposit, and, in the case of the Powers which ratify subsequently or adhere, sixty days after the notification of their ratification or of their adhesion has been received by the Netherlands Government.

Article 11

The present Convention shall remain in force for seven years, dating from the sixtieth day after the date of the first deposit of ratifications.

Unless denounced, it shall continue in force after the expiration of this period.

The denunciation shall be notified in writing to the Netherlands Government, which shall at once communicate a duly certified copy of the notification to all the Powers, informing them of the date on which it was received.

The denunciation shall only have effect in regard to the notifying Power, and six months after the notification has reached the Netherlands Government.

Article 12

The Contracting Powers undertake to reopen the question of the employment of automatic contact mines six months before the expiration of the period contemplated in the first paragraph of the preceding article, in the event of the question not having been already reopened and settled by the Third Peace Conference.

If the Contracting Powers conclude a fresh Convention relative to the employment of mines, the present Convention shall cease to be applicable from the moment it comes into force.

Article 13

A register kept by the Netherlands Ministry for Foreign Affairs shall give the date of the deposit of ratifications made in virtue of Article 8, paragraphs 3 and 4, as well as the date on which the notifications of adhesion (Article 9, paragraph 2) or of denunciation (Article 11, paragraph 3) have been received.

Each Contracting Power is entitled to have access to this register and to be supplied with duly certified extracts from it.

In faith whereof the Plenipotentiaries have appended their signatures to the present Convention.

Done at The Hague, 18 October 1907, in a single copy, which shall remain deposited in the archives of the Netherlands Government, and duly certified copies of which shall be sent, through the diplomatic channel, to the Powers which have been invited to the Second Peace Conference.

Appendix B

CONVENTION ON THE PROHIBITION OF THE USE, STOCKPILING, PRODUCTION AND TRANSFER OF ANTI-PERSONNEL MINES AND ON THEIR DESTRUCTION, 18 SEPTEMBER 1997

Preamble

The States Parties,

Determined to put an end to the suffering and casualties caused by anti-personnel mines, that kill or maim hundreds of people every week, mostly innocent and defenceless civilians and especially children, obstruct economic development and reconstruction, inhibit the repatriation of refugees and internally displaced persons, and have other severe consequences for years after emplacement,

Believing it necessary to do their utmost to contribute in an efficient and coordinated manner to face the challenge of removing anti-personnel mines placed throughout the world, and to assure their destruction,

Wishing to do their utmost in providing assistance for the care and rehabilitation, including the social and economic reintegration of mine victims,

Recognizing that a total ban of anti-personnel mines would also be an important confidence-building measure,

Welcoming the adoption of the Protocol on Prohibitions or Restrictions on the Use of Mines, Booby-Traps and Other Devices, as amended on 3 May 1996, annexed to the Convention on Prohibitions or Restrictions on the Use of Certain Conventional Weapons Which May Be Deemed to Be

Excessively Injurious or to Have Indiscriminate Effects, and calling for the early ratification of this Protocol by all States which have not yet done so,

Welcoming also United Nations General Assembly Resolution 51/45 S of 10 December 1996 urging all States to pursue vigorously an effective, legally-binding international agreement to ban the use, stockpiling, production and transfer of anti-personnel landmines,

Welcoming furthermore the measures taken over the past years, both unilaterally and multilaterally, aiming at prohibiting, restricting or suspending the use, stockpiling, production and transfer of anti-personnel mines,

Stressing the role of public conscience in furthering the principles of humanity as evidenced by the call for a total ban of anti-personnel mines and recognizing the efforts to that end undertaken by the International Red Cross and Red Crescent Movement, the International Campaign to Ban Landmines and numerous other non-governmental organizations around the world,

Recalling the Ottawa Declaration of 5 October 1996 and the Brussels Declaration of 27 June 1997 urging the international community to negotiate an international and legally binding agreement prohibiting the use, stockpiling, production and transfer of anti-personnel mines,

Emphasizing the desirability of attracting the adherence of all States to this Convention, and determined to work strenuously towards the promotion of its universalization in all relevant fora including, inter alia, the United Nations, the Conference on Disarmament, regional organizations, and groupings, and review conferences of the Convention on Prohibitions or Restrictions on the Use of Certain Conventional Weapons Which May Be Deemed to Be Excessively Injurious or to Have Indiscriminate Effects,

Basing themselves on the principle of international humanitarian law that the right of the parties to an armed conflict to choose methods or means of warfare is not unlimited, on the principle that prohibits the employment in armed conflicts of weapons, projectiles and materials and methods of warfare of a nature to cause superfluous injury or unnecessary suffering and on the principle that a distinction must be made between civilians and combatants,

Have agreed as follows:

Article 1
General obligations

1. Each State Party undertakes never under any circumstances:

a) To use anti-personnel mines;

b) To develop, produce, otherwise acquire, stockpile, retain or transfer to anyone, directly or indirectly, anti-personnel mines;

c) To assist, encourage or induce, in any way, anyone to engage in any activity prohibited to a State Party under this Convention.

2. Each State Party undertakes to destroy or ensure the destruction of all anti-personnel mines in accordance with the provisions of this Convention.

Article 2
Definitions

1. "Anti-personnel mine" means a mine designed to be exploded by the presence, proximity or contact of a person and that will incapacitate, injure or kill one or more persons. Mines designed to be detonated by the presence, proximity or contact of a vehicle as opposed to a person, that are equipped with anti-handling devices, are not considered anti-personnel mines as a result of being so equipped.

2. "Mine" means a munition designed to be placed under, on or near the ground or other surface area and to be exploded by the presence, proximity or contact of a person or a vehicle.

3. "Anti-handling device" means a device intended to protect a mine and which is part of, linked to, attached to or placed under the mine and which activates when an attempt is made to tamper with or otherwise intentionally disturb the mine.

4. "Transfer" involves, in addition to the physical movement of anti-personnel mines into or from national territory, the transfer of title to and control over the mines, but does not involve the transfer of territory containing emplaced anti-personnel mines.

5. "Mined area" means an area which is dangerous due to the presence or suspected presence of mines.

Article 3
Exceptions

1. Notwithstanding the general obligations under Article 1, the retention or transfer of a number of anti-personnel mines for the development of and training in mine detection, mine clearance, or mine destruction techniques is permitted. The amount of such mines shall not exceed the minimum number absolutely necessary for the above-mentioned purposes.

2. The transfer of anti-personnel mines for the purpose of destruction is permitted.

Article 4
Destruction of stockpiled anti-personnel mines

Except as provided for in Article 3, each State Party undertakes to destroy or ensure the destruction of all stockpiled anti-personnel mines it owns or possesses, or that are under its jurisdiction or control, as soon as possible but not later than four years after the entry into force of this Convention for that State Party.

Article 5
Destruction of anti-personnel mines in mined areas

1. Each State Party undertakes to destroy or ensure the destruction of all anti-personnel mines in mined areas under its jurisdiction or control, as soon as possible but not later than ten years after the entry into force of this Convention for that State Party.

2. Each State Party shall make every effort to identify all areas under its jurisdiction or control in which anti-personnel mines are known or suspected to be emplaced and shall ensure as soon as possible that all anti-personnel mines in mined areas under its jurisdiction or control are perimeter-marked, monitored and protected by fencing or other means, to ensure the effective exclusion of civilians, until all anti-personnel mines contained therein have been destroyed. The marking shall at least be to the standards set out in the Protocol on Prohibitions or Restrictions on the Use of Mines, Booby-Traps and Other Devices, as amended on 3 May 1996, annexed to the Convention on

Prohibitions or Restrictions on the Use of Certain Conventional Weapons Which May Be Deemed to Be Excessively Injurious or to Have Indiscriminate Effects.

3. If a State Party believes that it will be unable to destroy or ensure the destruction of all anti-personnel mines referred to in paragraph 1 within that time period, it may submit a request to a Meeting of the States Parties or a Review Conference for an extension of the deadline for completing the destruction of such anti-personnel mines, for a period of up to ten years.

4. Each request shall contain:

a) The duration of the proposed extension;

b) A detailed explanation of the reasons for the proposed extension, including:

(i) The preparation and status of work conducted under national demining programs;

(ii) The financial and technical means available to the State Party for the destruction of all the anti-personnel mines; and

(iii) Circumstances which impede the ability of the State Party to destroy all the anti-personnel mines in mined areas;

c) The humanitarian, social, economic, and environmental implications of the extension; and

d) Any other information relevant to the request for the proposed extension.

5. The Meeting of the States Parties or the Review Conference shall, taking into consideration the factors contained in paragraph 4, assess the request and decide by a majority of votes of States Parties present and voting whether to grant the request for an extension period.

6. Such an extension may be renewed upon the submission of a new request in accordance with paragraphs 3, 4 and 5 of this Article. In requesting a further extension period a State Party shall submit relevant additional information on what has been undertaken in the previous extension period pursuant to this Article.

Article 6
International cooperation and assistance

1. In fulfilling its obligations under this Convention each State Party has the right to seek and receive assistance, where feasible, from other States Parties to the extent possible.

2. Each State Party undertakes to facilitate and shall have the right to participate in the fullest possible exchange of equipment, material and scientific and technological information concerning the implementation of this Convention. The States Parties shall not impose undue restrictions on the provision of mine clearance equipment and related technological information for humanitarian purposes.

3. Each State Party in a position to do so shall provide assistance for the care and rehabilitation, and social and economic reintegration, of mine victims and for mine awareness programs. Such assistance may be provided, inter alia, through the United Nations system, international, regional or national organizations or institutions, the International Committee of the Red Cross, national Red Cross and Red Crescent societies and their International Federation, non-governmental organizations, or on a bilateral basis.

4. Each State Party in a position to do so shall provide assistance for mine clearance and related activities. Such assistance may be provided, inter alia, through the United Nations system, international or regional organizations or institutions, non-governmental organizations or institutions, or on a bilateral basis, or by contributing to the United Nations Voluntary Trust Fund for Assistance in Mine Clearance, or other regional funds that deal with demining.

5. Each State Party in a position to do so shall provide assistance for the destruction of stockpiled anti-personnel mines.

6. Each State Party undertakes to provide information to the database on mine clearance established within the United Nations system, especially information concerning various means and technologies of mine clearance, and lists of experts, expert agencies or national points of contact on mine clearance.

7. States Parties may request the United Nations, regional organizations, other States Parties or other competent intergovernmental or non-

governmental fora to assist its authorities in the elaboration of a national demining program to determine, inter alia:

a) The extent and scope of the anti-personnel mine problem;

b) The financial, technological and human resources that are required for the implementation of the program;

c) The estimated number of years necessary to destroy all anti-personnel mines in mined areas under the jurisdiction or control of the concerned State Party;

d) Mine awareness activities to reduce the incidence of mine-related injuries or deaths;

e) Assistance to mine victims;

f) The relationship between the Government of the concerned State Party and the relevant governmental, inter-governmental or non-governmental entities that will work in the implementation of the program.

8. Each State Party giving and receiving assistance under the provisions of this Article shall cooperate with a view to ensuring the full and prompt implementation of agreed assistance programs.

Article 7
Transparency measures

1. Each State Party shall report to the Secretary-General of the United Nations as soon as practicable, and in any event not later than 180 days after the entry into force of this Convention for that State Party on:

a) The national implementation measures referred to in Article 9;

b) The total of all stockpiled anti-personnel mines owned or possessed by it, or under its jurisdiction or control, to include a breakdown of the type, quantity and, if possible, lot numbers of each type of anti-personnel mine stockpiled;

c) To the extent possible, the location of all mined areas that contain, or are suspected to contain, anti-personnel mines under its jurisdiction or control, to include as much detail as possible regarding the type and quantity of each type of anti-personnel mine in each mined area and when they were emplaced;

d) The types, quantities and, if possible, lot numbers of all anti-personnel mines retained or transferred for the development of and training in mine detection, mine clearance or mine destruction techniques, or transferred for the purpose of destruction, as well as the institutions authorized by a State Party to retain or transfer anti-personnel mines, in accordance with Article 3;

e) The status of programs for the conversion or de-commissioning of anti-personnel mine production facilities;

f) The status of programs for the destruction of anti-personnel mines in accordance with Articles 4 and 5, including details of the methods which will be used in destruction, the location of all destruction sites and the applicable safety and environmental standards to be observed;

g) The types and quantities of all anti-personnel mines destroyed after the entry into force of this Convention for that State Party, to include a breakdown of the quantity of each type of anti-personnel mine destroyed, in accordance with Articles 4 and 5, respectively, along with, if possible, the lot numbers of each type of anti-personnel mine in the case of destruction in accordance with Article 4;

h) The technical characteristics of each type of anti-personnel mine produced, to the extent known, and those currently owned or possessed by a State Party, giving, where reasonably possible, such categories of information as may facilitate identification and clearance of anti-personnel mines; at a minimum, this information shall include the dimensions, fusing, explosive content, metallic content, colour photographs and other information which may facilitate mine clearance; and

i) The measures taken to provide an immediate and effective warning to the population in relation to all areas identified under paragraph 2 of Article 5.

2. The information provided in accordance with this Article shall be updated by the States Parties annually, covering the last calendar year, and reported to the Secretary-General of the United Nations not later than 30 April of each year.

3. The Secretary-General of the United Nations shall transmit all such reports received to the States Parties.

Article 8
Facilitation and clarification of compliance

1. The States Parties agree to consult and cooperate with each other regarding the implementation of the provisions of this Convention, and to work together in a spirit of cooperation to facilitate compliance by States Parties with their obligations under this Convention.

2. If one or more States Parties wish to clarify and seek to resolve questions relating to compliance with the provisions of this Convention by another State Party, it may submit, through the Secretary-General of the United Nations, a Request for Clarification of that matter to that State Party. Such a request shall be accompanied by all appropriate information. Each State Party shall refrain from unfounded Requests for Clarification, care being taken to avoid abuse. A State Party that receives a Request for Clarification shall provide, through the Secretary-General of the United Nations, within 28 days to the requesting State Party all information which would assist in clarifying this matter.

3. If the requesting State Party does not receive a response through the Secretary-General of the United Nations within that time period, or deems the response to the Request for Clarification to be unsatisfactory, it may submit the matter through the Secretary-General of the United Nations to the next Meeting of the States Parties. The Secretary-General of the United Nations shall transmit the submission, accompanied by all appropriate information pertaining to the Request for Clarification, to all States Parties. All such information shall be presented to the requested State Party which shall have the right to respond.

4. Pending the convening of any meeting of the States Parties, any of the States Parties concerned may request the Secretary-General of the United Nations to exercise his or her good offices to facilitate the clarification requested.

5. The requesting State Party may propose through the Secretary-General of the United Nations the convening of a Special Meeting of the States Parties to consider the matter. The Secretary-General of the United Nations shall thereupon communicate this proposal and all information submitted by the

States Parties concerned, to all States Parties with a request that they indicate whether they favour a Special Meeting of the States Parties, for the purpose of considering the matter. In the event that within 14 days from the date of such communication, at least one-third of the States Parties favours such a Special Meeting, the Secretary-General of the United Nations shall convene this Special Meeting of the States Parties within a further 14 days. A quorum for this Meeting shall consist of a majority of States Parties.

6. The Meeting of the States Parties or the Special Meeting of the States Parties, as the case may be, shall first determine whether to consider the matter further, taking into account all information submitted by the States Parties concerned. The Meeting of the States Parties or the Special Meeting of the States Parties shall make every effort to reach a decision by consensus. If despite all efforts to that end no agreement has been reached, it shall take this decision by a majority of States Parties present and voting.

7. All States Parties shall cooperate fully with the Meeting of the States Parties or the Special Meeting of the States Parties in the fulfilment of its review of the matter, including any fact-finding missions that are authorized in accordance with paragraph 8.

8. If further clarification is required, the Meeting of the States Parties or the Special Meeting of the States Parties shall authorize a fact-finding mission and decide on its mandate by a majority of States Parties present and voting. At any time the requested State Party may invite a fact-finding mission to its territory. Such a mission shall take place without a decision by a Meeting of the States Parties or a Special Meeting of the States Parties to authorize such a mission. The mission, consisting of up to 9 experts, designated and approved in accordance with paragraphs 9 and 10, may collect additional information on the spot or in other places directly related to the alleged compliance issue under the jurisdiction or control of the requested State Party.

9. The Secretary-General of the United Nations shall prepare and update a list of the names, nationalities and other relevant data of qualified experts provided by States Parties and communicate it to all States Parties. Any expert included on this list shall be regarded as designated for all fact-finding missions unless a State Party declares its non-acceptance in writing. In the event of non-acceptance, the expert shall not participate in fact-finding missions on the territory or any other place under the jurisdiction or control of the objecting State Party, if the non-acceptance was declared prior to the appointment of the expert to such missions.

10. Upon receiving a request from the Meeting of the States Parties or a Special Meeting of the States Parties, the Secretary-General of the United Nations shall, after consultations with the requested State Party, appoint the members of the mission, including its leader. Nationals of States Parties requesting the fact-finding mission or directly affected by it shall not be appointed to the mission. The members of the fact-finding mission shall enjoy privileges and immunities under Article VI of the Convention on the Privileges and Immunities of the United Nations, adopted on 13 February 1946.

11. Upon at least 72 hours notice, the members of the fact-finding mission shall arrive in the territory of the requested State Party at the earliest opportunity. The requested State Party shall take the necessary administrative measures to receive, transport and accommodate the mission, and shall be responsible for ensuring the security of the mission to the maximum extent possible while they are on territory under its control.

12. Without prejudice to the sovereignty of the requested State Party, the fact-finding mission may bring into the territory of the requested State Party the necessary equipment which shall be used exclusively for gathering information on the alleged compliance issue. Prior to its arrival, the mission will advise the requested State Party of the equipment that it intends to utilize in the course of its fact-finding mission.

13. The requested State Party shall make all efforts to ensure that the fact-finding mission is given the opportunity to speak with all relevant persons who may be able to provide information related to the alleged compliance issue.

14. The requested State Party shall grant access for the fact-finding mission to all areas and installations under its control where facts relevant to the compliance issue could be expected to be collected. This shall be subject to any arrangements that the requested State Party considers necessary for:

a) The protection of sensitive equipment, information and areas;

b) The protection of any constitutional obligations the requested State Party may have with regard to proprietary rights, searches and seizures, or other constitutional rights; or

c) The physical protection and safety of the members of the fact-finding mission.

In the event that the requested State Party makes such arrangements, it shall make every reasonable effort to demonstrate through alternative means its compliance with this Convention.

15. The fact-finding mission may remain in the territory of the State Party concerned for no more than 14 days, and at any particular site no more than 7 days, unless otherwise agreed.

16. All information provided in confidence and not related to the subject matter of the fact-finding mission shall be treated on a confidential basis.

17. The fact-finding mission shall report, through the Secretary-General of the United Nations, to the Meeting of the States Parties or the Special Meeting of the States Parties the results of its findings.

18. The Meeting of the States Parties or the Special Meeting of the States Parties shall consider all relevant information, including the report submitted by the fact-finding mission, and may request the requested State Party to take measures to address the compliance issue within a specified period of time. The requested State Party shall report on all measures taken in response to this request.

19. The Meeting of the States Parties or the Special Meeting of the States Parties may suggest to the States Parties concerned ways and means to further clarify or resolve the matter under consideration, including the initiation of appropriate procedures in conformity with international law. In circumstances where the issue at hand is determined to be due to circumstances beyond the control of the requested State Party, the Meeting of the States Parties or the Special Meeting of the States Parties may recommend appropriate measures, including the use of cooperative measures referred to in Article 6.

20. The Meeting of the States Parties or the Special Meeting of the States Parties shall make every effort to reach its decisions referred to in paragraphs 18 and 19 by consensus, otherwise by a two-thirds majority of States Parties present and voting.

Article 9
National implementation measures

Each State Party shall take all appropriate legal, administrative and other measures, including the imposition of penal sanctions, to prevent and suppress any activity prohibited to a State Party under this Convention undertaken by persons or on territory under its jurisdiction or control.

Article 10
Settlement of disputes

1. The States Parties shall consult and cooperate with each other to settle any dispute that may arise with regard to the application or the interpretation of this Convention. Each State Party may bring any such dispute before the Meeting of the States Parties.

2. The Meeting of the States Parties may contribute to the settlement of the dispute by whatever means it deems appropriate, including offering its good offices, calling upon the States parties to a dispute to start the settlement procedure of their choice and recommending a time-limit for any agreed procedure.

3. This Article is without prejudice to the provisions of this Convention on facilitation and clarification of compliance.

Article 11
Meetings of the States Parties

1. The States Parties shall meet regularly in order to consider any matter with regard to the application or implementation of this Convention, including:

a) The operation and status of this Convention;

b) Matters arising from the reports submitted under the provisions of this Convention;

c) International cooperation and assistance in accordance with Article 6;

d) The development of technologies to clear anti-personnel mines;

e) Submissions of States Parties under Article 8; and

f) Decisions relating to submissions of States Parties as provided for in Article 5.

2. The First Meeting of the States Parties shall be convened by the Secretary-General of the United Nations within one year after the entry into force of this Convention. The subsequent meetings shall be convened by the Secretary-General of the United Nations annually until the first Review Conference.

3. Under the conditions set out in Article 8, the Secretary-General of the United Nations shall convene a Special Meeting of the States Parties.

4. States not parties to this Convention, as well as the United Nations, other relevant international organizations or institutions, regional organizations, the International Committee of the Red Cross and relevant non-governmental organizations may be invited to attend these meetings as observers in accordance with the agreed Rules of Procedure.

Article 12
Review Conferences

1. A Review Conference shall be convened by the Secretary-General of the United Nations five years after the entry into force of this Convention. Further Review Conferences shall be convened by the Secretary-General of the United Nations if so requested by one or more States Parties, provided that the interval between Review Conferences shall in no case be less than five years. All States Parties to this Convention shall be invited to each Review Conference.

2. The purpose of the Review Conference shall be:

a) To review the operation and status of this Convention;

b) To consider the need for and the interval between further Meetings of the States Parties referred to in paragraph 2 of Article 11;

c) To take decisions on submissions of States Parties as provided for in Article 5; and

d) To adopt, if necessary, in its final report conclusions related to the implementation of this Convention.

3. States not parties to this Convention, as well as the United Nations, other relevant international organizations or institutions, regional organizations, the International Committee of the Red Cross and relevant non-governmental organizations may be invited to attend each Review Conference as observers in accordance with the agreed Rules of Procedure.

Article 13
Amendments

1. At any time after the entry into force of this Convention any State Party may propose amendments to this Convention. Any proposal for an amendment shall be communicated to the Depositary, who shall circulate it to all States Parties and shall seek their views on whether an Amendment Conference should be convened to consider the proposal. If a majority of the States Parties notify the Depositary no later than 30 days after its circulation that they support further consideration of the proposal, the Depositary shall convene an Amendment Conference to which all States Parties shall be invited.

2. States not parties to this Convention, as well as the United Nations, other relevant international organizations or institutions, regional organizations, the International Committee of the Red Cross and relevant non-governmental organizations may be invited to attend each Amendment Conference as observers in accordance with the agreed Rules of Procedure.

3. The Amendment Conference shall be held immediately following a Meeting of the States Parties or a Review Conference unless a majority of the States Parties request that it be held earlier.

4. Any amendment to this Convention shall be adopted by a majority of two-thirds of the States Parties present and voting at the Amendment Conference. The Depositary shall communicate any amendment so adopted to the States Parties.

5. An amendment to this Convention shall enter into force for all States Parties to this Convention which have accepted it, upon the deposit with the Depositary of instruments of acceptance by a majority of States Parties. Thereafter it shall enter into force for any remaining State Party on the date of deposit of its instrument of acceptance.

Article 14
Costs

1. The costs of the Meetings of the States Parties, the Special Meetings of the States Parties, the Review Conferences and the Amendment Conferences shall be borne by the States Parties and States not parties to this Convention participating therein, in accordance with the United Nations scale of assessment adjusted appropriately.

2. The costs incurred by the Secretary-General of the United Nations under Articles 7 and 8 and the costs of any fact-finding mission shall be borne by the States Parties in accordance with the United Nations scale of assessment adjusted appropriately.

Article 15
Signature

This Convention, done at Oslo, Norway, on 18 September 1997, shall be open for signature at Ottawa, Canada, by all States from 3 December 1997 until 4 December 1997, and at the United Nations Headquarters in New York from 5 December 1997 until its entry into force.

Article 16
Ratification, acceptance, approval or accession

1. This Convention is subject to ratification, acceptance or approval of the Signatories.

2. It shall be open for accession by any State which has not signed the Convention.

3. The instruments of ratification, acceptance, approval or accession shall be deposited with the Depositary.

Article 17
Entry into force

1. This Convention shall enter into force on the first day of the sixth month after the month in which the 40th instrument of ratification, acceptance, approval or accession has been deposited.

2. For any State which deposits its instrument of ratification, acceptance, approval or accession after the date of the deposit of the 40th instrument of ratification, acceptance, approval or accession, this Convention shall enter into force on the first day of the sixth month after the date on which that State has deposited its instrument of ratification, acceptance, approval or accession.

Article 18
Provisional application

Any State may at the time of its ratification, acceptance, approval or accession, declare that it will apply provisionally paragraph 1 of Article 1 of this
Convention pending its entry into force.

Article 19
Reservations

The Articles of this Convention shall not be subject to reservations.

Article 20
Duration and withdrawal

1. This Convention shall be of unlimited duration.

2. Each State Party shall, in exercising its national sovereignty, have the right
to withdraw from this Convention. It shall give notice of such withdrawal to
all other States Parties, to the Depositary and to the United Nations Security
Council. Such instrument of withdrawal shall include a full explanation of the
reasons motivating this withdrawal.

3. Such withdrawal shall only take effect six months after the receipt of the
instrument of withdrawal by the Depositary. If, however, on the expiry of that
six- month period, the withdrawing State Party is engaged in an armed conflict, the withdrawal shall not take effect before the end of the armed conflict.

4. The withdrawal of a State Party from this Convention shall not in any way
affect the duty of States to continue fulfilling the obligations assumed under
any relevant rules of international law.

Article 21
Depositary

The Secretary-General of the United Nations is hereby designated as the
Depositary of this Convention.
Article 22
Authentic texts

The original of this Convention, of which the Arabic, Chinese, English,
French, Russian and Spanish texts are equally authentic, shall be deposited
with the Secretary-General of the United Nations.

Notes

Introduction

1. Statistics are from International Committee of the Red Cross, *Overview 1999: Landmines Must Be Stopped* (Geneva: ICRC, 1999), 10.

Chapter 1

1. An orthostat is an upright stone slab used to form the lower section of the wall in ancient buildings. For the purposes of this chapter, the term "mining" refers to tunneling underneath an enemy's wall in an effort to collapse it. Photographs and drawings of the orthostats can be found in Yigael Yadin, *The Art of Warfare in Biblical Lands in the Light of Archeaological Discovery,* trans. M. Pearlman (London: Weidenfeld and Nicolson, 1963), 313–17, 388–93.

2. Diodorus Siculus, *The Library of History,* trans. C. H. Oldfather (Cambridge, MA: Harvard University Press, 1950), 10:287–88. Diodorus lived between 80–20 B.C.E.

3. Ibid.

4. Ibid., 393. Aeneas Tacticus's writings can be found in T. E. Page, ed., *Aeneas Tacticus, Asclepiodotus, Onsander,* trans. Illinois Greek Club (Cambridge, MA: Harvard University Press, 1943), 187. Vitruvius, *On Architecture*, trans. Frank Granger (Cambridge, MA: Harvard University, 1956), 2:367. F. E. Winter, *Greek Fortifications* (Toronto: University of Toronto Press, 1971), 133.

5. Much of Philo's work is translated in A. W. Lawrence, *Greek Aims in Fortification* (Oxford: Clarendon Press, 1979). Lawrence described Philo's work as "An essential key to understanding Greek fortifications." Ibid., 67. Philo discussed mining in Ibid., 103, and the use of pots in Ibid., 87.

6. Publius Flavius Vegetius Renatus, *Epitome of Military Science,* trans. N. P. Miller (Liverpool: Liverpool University Press, 1993), 124, 128. Quotation is from Ibid., 128.

7. Julius Caesar, *The Gallic War,* trans. Carolyn Hammond (Oxford: Oxford University Press, 1996), 156. Descriptions are from Ibid., 185. Translation notes are from Ibid., 241.

8. Vegetius, *Epitome of Military Science,* xiii. A more thorough discussion of the state of military education in Middle Ages and the significance of Vegetius can be found in Philippe Contamine, *War in the Middle Ages,* trans. Michael Jones (Cambridge, MA: Blackwell Publishers, 1984), 210–18.

9. Origins of gunpowder in Europe are discussed in Bert S. Hall, *Weapons and Warfare in Renaissance Europe: Gunpowder, Technology, and Tactics* (Baltimore: Johns Hopkins University, 1997), 41–43. Robert Temple, *The Genius of China* (New York: Simon and Schuster, 1986), 224–28, 232–33. Temple provides an intriguing discussion of the development of Chinese technology, including military technology, and gives the reader numerous block quotations from period Chinese military manuals.

10. Ibid., 234.

11. Ibid., 235–36. Quotation is from Ibid., 235.

12. Ibid., 236–37.

13. Ibid., 237.

14. Ibid., 226. William C. Schneck, "The Origins of Military Mines: Part 1," *Engineer Bulletin* 28, no. 3 (July 1998): 50. Contamine, *War in the Middle Ages,* 256, 270–80, 305.

15. Mike Croll, *The History of Landmines* (Barnsley, UK: Pen & Sword Books Ltd., 1998), 15. Schneck, "The Origins of Military Mines: Part 1," 54. Ulrich Kreuzfeld, "Mine Warfare, Land," *International Military and Defence Encyclopedia* (Washington, DC: Brassey's Inc., 1993), 4:1756–1757. Interestingly, Croll and Schneck both cite Kreuzfeld's work for Flemming's description, yet both include information not in Kreuzfeld's article. The description above includes information from all three.

16. John Lothrop Motley, *History of the United Netherlands* (New York: Harper and Brothers Publishers, 1888), 1:188–92. This occurred during the Eighty Years' War, also known as the Dutch War for Independence.

17. Ibid., 189–99. Quotation is from Ibid., 191.

18. Michael Lewis, *The Spanish Armada* (New York: Thomas Y. Crowell Company, 1960), 153–54. Colin Martin and Geoffrey Parker, *The Spanish Armada* (New York: W. W. Norton and Company, 1988), 186–87.

19. Motley, *History of the United Netherlands,* 192.

20. Details of Vauban's life are from Daniel Halévy, *Vauban: Builder of Fortresses,* trans. C. J. C. Street (London: Geoffrey Bles, 1924), 15, 17, 27, 184.

21. Sebastien LePreste de Vauban, *A Manual of Siegecraft and Fortification,* trans. George A. Rothrock (Ann Arbor: University of Michigan Press, 1968), 108–9, 122, 129.

22. In large part, the French dominance in mining was due to their possession of a separate engineering corps. Christopher Duffy, *The Fortress in the Age of Vauban and Fredrick the Great 1660–1789* (London: Routledge and Kegan Paul, 1988), 2:128. Definition is from Simon Francis Gay de Vernon, *A Treatise on the Science of War and*

Fortification, trans. John Michael O'Conner (New York: J. Seymour, 1817), 2:263. Second quotation is from Ibid., 279–80.

23. Ibid., 285–86.

24. Ibid., 285.

25. Quotation is from Ibid., 288. Gay de Vernon provided the reader with all of the mathematical equations necessary to calculate not only the amount of charge needed to detonate a specific shell, but the size of the crater the explosion would generate and the distance that was needed between mines to prevent the explosion of one from triggering the explosion of another.

26. Gay de Vernon's work was one of the earliest texts used at West Point, along with C. Hutton's *Mathematics,* W. Enfield's *Natural Philosophy,* and H. O. de Scheel's *Treatise of Artillery.* Stephen E. Ambrose, *Duty, Honor, Country: A History of West Point* (Baltimore: Johns Hopkins Press, 1966), 26. West Point continued to use Gay de Vernon's book through 1830. Perry David Jamieson, "The Development of Civil War Tactics" (Ph.D. diss., Wayne State University, 1979), 5–6, and Edward Hagerman, *The American Civil War and the Origin of Modern Warfare* (Bloomington: Indiana University Press, 1988), 5–7.

27. Dennis Hart Mahan, *A Complete Treatise on Field Fortification, with the General Outlines of the Principles Regulating the Arrangement, the Attack, and the Defense of Permanent Works* (New York: Wiley and Long, 1836; reprint, New York: Greenwood Press, 1968), 75. Mahan's debt to Gay de Vernon is referred to in Jamieson, "The Development of Civil War Tactics," 7, and in Hagerman, *The American Civil War and the Origin of Modern Warfare,* 6–7.

28. Mahan, *A Complete Treatise on Field Fortification, with the General Outlines of the Principles Regulating the Arrangement, the Attack, and the Defense of Permanent Works,* 75–76. Mahan does not explicitly state why the stone fougasse would be effective.

29. The Confederate version was published by West and Johnson, Richmond, Virginia in 1862. William Warner Bishop et al., *A Catalog of Books Represented by Library of Congress Printed Cards* (Paterson, NJ: Rowman and Littlefield Inc.), 94:31.

30. J. E. Kaufmann and H. W. Kaufmann, *Fortress America: The Forts that Defended America, 1800 to the Present* (Cambridge, MA: Da Cappo Press, 2004), 124, 135.

Chapter 2

1. Quotation is from William Dudley, ed. *The Naval War of 1812* (Washington, DC: Naval Historical Center Department of the Navy, 1992), 2:162.

2. Fulton discusses his work with the British in "Use of the Torpedo in the Defense of Ports and Harbors," which he submitted to the Senate on February 26, 1810. A copy of this report can be found in Thomas Cochran, ed., *The New American State Papers 1789–1860* (Wilmington, DE: Scholarly Resources, Inc., 1973), 9:21–42.

3. These ideas are echoed by both Fulton and members of Congress in Ibid.

4. Bushnell provided a detailed description of the Turtle in a 1787 letter to Thomas Jefferson. A copy of this can be found in William Morgan, ed., *Naval Documents of the American Revolution* (Washington, DC: Naval History Division, Department of the Navy, 1972), 6:1501–1507. Quotation is from Ibid., 1502. A detailed discussion of the development of submarines leading up to Bushnell's craft can be found in Alex Roland, *Underwater in the Age of Sail* (Bloomington: Indiana University Press, 1978).

5. Ezra Lee discussed his adventures in a February 20, 1815 letter to David Humphreys. The text of the letter can be found in Ibid., 1507–1510. Quotation is from Ibid., 1509.

6. Information and quotations are from Bushnell to Jefferson, Ibid., 1506, 1507.

7. Quotations are from the Journal of the Connecticut Council of Safety, April 23, 1777, included in William Morgan, ed., *Naval Documents of the American Revolution* (Washington, DC: Naval History Division, Department of the Navy, 1980), 8:407

8. Bushnell briefly discusses the weapon in his letter to Jefferson. Morgan, ed., *Naval Documents of the American Revolution,* 6:1507. Roland provides a more succinct discussion of the mine in Roland, *Underwater in the Age of Sail,* 82–83.

9. Captain Symons's August 15, 1777, report to Rear Admiral Sir Peter Parker can be found in Willam Morgan, ed., *Naval Documents of the American Revolution* (Washington, DC: Naval Historical Center, Department of the Navy, 1986), 9:746–47. Quotation is from the Captain's journal entry of August 13, 1777, found in Ibid., 741.

10. Symons's report is the previously cited one found in Ibid., 746–47. Quotation is from Ibid., 747.

11. Most of the above information can be found in Bushnell to Jefferson, Morgan, ed., *Naval Documents of the American Revolution,* 6:1507. Additional information is from Royal Bradford, *History of Torpedo Warfare* (Newport, RI: U.S. Torpedo Station, 1882), 7–8. There is some debate as to the exact shape of Bushnell's second mines.

12. Biographical information is from Roland, *Underwater in the Age of Sail,* 84–91.

13. Craig L. Symonds, *Navalists and Antinavalists: The Naval Policy Debate in the United States, 1785–1827* (Newark: University of Delaware Press, 1980), 11–13, 105–7. Jefferson's promotion of gunboats is discussed in Allen Millett and Peter Maslowski, *For the Common Defense, A Military History of the United States* (New York: The Free Press, 1994), 105.

14. Alex Roland is particularly critical of Fulton on this account and provides an excellent discussion of the relationship between Fulton's and Bushnell's research, speculating that the former borrowed a good deal more from the latter than Fulton ever chose to admit. Roland, *Underwater in the Age of Sail,* 89–105.

15. Fulton related his experiment in a February 26 report to the United States Senate titled "Use of the Torpedo in the Defense of Ports and Harbors." A copy of the report can be found in Thomas Cochran, ed., *The New American State Papers 1789–1860* (Wilmington, DE: Scholarly Resources, 1973), 8:22–23.

16. Quotations are from Ibid., 23.

17. Report from Mr. Bradley to the Senate February 26, 1810. "Use of the Torpedo in the Defense of Ports and Harbors." Ibid., 23.

18. Information is from Ibid., 24–25.

19. All information is from Ibid., 26–29.

20. Chart concerning costs is from Ibid., 32. Figures on the USS Wasp are from Ibid., 42.

21. Communications on the experiments, as well as Fulton's report on the experiments, are part of a February 14, 1811, report to Congress titled "Experiments on the Practical Use of Torpedoes," which can be found in Ibid., 43–56.

22. Quotations are from a June 22, 1812, letter from Robert Fulton to Secretary of the Navy Hamilton. A copy of the letter can be found in William Dudley, ed., *The Naval War of 1812* (Washington, DC: Naval Historical Center Department of the Navy, 1985), 1:146.

23. Note that Fulton would benefit handsomely if the first policy were adopted and his mines proved even marginally successful. Quotations are from Ibid., 147. The policy was approved on March 3. The first letter to Jones is dated April 27, 1813. The second was written on May 8. Jones is quoted from a letter to Lewis dated May 16. All information is from Dudley, ed., *The Naval War of 1812,* 2:111–13.

24. Two reports from Lewis, dated June 20 and 28, can be found in Ibid., 113–14. Fulton discusses steam propulsion in an August 5 letter to Commodore Stephen Decatur in Ibid., 210–12. Oddly, both Roland and Bradford mistakenly claim Fulton received no assistance from the government during the war. Bradford, *History of Torpedo Warfare,* 23, and Roland, *Underwater in the Age of Sail,* 118.

25. Secretary of the Navy Jones ordered Captain Charles Jordan to provide Mix with supplies and commented that "His plan is that of Fulton's Torpedo." Jones to Jordan, May 16, 1813, Dudley, ed., *The Naval War of 1812,* 2:355. Cockburn's June 16, 1813, letter to Warren can also be found in Ibid., 355–56.

26. Bradford, *History of Torpedo Warfare,* 28–30.

27. Ibid., 30–31.

28. Totten's report can be found in Cochran, *The New American State Papers 1789–1860,* 9:299–304. Roland provides an in-depth look at Colt and his work in Roland, *Underwater in the Age of Sail,* 134–49. See also Philip K. Lundelberg, *Samuel Colt's Submarine Battery: The Secret and the Enigma* (Washington, DC: Smithsonian Institute Press, 1974).

29. Biographical information from Werner von Siemens, *Inventor and Entrepreneur: Recollection* (New York: Augustus M. Kelley, 1968), 11, 20–23, 50–56. Early investigations on friction fuses for firing cannons left him partially deaf when a compound he was working with exploded in his hands. Ibid., 31. Quotation is from Ibid., 53. The war is also sometimes referred to as the Schleswig-Holstein War.

30. Ibid., 56.

31. Siemens's sojourn in Kiel is discussed in Ibid., 57–70. Of particular interest are his discussion of his submarine mines in Ibid., 57, and his ersatz landmine in Ibid., 62–63. Bradford describes the mines as being filled with around 300 pounds of gunpowder each and places them at a depth of 30 feet rather than 20. Bradford also

disagrees with Siemens's assessment of the success of the mines, saying, "It does not appear …that their presence prevented the Danes from entering the harbor at Keil." Interestingly Bradford does not mention Siemens in his report and instead credits the mines solely to Himly. Bradford, *History of Torpedo Warfare*, 35–36.

32. Information on Halleck's book is from Jamieson, "The Development of Civil War Tactics," 14. Quotation is from Henry Wagner Halleck, *Elements of Military Art and Science*, 3rd ed. (New York: D. Appleton and Co., 1863), 374–75.

33. Construction information is from Ibid., 363.

34. Ibid., 363–64.

35. George W. Cullum, *Biographical Register of the Officers and Graduates of the United States Military Academy at West Point: From Its Establishment, in 1802, to 1890. With the Early History of the United States Military Academy* (Boston: Houghton Mifflin and Company, 1891), 393.

36. The Indian village near Fort King was surrounded by swamps, making it difficult to attack. Gabriel J. Rains, "Torpedoes," *Southern Historical Society Papers* 3, nos. 5 and 6 (May and June 1877): 255–60.

37. Rains, "Torpedoes," 256–27; another writer varies from Rains and claims that there were two mines, and that a number of Indians died from the explosion of the first mine. As Rains was a participant in the event and the other author not, Rains's account seems by far the more credible; E. P. Alexander, "Sketch of Longstreet's Division—Yorktown and Williamsburg," *Southern Historical Society Papers* 10, nos. 1 and 2 (January and February, 1882): 38.

38. Rains discusses the newspaper accounts of the action in Rains, "Torpedoes," 257. Quote is from Cullum, *Biographical Register of the Officers and Graduates of the United States Military Academy at West Point: From Its Establishment, in 1802, to 1890. With the Early History of the United States Military Academy*, 393. See also Clement A. Evans, ed., *Confederate Military History, vol. 4, D. H. Hill Jr., North Carolina* (Atlanta, GA: Confederate Publishing Company, 1899), 339.

39. Rains's promotion is discussed in John K. Mahon, *History of the Second Seminole War: 1835–1842* (Gainesville, FL: University of Florida Press, 1967), 275. This work also provides perhaps the best secondary account of Rains's activities in Florida. Quotation is from *War of the Rebellion: Official Records of the Union and Southern Armies,* series I, vol. 11, pt. 1 (Washington, DC: Government Printing Office, 1897–1900), 350. Work is hereafter cited as *ORA,* series/volume. It should be noted that Berry's comments were made during the Civil War and not during the Seminole War. This fact probably colored Berry's view of Rains's Seminole War activities.

40. For a discussion of the Mexican defenses at Chapultepec, especially the placement of the mines, see Don Ramon Alcaraz et al., *The Other Side,* trans. Albert Ramsey (n.p.: 1850; reprint, New York: Burt Franklin and Co., 1970), 333, and Nathan Convington Brooks, *A Complete History of the Mexican War 1846–1848* (Baltimore: Hutchinson and Seebold, 1849; reprint, Chicago: The Rio Grande Press Inc., 1965), 412.

41. For a discussion of the battle of Chapultepec and the failure of the Mexican army to set off their fougasses, see Alcaraz, *The Other Side,* 363, and K. Jack Bauer,

The Mexican War 1846–1848 (New York: Macmillan Publishing Company, 1974), 317. Quotation is from T. Harry Williams, ed., *With Beauregard in Mexico* (Baton Rouge: Louisiana State University Press, 1956), 81. The roles of the above-mentioned officers at the battle of Chapultepec are discussed in Robert Selph Henry, *The Story of the Mexican War* (New York: The Bobbs-Merrill Company Inc., 1950), 357, 361, 366. Armistead Long, ed., *The Memoirs of Robert E. Lee* (New York: J. M. Stoddart & Company, 1886). William Star Myers, ed., *The Mexican War Diary of George B. McClellan* (Princeton: Princeton University Press, 1917).

42. Robert W. Tolf, *The Russian Rockefellers* (Standford, CA: The Hoover Institute Press, 1976), 8–9, 11. The committee is described as the first of its kind; Roland, *Underwater Warfare in the Age of Sail,* 129. Schilder was also involved in designing early Russian submarines. Tolf, *The Russian Rockefellers* 9. It was common during this period for officers in both Europe and the United States to be closely involved in developing new technologies.

43. Tolf, *The Russian Rockefellers,* 9–11.

44. Ibid., 17–18.

45. Ibid.

46. Tolf, *The Russian Rockefellers,* 19. Trevor Royle, *Crimea: The Great Crimean War* (New York: St. Martin's Press, 2000), 158–59, for a more detailed account see D. Bonner-Smith and A. C. Dewar, eds., *Russian War, 1854: Baltic and Black Sea Official Correspondence* (n.p.: Navy Records Society, 1943).

47. First quotation is from D. Bonner-Smith, ed., *Russian War, 1855: Baltic Official Correspondence* (n.p.: Navy Records Society, 1944), 60. Royle, *Crimea: The Great Crimean War,* 379. Block quotation is from Bradford, *History of Torpedo Warfare,* 38–39.

48. Bonner-Smith, ed., *Russian War, 1855: Baltic Official Correspondence,* 155. Winfried Baumgart, *The Crimean War 1853–1856* (New York: Oxford University Press, 1999), 173. Tolf, *The Russian Rockefellers,* 17–18. Bradford, *History of Torpedo Warfare,* 39.

49. Bradford, *History of Torpedo Warfare,* 38.

50. The earthworks at Sebastopol are discussed in John Fox Burgoyne, *The Military Opinions of General John Fox Burgoyne* (London: R, Bentley, 1859), 191. Problems posed by Russian mines are discussed in Nicholas Bentley, ed., *Russell's Dispatches from the Crimea 1854–1856* (New York: Hill and Wang, 1966), 221–22.

51. Jacobi was also known as Boris Semenovich Iakobi. For more information on Jacobi, see A. M. Prokhorov, ed., *Great Soviet Encyclopeadia,* 3rd ed., trans. Lawrence W. Cannon et al. (New York: Macmillian Inc., 1977), 30:410. Not surprisingly, this source makes no mention of Nobel.

52. Delafield, *Report on the Art of War in Europe,* 109. Delafield also attributes the fuse design to Jacobi.

53. First description is from Ibid., 110. Russell's description is quoted from Bentley, *Russell's Dispatches from the Crimea 1854–1856,* 221–22.

54. Royle, *Crimea: The Great Crimean War,* 357.

55. Composition of the Commission is discussed in Delafield, *Report on the Art of War in Europe,* iii–iv. Quotation is from Ibid., 109.

56. Mordecai makes reference to his illness in his report to Congress. Alfred Mordecai, *Military Commission to Europe, in 1855 and 1856* (Washington, DC: George W. Bowman, 1860), 1. McClellan is quoted from United States War Department, *Report of the Secretary of War, Communicating the Report of Captain George B. McClellan (First Regiment United States Cavalry)* (Washington, DC: A. O. P. Nicholson, 1857), 15. McClellan's report also included a new manual for the United States Cavalry written by McClellan. McClellan's full report was reprinted four years later as George B. McClellan, *Armies of Europe* (Philadelphia: J. B. Lippincott and Co., 1861), with an added preface. Land mines remained of interest more to engineers than ordnance until the end of World War I.

57. Quotations are from James Saint Claire Morton, *Memoir on American Fortification* (Washington, DC: William A. Harris, 1859), 50, 66. Morton discussed his plans for New York in detail in Ibid., Chaps. 6–8, passim. Morton's ideas were not completely accepted by mainstream military; Ibid., 77. In his work, Morton drew a number of parallels between the defenses of Sebastopol and his planned defense of New York; Ibid., 82–85.

58. Ibid., 496–97.

59. Quotation is from James Saint Claire Morton, *Letter to the Hon. John B. Floyd, Secretary of War, Presenting for his consideration a new plan for the fortifications of certain points of the seacoast of the United States* (Washington, DC: William A. Harris, 1858), 10. Morton's career and death are discussed in Hagerman, *The American Civil War and the Origins of Modern Warfare,* 24–25.

Chapter 3

1. Civil War as the first modern war, Hagerman, *The American Civil War and the Origins of Modern Warfare,* xi.

2. Maury's life is chronicled in several biographies, including Charles Lee Lewis, *Matthew Fontaine Maury, Pathfinder of the Sea* (Annapolis: United States Naval Institute, 1927); John Wayland, *The Pathfinder of the Seas* (Richmond: Garret & Massie Inc., 1930); Hildegarde Hawthorne, *Matthew Fontaine Maury* (New York: Longmans, Green and Co, 1943). The connection between Colt and Maury is discussed in Roland, *Underwater Warfare in the Age of Sail,* 151–52. Maury held the rank of Commander in the Confederate Navy and Commodore in the Virginia Navy. Lewis, *Matthew Fontaine Maury, Pathfinder of the Sea,* 112.

3. The above information is from Milton F. Perry, *Infernal Machines* (Kingsport, TN: Kingsport Press, Inc., 1965), 5–6. This work is perhaps the best secondary source on mine warfare during the American Civil War, although it is primarily concerned with Naval warfare.

4. Ibid., 6.

5. Ibid., 6–8.

6. Patricia Jahns, *Matthew Fontaine Maury and Joseph Henry, Scientists of the Civil War* (New York: Hasting House, 1961), 243. The author cites a letter written by Maury to Captain Jansen on July 23, 1864. Maury's return is discussed in some detail in Lewis, *Matthew Fontaine Maury, Pathfinder of the Sea*, 183.

7. Perry, *Infernal Machines*, 191. Perry refers to Maury's mines as "without question the most advanced system of mines in the world at that time." This system is described in Ibid., and in block quotation from Maury's writings in Lewis, *Matthew Fontaine Maury, Pathfinder of the Sea*, 181–82.

8. Lewis, *Matthew Fontaine Maury, Pathfinder of the Sea*, 10–12.

9. *ORA*, 1/51 pt. 2, 306, 325; *ORA*, 1/11 pt. 3, 482.

10. Stephen W. Sears, *George B. McClellan, the Young Napoleon* (New York: Ticknor and Fields, 1988), 178–79. Italics are in the original.

11. David Herbert Donald, ed., *Gone For a Soldier: Memoirs of Private Alfred Bellard* (Boston: Little, Brown and Company, 1975), 64.

12. Rains's figures are from Joseph T. Durkin, *Stephen R. Mallory: Confederate Navy Chief* (Chapel Hill, NC: The University of North Carolina Press, 1954), 283. Quote is from *ORA*, 1/11 pt. 3, 516. Description is from General Berry in *ORA*, 1/11 pt. 1, 349.

13. Wainwright is quoted from Allan Nevins, ed., *A Diary of Battle: The Personal Journals of Colonel Charles S. Wainwright 1861–1865* (New York: Harcourt Brace and World, Inc., 1962), 45. S. A. Cunningham, "More of Gen. Rains and His Torpedoes," *Confederate Veteran* 2, no. 9 (September 1894): 283.

14. The term torpedo was frequently used to describe both land and sea mines during this period. First quotation and information on telegraph operator are from General William Berry's report, *ORA*, 1/11 pt. 1, 349–50. Second quotation is from Stephen Sears, ed., *The Civil War Papers of George B. McClellan: Selected Correspondence, 1860–1865* (New York: Ticknor and Fields, 1989), 254.

15. For the Confederate correspondence concerning the mining at Yorktown, see *ORA*, 1/11 pt. 3, 509–511, 516–17. Rains's arrest is mentioned in Cunningham's writings on Rains, though no mention of the arrest appears in *ORA*. Cunningham, "More of Gen. Rains and His Torpedoes," 283. McClellan in his letter to Stanton listed 4 or 5 killed and a dozen wounded; Sears, ed., *The Civil War Papers of George B. McClellan: Selected Correspondence, 1860–1865*, 254. After the war Cunningham claimed the mines had incurred about 30 Union casualties; Cunningham, "More of Gen. Rains and His Torpedoes," 283.

16. First quotation is from Nicholas A. Davis, *The Campaign from Texas to Maryland with the Battle of Fredericksburg* (Austin, TX: The Steck Company, 1961), 30. Second quotation is from Mary Laswell, ed., *Rags and Hope: The Memoirs of Val C. Giles, Four Years with Hood's Brigade. Fourth Texas Infantry, 1861–1865* (New York: Coward McCann, 1961), 76.

17. James A. Longstreet, *From Manassas to Appomattox: Memoirs of the Civil War in America* (Bloomington: Indiana University Press, 1960), 79. *ORA*, 1/11 pt. 3, 516.

18. *ORA*, 1/11 pt. 3, 516.

19. Jefferson Davis, *Rise and Fall of the Confederate Government* (New York: D. Appleton and Company, 1881), 2:97–98. Deaths from subterras seem to have been only four or five, Donald, *Gone for a Soldier,* 64, and Sears, ed., *The Civil War Papers of George B. McClellan: Selected Correspondence, 1860–1865,* 254.

20. Quotations are from *ORA,* 1/11 pt. 3, 509, and G. Moxley Sorrel, *Recollections of a Confederate Staff Officer* (New York: The Neale Publishing Company, 1905), 67. The second quotation, however, does not appear in *ORA.*

21. *ORA,* 1/11 pt. 3, 510. General Hill was General Longstreet's subordinate.

22. First quotation is from Stephen W. Sears, ed., *The Civil War Papers of George B. McClellan: Selected Correspondence, 1860–1865* (New York: Ticknor and Fields, 1989), 254. Second quotation is from G. B. McClellan, *McClellan's Own Story* (New York: C. L. Webster and Co., 1887), , 326–37.

23. First quotation is from *ORA,* 1/11 pt. 1, 349. Reference to "infernal machines" is from Donald, *Gone for a Soldier,* 64. Second quotation is from J. W. Minnich, "Incidents of the Peninsular Campaign," *Confederate Veteran* 30, no. 2 (February 1922): 53.

24. The first quotation is from *ORA,* 1/11 pt. 3, 516–17. The second quotation is from J. B. Jones, *Diary of a Rebel Clerk* (New York: Old Hickory Bookshop, 1935), 1:246.

25. Ibid., 510.

26. Rains ordered to James, *ORA,* 1/11 pt. 3, 608. Rains ordered to turn over command to Lt. Davidson, *ORA,* 1/18, 743. Rains assigned to Conscription Service, *ORA,* 4/2, 241. Durkin, *Stephen R. Mallory: Confederate Navy Chief,* 265–66. Unfortunately, only the last of the appropriation figures, cited in Rains, "Torpedoes," 256, can be firmly assigned to the Torpedo Bureau. Durkin's footnote on the matter is, alas, somewhat incomplete. According to John Thomas Scharf, *History of the Confederate States Navy from its Organization to the Surrender of its Last Vessel* (New York: Rodgers and Sherwood, 1887), 753, however, it appears that Durkin's figures were probably the amount destined for the Submarine Battery Service. The appropriations for 1864 were made on February 17 ($100,000) and July 13 ($250,000). Scharf, *History of the Confederate States Navy from its Organization to the Surrender of its Last Vessel,* 753, and Durkin, *Stephen R. Mallory: Confederate Navy Chief,* 265. Rains, for his part, commented that the $6,000,000 was appropriated "too late, and the delay was not shortened by this enormous appropriation." Rains, "Torpedoes," 256.

27. Durkin, *Stephen R. Mallory: Confederate Navy Chief,* 266. R. O. Crowley, "The Confederate Torpedo Service," *Century Magazine* 51, no. 1 (May 1898): 290.

28. *Official Records of the Union and Confederate Navies in the War of the Rebellion,* series I, vol. 10 (Washington, DC: Government Printing Office), 11. Hereafter cited as *ORN.*

29. Isaac N. Brown, "Confederate Torpedoes in the Yazoo," in *Battles and Leaders of the Civil War,* vol. 3, Retreat from Gettysburg (New York: Castle Books, 1956), 580.

30. *ORN,* 23:544–555.

31. Maury quoted in Arthur William Bergeron Jr., "The Confederate Defense of Mobile, 1861–1865" (Ph.D. diss., Louisiana State University and Agricultural and

Mechanical College, 1980), 1:164–165. See also *ORA,* 1/26 pt. 2, 136, 179–80 and Ibid., 1/28 pt. 2, 297.

32. W. R. King, *Torpedoes: Their Invention and Use from the First Application of the Art of War to the Present Time* (Washington, DC: n.p., 1866), 4.

33. Rains replaced, *ORA,* 4/2, 1074. Quotation is from *ORA,* 1/18, 1082–1083. Unfortunately no copy of the book seems to have survived.

34. Seddon quoted from *ORA,* 1/23 pt. 1, 220. Seddon was appointed Secretary of War in November 1862 and held that post until January 1865.

35. Davis quoted from Jefferson Davis, *Rise and Fall,* 424–25.

36. The chlorate of potash and white sugar were mixed in about a 50/50 ratio. J. S. Barnes, *Submarine Warfare, Offensive and Defensive* (New York: D. Van Nostrand, 1869), 68. Available sources do not indicate if Rains was familiar with Nobel's work. Given the similarities between Rains's early fuses and Nobel's, however, it seems logical to infer that Rains had at least some knowledge of mine warfare in the Crimea, either from Delafield's writings or from the discussion of Jacobi's (Nobel's) mines in H. L. Scott, *Military Dictionary* (New York: D. Van Nostrand, 1861; reprint, New York: Greenwood Press, 1968), 318.

37. Information on sulfuric acid fuse and pressure necessary to set off a mine is from Bradford, *History of Torpedo Warfare,* 51–52. Other information is from Viktor Ernst Karl Rudolf Von Scheliha, *A Treatise on Coast-Defense* (London: E. and F. N. Spoon, 1868; reprint Westport, CT: Greenwood Press, 1971), 231, 234, 235.

38. Von Scheliha, *A Treatise on Coast-Defense,* 231–35. Most of this information is available in other sources, especially the studies conducted following the Civil War. However, almost all sources cite Von Scheliha. Unfortunately, Von Scheliha does not provide a chronology on the development of the mines.

39. The frame torpedo is discussed in Scharf, *History of the Confederate States Navy,* 751, and an excellent drawing of one can be found in *ORN,* 1/16, 393. Information on modified shells from King, *Torpedoes: Their Invention and Use from the First Application of the Art of War to the Present Time,* 14, and *ORA,* 1/42 pt. 3, 1219–1221.

40. It appears that there were only two copies of Rains's book, one in Davis's possession and the other in Rains's. Rains had desired to make copies of the work for distribution, but Davis overruled this, telling Rains that "no printed paper could ever be kept secret," and that "Your invention would be deprived of a great part of its value if its peculiarities were known to the enemy." *ORA,* 1/52 pt. 2, 487. Rains's letter to Seddon is in *ORA,* 1/42 pt. 3, 1219. Unfortunately, virtually no information is available as to the content of Rains's book.

41. *ORA,* 1/42 pt. 3, 1219–1220.

42. Report of Major Brooks in Q. A. Gilmore, *Engineering and Artillery Operations Against the Defenses of Charleston Harbor in 1863* (New York: D. Van Nostrand, 1865), 163, 216–17. Northern sources generally refer to Battery Wagner as Fort Wagner.

43. Ibid., 235–37.

44. Perry, *Infernal Machines,* 60. The Federal Navy also used Confederate prisoners to help navigate torpedo infested waterways. Ibid., 113.

45. Quotations are from *ORA*, 1/28 pt. 2, 324. Beauregard referred to the land mines at Battery Wagner as the "watch dogs of the battery" and stated that the mines were "perfectly accredited in civilized warfare." P. T. Beauregard, "Defense of Charleston," *North American Review* 143 (July 1886): 44, 50, 51.

46. For more on torpedo boats see Perry, *Infernal Machines*, 81–88. For more on *Hunley* see Ibid., 90–108.

47. Ibid., 44. King, *Torpedoes: Their Invention and Use from the First Application of the Art of War to the Present Time*, 6. Von Scheliha, *A Treatise on Coast-Defense*, 225–29.

48. Description is from *ORA*, 1/34 pt. 2, 854. The mines were of the type designed and manufactured by E. C. Singer. King, *Torpedoes: Their Invention and Use from the First Application of the Art of War to the Present Time*, 6. Shea's first name is not listed in *ORA*.

49. Bradbury quoted from *ORA*, 1/34 pt. 2, 884. Baker's findings are disclosed in a letter from Baker in King, *Torpedoes: Their Invention and Use from the First Application of the Art of War to the Present Time*, 6. The description of the sea version of the Singer torpedo is from Von Scheliha, *A Treatise on Coast-Defense*, 228.

50. Perry, *Infernal Machines*, 158–63; *Battles and Leaders of the Civil War*, 4:384–87; Von Scheliha, *A Treatise on Coast-Defense*, 106–108, 120–22.

51. *Battles and Leaders of the Civil War*, 4:412. King, *Torpedoes: Their Invention and Use from the First Application of the Art of War to the Present Time*, 3–4. During World War II it was considered crucial for landmines to be covered by artillery fire if they were to be effective.

52. Quotation is from King, *Torpedoes: Their Invention and Use from the First Application of the Art of War to the Present Time*, 4. The Union officer also felt that the rebel torpedoes would have been more effective had the chance that they exploded been increased, perhaps by connecting them to wire entanglements on the land face of the fort so that "any step or pressure on the wire would explode the shell." Ibid., 5.

53. Johnston's use of mines is discussed in Jones, *Diary of a Rebel Clerk*, 2:8. A new method of planting mines is discussed in *ORA*, 1/28 pt. 2, 371.

54. Information and quotation are from P. H. Sheridan, *Personal Memoirs of P. H. Sheridan* (New York: Charles L. Webster and Company, 1888), 2:380.

55. Information and quotations are from Underwood Johnson and Clarence Clough Buel, *Battles and Leaders of the Civil War* (New York: The Century Company, 1888), 4:684–85.

56. Sherman's early thoughts on torpedoes are mentioned in Joseph T. Glatthar, *The March to the Sea and Beyond* (New York: New York University Press, 1985), 108. Sherman's comments are from a letter to Major General James B. Steedman and are quoted from *ORA*, 1/38 pt. 4, 579.

57. Union dispatch is from *ORA*, 1/42 pt. 3, 1180. Dispatch from Torpedo Bureau is from Ibid., 1181.

58. Plans to arm Mosby with subterras, *ORA*, 1/29 pt. 2, 653–64. Gorgas cited in Ibid., 1/42 pt. 3, 1181. Reaction of Union forces to Mosby discussed in James

McPherson, *Battle Cry of Freedom: The Civil War Era* (New York: Oxford University Press, 1988), 737–38. Lee's recommendation of arming Mosby with subterras is from *ORA*, 1/42 pt. 3, 1181.

59. First quotation is from Colonel Lamb quoted in Benjamin Butler, *Butler's Book* (Boston: A. M. Thayer and Company, 1892), 815. Information on construction of torpedoes is from Crowley, "Confederate Torpedo Service," 295, and from C. B. Denson, "William Henry Chase Whiting, Major-General C. S. Army," *Southern Historical Society Papers* 26 (1898): 160.

60. Quotations and design of fortification are from William Lamb, *Colonel Lamb's Story of Fort Fisher* (Carolina Beach, NC: The Blockade Runner Museum, 1966), 2, 5. The correction in the second quotation is based on an excerpt from an earlier printing found in W. Buck Yearns and John G. Barret, ed., *North Carolina Civil War Documentary* (Chapel Hill, NC: University of North Carolina Press, 1980), 80. Lamb mentions a number of officers who were involved in the planning of Fort Fisher, including Generals Rains, Beauregard, Longstreet, French, and Whiting, Ibid. Lamb spells Rains "Raines," but this misspelling can be found frequently, including in *ORA*.

61. First quotation is from James McPherson, *Battle Cry of Freedom: The Civil War Era* (New York: Oxford University Press, 1988), 820–21. Butler is quoted from Butler, *Butler's Book,* 813. Butler was removed from command of the expedition against Fort Fisher and did not command the final assault on the fort. McPherson, *Battle Cry of Freedom,* 820–21.

62. The battle was also significant because of the heavy casualties among African American troops in the battle. Alfred P. James, "The Battle of the Crater," *Military Affairs* 2, no. 1 (Spring 1938): 3–25 is helpful.

63. King, *Torpedoes: Their Invention and Use from the First Application of the Art of War to the Present Time,* 29. Perhaps the only real reference to Union land mine activity can be found in a pair of letters dated July 26, 1864, neither of which indicate the Union's successful use of torpedoes, *ORA*, 1/35 pt. 2, 188–89.

64. King, *Torpedoes: Their Invention and Use from the First Application of the Art of War to the Present Time,* 32–33.

65. Ibid.

66. Ibid.

67. Ibid., 29.

68. *ORA*, 1/42 pt. 3, 1219.

69. Jefferson Davis and Hunter Davidson, "Davis and Davidson, A Chapter of War History Concerning Torpedoes," *Southern Historical Society Papers* 24 (1896): 284–91.

70. Perry, *Infernal Machines,* 193, and Cullum, *Biographical Register of the Officers and Graduates of the United States Military Academy at West Point: From Its Establishment, in 1802, to 1890. With the Early History of the United States Military Academy,* 393.

71. Information on Davidson is from Perry, *Infernal Machines,* 193. Perry states in his bibliographic section that the records of the Torpedo Bureau were destroyed,

"some intentionally." For an example of the debate between Davis and Davidson see Jefferson Davis and Hunter Davidson, "Davis and Davidson," 284–91.

72. Figures from Perry, 199–201.

Chapter 4

1. Text of treaties and conferences are from *International Humanitarian Law*. CD-ROM. International Committee of the Red Cross, Geneva, 1999. This database is extremely valuable in that it includes the full text of over 90 treaties and documents concerning the laws of war, as well as a complete list of signatories.

2. Bradford, *History of Torpedo Warfare*, 77–78.

3. Ibid., 79–80. "Torpedoes," *The Manufacturer and Builder* 9 (1877): 181–82. Austria was allied with a number of the German states including Baden, Hanover, Saxony, and Wurttemberg. Prussia was allied with the recently formed Kingdom of Italy.

4. Ruddock F. Mackay, *Fisher of Kilverstone* (Oxford: Clarendon Press, 1973), 57–58.

5. R. Thomas Campbell, ed., *Engineer in Gray: Memoirs of Chief Engineer James H. Tomb, CSN* (Jefferson, NC: McFarland and Company, Inc., 2005), 133, 139–140. Darryl E. Brock, "Naval Technology from Dixie," *Americas*, 03790940, Vol. 46, No. 4 (July/August 1994): 6. The War of the Triple Alliance is also referred to as the Paraguayan War.

6. Campbell, *Engineer in Gray: Memoirs of Chief Engineer James H. Tomb, CSN*, 140, 150–51.

7. Ibid., 142–49. Bradford, *History of Torpedo Warfare*, 84.

8. Campbell, *Engineer in Gray: Memoirs of Chief Engineer James H. Tomb, CSN*, 149. Bradford, *History of Torpedo Warfare*, 84.

9. Bradford, *History of Torpedo Warfare*, 85–86. "Torpedoes and Torpedo Boats," *Harper's New Monthly Magazine* LXV (June–November, 1882): 45.

10. Edwyn Gray, *The Devil's Device: The Story of Robert Whitehead, Inventor of the Torpedo* (London: Seeley, Service and Co. Ltd., 1975), 80–81.

11. Isaac Newton, "Has the Day of the Great Navies Passed?" *The Galaxy* 24, no. 3 (September 1877): 294. F. V. Greene, "Our Defenseless Coasts," *Scribner's Magazine* 1 (January–June 1887): 51. Eugene Griffin, "Our Sea-Coast Defenses," *The North American Review* CXLVII, no. 380 (1888): 75.

12. H. G. Rickover, *How the Battleship Maine was Destroyed* (Washington, DC, 1976), 1, 5, 69–70, 127–28.

13. David F. Trask, *The War with Spain* (Lincoln, NB: University of Nebraska Press, 1996), 69–70, 97–99.

14. Ibid., 96–99, 101. Joseph L. Stickney, *Harper's New Monthly Magazine* 98, no. 585 (February 1899): 481.

15. Trask, *The War with Spain*, 99–101. Stickney, "With Dewey at Manila," 481.

16. Trask, *The War with Spain*, 196–203.

17. Ibid., 195–269, passim. Quotation and discussion of mine-clearing equipment, A. B. Feuer, *The Spanish American War at Sea: Naval Action in the Atlantic* (Westport, CT: Praeger Publisher, 1995), 170–71.

18. A. B. Feuer, *The Spanish American War at Sea: Naval Action in the Atlantic,* 131, 134–35.

19. See Barnes, *Submarine Warfare,* 58–59, 67–68, and Bradford, *History of Torpedo Warfare,* 37, 51–52, 55–56. The latter work is especially useful to anyone studying sea mine warfare before 1882 as it has information on sea mines from all parts of the world. See also King, *Torpedoes: Their Invention and Use from the First Application of the Art of War to the Present Time.* Bradford, later a Rear Admiral, wrote at least three additional works on torpedoes: *Notes on the Spar Torpedo* (1882), *Notes on Movable Torpedoes* (1882), and *Notes on Towing Torpedoes* (1882). William B. Cogar, *Dictionary of Admirals of the U.S. Navy* (Annapolis, MD: Naval Institute Press, 1991), 2:34–35.

20. King, *Torpedoes: Their Invention and Use from the First Application of the Art of War to the Present Time,* 86–87.

21. Ibid., 87–89.

22. Ibid., 86–89.

23. Information and quotations are from O. H. Ernest, *A Manual of Practical Military Engineering, Prepared for the Use of the Cadets of the U.S. Military Academy, and for Engineering Troops* (New York: D. Van Nostrand, 1873), 223–24.

24. Quotations and information from the 1894 edition are from William D. Beach, *A Manual or Military Field Engineering for the Use of Officers and Troops of the Line* (Fort Leavenworth, KS: United States Infantry and Cavalry School, 1894), 42. In his discussion of the landmine, Beach unfortunately did not discuss the effects of various types of soil on the effectiveness of the mine. Beach also included a discussion of the more traditional fougasse.

25. Croll, *The History of Landmines,* 20–21.

26. Joseph E. Kuhn, *Reports of Military Observers Attached to the Armies in Manchuria during the Russo-Japanese War,* Pt. 3. Report of Major Joseph E. Kuhn, Corps of Engineers (Washington, DC: Government Printing Office, 1906), 227.

27. The defenses at Nanshan are discussed in G. J. Fiebeger, *A Text-book on Field Fortification,* 3rd. ed. (New York: John Wiley and Sons, 1913), 91–92. Construction of mines is discussed in Kuhn, *Reports of Military Observers Attached to the Armies in Manchuria during the Russo-Japanese War,,* 189, and in Carl Toepfer, "Technics in the Russo-Japanese War," *Professional Memoirs. Corps of Engineers* 2, no. 6 (April–June 1910): 196–97. Russian use of mines in ravines is from Committee of Imperial Defense, *Official History of the Russo-Japanese War,* Pt. 3, The Siege of Port Arthur (London: Wyman and Sons, 1909), 31. A *troups-de-loups* is a pit with a sharpened stake or stakes in the bottom of it, similar to the Roman *lilia.*

28. Kuhn, *Reports of Military Observers Attached to the Armies in Manchuria during the Russo-Japanese War,* 189, Plate XXXIV. The Russians continued to use a Nobel-style fuse for their sea mines. For a discussion of the mines and their construction, see Newton A. McCully, *The McCully Report: The Russo-Japanese War, 1904–05*

(Annapolis, MD: Naval Institute Press, 1977), 157–58. McCully was a naval observer during the war.

29. Tadayoshi Sakurai, *Human Bullets*, trans. Masujiro Honda and Alice Bacon (Tokyo: Teibi Publishing Co., 1907), 36, 149, 176, 202.

30. Sakurai quotation is from Ibid., 147–48. Kuhn, *Reports of Military Observers Attached to the Armies in Manchuria during the Russo-Japanese War,* 189. Toepfer, "Technics in the Russo-Japanese War," 197. British source is from Committee of Imperial Defense, *Official History of the Russo-Japanese War,* 31.

31. Newton A. McCully, *The McCully Report: The Russo-Japanese War, 1904-05,* 77–80. Lt. Commander McCully was an observer during the war and was present for much of what went on at Port Arthur.

32. Ibid., 82.

33. Ibid., 158–59.

34. Ibid., 67.

35. Ibid., 157, 195, 99.

36. Ibid., 258.

37. David C. Evans and Mark R. Peattie, *Kaigun: Strategy, Tactics, and Technology in the Imperial Japanese Navy, 1887–1941* (Annapolis, MD: Naval Institute Press, 1997), 114, 118, 131, 557–58.

38. Calvin DeArmond Davis, *The United States and the Second Hague Peace Conference* (Durham, NC: Duke University Press, 1975), 244–45. Quotation is from James Brown Scott, ed., *The Proceedings of the Hague Peace Conferences: The Conference of 1907* (New York: Oxford University Press, 1921), 3:665.

39. Davis, *The United States and the Second Hague Peace Conference,* 5, 33–34.

40. Ibid., 244–46. James Brown Scott, *The Hague Peace Conferences of 1899 and 1907: A Series of Lectures Delivered Before the Johns Hopkins University in the Year 1908* (New York: Garland Publishing, Inc., 1972), 1:579–80.

41. Davis, *The United States and the Second Hague Peace Conference,* 245–47. The full text of the agreement can be found in James Brown Scott, *The Hague Peace Conferences of 1899 and 1907: A Series of Lectures Delivered Before the Johns Hopkins University in the Year 1908* (New York: Garland Publishing, Inc., 1972), 2:429–37.

42. Prohibitions on poison gas and the dropping of bombs were also part of the Hague Convention of 1899. James Scott Brown, *The Hague Conventions and Declarations of 1899 and 1907,* 3rd ed. (New York: Oxford University Press, 1918), 157, 220–22, 225–26. Prohibitions on poison gas and the dropping of bombs were also part of the Hague Convention of 1899.

43. Quotation is from Scott, *The Hague Peace Conferences of 1899 and 1907,* 429–37. Douglas MacArthur, *Military Demolitions* (n.p.: Staff College Press, 1909), 30–32. Large sections of *The Engineer Field Manual* are included in the *Complete U.S. Infantry Guide,* comprising some 269 pages of the work. *Complete U.S. Infantry Guide* (Philadelphia: J. B. Lippincott, 1917), 1009–1278. Mining section quoted in Ibid., 1237.

Chapter 5

1. Robert K. Massie, *Castles of Steel* (New York: Random House, 2003), 141–43.

2. The number of mines in the Northern Barrage is discussed in Massie, *Castles of Steel*, 761.

3. Massie, *Castles of Steel*, 77–78. A. C. Bell, *A History of the Blockade of Germany* (1931; reprint, London: Her Majesty's Stationary Office, 1961), 37.

4. Massie, *Castles of Steel*, 77–78.

5. Bell, *A History of the Blockade of Germany*, 37–39. First quotation is from Bell, Ibid., 37. The author does not let the Germans off the hook entirely and points out that the admiralty should instead have accused them "of violating a custom of war." Second quotation is from Louis Guichard, *The Naval Blockade 1914–1918*, trans. Christopher R. Turner (New York: D. Appleton and Company, 1930), 27.

6. Massie, *Castles of Steel*, 73–77. Arthur J. Marder, *From the Dreadnought to Scapa Flow* (Oxford: Oxford University Press, 1961), 1:369–72. Quotations are from Ibid., 371, and Massie, *Castles of Steel*, 73. The former is the more complete.

7. Mine information is from Reinhard Scheer, *Germany's High Sea Fleet in the World War* (New York: Peter Smith, 1934), 199–201, 286–88. Scheer was appointed Command-in-Chief of the High Seas Fleet in January 1916 and was the German navy's Chief of Staff from August 1918 until the end of the war. The German spelling of Heliogoland is Helgoland.

8. Hartmann, *Weapons That Wait, Mine Warfare in the U.S. Navy*, 43. John Jellicoe, *The Crisis of the Naval War* (New York: George H. Doran Co., 1920), 186–87. Howard S. Levie, *Mine Warfare at Sea* (Dordrecht, Netherlands: Martinus Nijhoff Publishers, 1992), 72. Scheer, *Germany's High Sea Fleet in the World War*, 288.

9. An example of the admiralty's disinterest in sea mines was the order to end research on blockade mines at a time when many other nations, including Germany, were actively developing them. Nicholas Lambert, ed., *The Submarine Service, 1900–1918* (Hants, UK: Ashgate Publishing Ltd., 2001), 5. Peter F. Halvorsen, "The Royal Navy and Mine Warfare, 1868–1914," *The Journal of Strategic Studies* 27, no. 4 (December 2004):686–88.

10. Halvorsen, "The Royal Navy and Mine Warfare, 1868–1914," 691.

11. Ibid., 697. Mackay, *Fisher of Kilverstone*, 378.

12. Halvorsen, "The Royal Navy and Mine Warfare, 1868–1914," 700–703. Quotation is from Nicholas Lambert, *Sir John Fisher's Naval Revolution* (Columbia, SC: University of South Carolina Press, 1999), 271.

13. Halvorsen, "The Royal Navy and Mine Warfare, 1868–1914," 700–703.

14. Hartmann, *Weapons That Wait, Mine Warfare in the U.S. Navy*, 37, 43. Figures are from Mackay, *Fisher of Kilverstone*, 377.

15. Massie, *Castles of Steel*, 161.

16. Massie, *Castles of Steel*, 345. Scheer, *Germany's High Sea Fleet in the World War*, 215.

17. Massie, *Castles of Steel*, 428, 432–33.

18. Ibid., 432–33. Richard Hough, *The Great War at Sea, 1914–1918* (Oxford: Oxford University Press, 1983), 151. Paul Halpern, *The Naval War in the Mediterranean, 1914–1918* (Annapolis, MD: Naval Institute Press, 1987), 54. For a detailed discussion of British intelligence on the Dardanelles, see Yigal Sheffy, *British Military Intelligence in the Palestine Campaign* (London: Frank Cass and Company, Ltd., 1998).

19. Arthur J. Marder, *From the Dardanelles to Oran: Studies of the Royal Navy in War and Peace 1915–1940* (London: Oxford University Press, 1974), 2. Massie, *Castles of Steel,* 50, 444–45.

20. Ibid., 445–51.

21. Ibid. Marder, *From the Dardanelles to Oran,* 24.

22. Massie, *Castles of Steel,* 453–55.

23. Carden's health is discussed in Ibid., 456.

24. Marder, *From the Dardanelles to Oran,* 15–21. Figures are from Massie, *Castles of Steel,* 502. While the mines in the Dardanelles were indirectly responsible for ending many careers, a mine in the Atlantic took a much greater toll, sinking the British cruiser *Hampshire* and drowning Secretary of War Kitchener on June 5, 1916. Halpern, *The Naval War in the Mediterranean, 1914–1918,* 329.

25. Jellicoe, *The Crisis of the Naval War,* 200–202. Arthur J. Marder, *From Dreadnaught to Scapa Flow* (London: Oxford University Press, 1969), 4:316–18.

26. Marder, *From Dreadnaught to Scapa Flow,* 4:316–318. Keyes would have been well aware of the effectiveness of mines given his experience as the Chief of Staff for the Eastern Mediterranean Squadron in 1915 during the efforts to breach the Dardanelles minefields. Levie, *Mine Warfare at Sea,* 72.

27. Levie, *Mine Warfare at Sea,* 72. Marder, *From Dreadnaught to Scapa Flow,* 4:320–22, 347–48.

28. The firing device was the work of Ralph Browne. Hartmann, *Weapons That Wait, Mine Warfare in the U.S. Navy,* 48–50.

29. Ibid., 51–55.

30. Hartmann, *Weapons That Wait, Mine Warfare in the U.S. Navy,* 55.

31. Paul Halpern, *A Naval History of World War I* (Annapolis, MD: Naval Institute Press, 1994), 179.

32. Ibid., 181–83.

33. Ibid., 213–21.

34. Figures on Northern Barrage clearance are from Levie, *Mine Warfare at Sea,* 74.

35. For an example of one of the attacks following the explosion of the mines see Peter H. Liddle, *The 1916 Battle of the Somme: A Reappraisal* (Hertfordshire, UK: Wordsworth Editions Ltd., 2001), 58–60. Robert Cowley and Geoffrey Parker, eds., *The Reader's Companion to Military History* (New York: Houghton Mifflin Co., 1996), 433. Information on the evolution of the tank is from David Childs, *A Peripheral Weapon? The Production and Employment of British Tanks in the First World War* (London: Greenwood Press, 1999), 3–4.

36. Early tanks were notoriously unreliable. Historian J. P. Harris suggests that as few as 21 of the tanks actually participated in the fighting. J. P. Harris, *Men, Ideas, and Tanks: British Military Thought and Armoured Forces 1903–1939* (Manchester, UK: Manchester University Press, 1995), 65–66. Cambrai is discussed in Ibid., 120–26. Figures for Cambrai are from Martin Gilbert, *The First World War: A Complete History* (New York: Henry Holt and Company, 1994), 378–81. For a concise discussion of the armored forces of both sides see Armin Halle, *Tanks: An Illustrated History of Fighting Vehicles* (New York: Crescent Books, 1971), 33–68.

37. "German Traps and Land Mines. From a captured German Document," *Professional Memoirs, Corps of Engineers* 11 (1919): 277–78.

38. Artillery Inspector, Ministry of War, French Army. "German Mine for Wrecking Tanks," *Professional Memoirs, Corps of Engineers* 11 (1919): 305–307.

39. "Anti-Tank Defenses," *Professional Memoirs, Corps of Engineers* 11 (1919): 422–23. This article includes segments from the A. E. F. Ordnance Report as well as translations of comments on antitank mines from two German officers.

40. "The Barrier Type of Tank Defenses," *Professional Memoirs, Corps of Engineers* 11 (1919): 302–304. Quotation is from "Anti-Tank Defenses," 425. The officer's last name is Von Hofacker; unfortunately the article does not provide a first name. The use of rollers is discussed in Childs, *A Peripheral Weapon? The Production and Employment of British Tanks in the First World War,* 81.

41. The British box mine is discussed in Croll, *The History of Landmines,* 31. Mortar-based mines and the American tanks are discussed in Ibid., 32, and in Childs, *A Peripheral Weapon? The Production and Employment of British Tanks in the First World War,* 175, 186. Childs's discussion is particularly useful as he addressed conflicting accounts of the battle.

42. *German Traps and Mines, E.-in-C. Fieldwork Notes no. 59* (September 29, 1918): 1–2. This document is located at the Institute of Military History, Carlisle, PA.

43. Albert A. Hopkins, *The Scientific American War Book; The Mechanism and Technique of Warfare* (New York: Munn & Company, Inc., 1916), 160–62.

44. Information and quotations are from William A. Mitchell, *Fortification*, 2nd ed. (Washington, DC: The Society of American Military Engineers, 1928), 43. At the time *Fortification* was written, Mitchell was a professor of Civil and Military Engineering at West Point. Mitchell's work remained in print, and probably in use, through at least 1937. William Warner Bishop et al., *A Catalog of Books Represented by Library of Congress Printed Cards* (Paterson, NJ: Rowman and Littlefield Inc., 1963), 101:372. An example of one of the Army's studies in the 1930s is William C. Baker, Jr., Subproject SP 220, "Mines and Obstacles for Use Against Mechanized Units," Report No. 571, March 31, 1939, Fort Belvoir, Virginia. United States Army War College Library, Carlisle Barracks, PA. Like Mitchell, Baker did not seem to place any restrictions on the use of mines.

45. First United States Army landmine is discussed in Jackson M. Abbot and Logan Cassedy, "Landmines: Past and Present," *Military Engineer* 54 (September to October 1962): 367–68. Detailed descriptions of both mines can be found in Ernest

R. Gilliespie, *Ammunition Manual for General Training* (Raritan Arsenal, n.p.: Ordnance Department, 1943), 67–68.

46. For the text of these treaties, see Treaty Relating to the Use of Submarines and Noxious Gases in Warfare. Washington, February 6, 1922; Protocol for the Prohibition of the Use of Asphyxiating, Poisonous or Other Gases, and of Bacteriological Methods of Warfare. Geneva, June 17, 1925; Convention Relative to the Treatment of Prisoners of War, Geneva, July 27, 1929; Draft International Convention on the Condition and Protection of Civilians of Enemy Nationality who are on Territory Belonging to or Occupied by a Belligerent. Tokyo, 1934; and the Draft Convention for the Protection of Civilian Populations Against New Engines of War. Amsterdam, 1938. The text of these treaties can be found in *International Humanitarian Law.* CD-ROM.

Chapter 6

1. The French used antitank mines and booby-trap style antipersonnel weapons in the defenses of some of their fortifications including the Maginot Line. They do not appear to have had antipersonnel mines available for use. J. E. Kaufmann and Robert M. Jurga, *Fortress Europe: European Fortifications of World War II* (Cambridge, MA: Da Capo Press, 1999), 25. Mining on the German West Wall is discussed in J. E. Kaufmann and H. W. Kaufmann, *Fortress Third Reich: German Fortifications and Defense Systems in World War II* (Cambridge, MA: Da Capo Press, 2003), 100–101. Information on German mines is drawn from U.S. War Department, *Handbook on German Military Forces, TME-30-451* (Washington, DC: Military Intelligence Service, March 15, 1945; reprint, Baton Rouge: Louisiana State University Press, 1990), 486–499 (page references are to reprint edition). Heinz Guderian, *Achtung—Panzer!* trans. Christopher Duffy (London: Arms and Armour Press, 1992), 157.

2. Analysis of Japanese use of landmines is from U.S. War Department, *Handbook on Japanese Military Forces, TME-30-480* (Washington, DC: Military Intelligence Service, July 1, 1945), VII A-57. This work is hereafter cited as *Handbook on Japanese Military 1945 ed.* American lack of interest in landmines is discussed in Constance Green, Harry Thompson, and Peter Root, *The Ordnance Department: Planning Munitions for War,* The United States Army in World War II (Washington, DC: Office of the Chief of Military History, Department of the Army, 1955), 381–84.

3. U.S. War Department, *Enemy Landmines and Booby Traps, TM 5-325* (April 19, 1943), 67–69, and U.S. War Department, *Handbook on German Military Forces,* 491–95.

4. U.S. War Department, *Handbook on German Military Forces,* 486–99.

5. Quotations are from Guderian, *Achtung—Panzer!* 157, 178.

6. Hermann Balck, Interview from the U.S. Air Force Oral History Program, transcript, U.S. Air Force Historical Resource Center, Maxwell AFB, AL.

7. Technical information is from the U.S. War Department, *Handbook on German Military Forces,* 487–88. Firsthand account is from Richard D. Courtney, *Normandy to*

the Bulge: An American Infantry GI in Europe During World War II (Carbondale: Southern Illinois University Press, 1997), 75.

8. U.S. War Department, *Handbook on German Military Forces,* 487–48.

9. U.S. War Department, "Mines in the Spotlight," *Intelligence Bulletin* III, no. 8 (April 1945): 26–29.

10. Ibid., 30–33, 38–41.

11. Ibid. Concrete mines are discussed in detail in U.S. War Department, *Engineer Intelligence Bulletin, Mine Series no. 2,* 1–7.

12. Tactics are discussed in U.S. War Department, *Handbook on German Military Forces,* 243–52. Quotation is from Belton Y. Cooper, *Death Traps, The Survival of an American Armored Division in World War II* (Novato, CA: Presidio Press, 1998), 148.

13. U.S. War Department, *Handbook on German Military Forces*, 243–52, and U.S. War Department, *German Mine Warfare in Winter* (n.p.: Information Section, Intelligence Division, OCE, HQ, ETOUSA, January 7, 1945), 6. This manual is of particular interest as it is basically a translation of the German Field Manual, *Minensparren im Winter,* published August 1, 1943.

14. The Italian B2 and N5 are discussed in detail in U.S. War Department, *Handbook on the Italian Military Forces, TME-30-420* (Washington, DC: Military Intelligence Service), 288–300. Riegel mine is described in U.S. War Department, *Handbook on German Military Forces,* 495–97.

15. Ibid., 505.

16. Figures are from The Dupuy Institute, "A Measure of the Real-World Value of Mixed Mine Systems" (McLean, VA: The Dupuy Institute, June 20, 2001), 7, 36. The article provides an extremely detailed analysis of the use of landmines in both battles and is based on extensive primary source research.

17. Ibid., 16–17.

18. Scorpion described in Ibid., 17.

19. Ibid.

20. Ibid., 15.

21. Zhukov describes his plans in Georgi Zhukov, *Marshal Zhukov's Greatest Battles,* trans. Theodore Shabad (New York: Harper and Row, 1969), 199. Troop figures are from The Dupuy Institute, "A Measure of the Real-World Value of Mixed Mine Systems," 15.

22. Percentages are from The Dupuy Institute, "A Measure of the Real-World Value of Mixed Mine Systems," 64. Snipers and the use of mines to shape attacks are discussed in Martin Caiden, *The Tigers are Burning* (New York: Hawthorn Books, 1974), 185, 191. The mobile obstacle corps is discussed in David Glantz and Jonathan House, *The Battle of Kursk* (Lawrence, KS: University of Kansas Press, 1999), 68, and Zhukov, *Marshal Zhukov's Greatest Battles*, 231.

23. Information on Soviet landmines is from U.S. War Department, *Handbook on U.S.S.R. Military Forces* (Washington, DC: GPO, November 1945), VI-25; Edward Emering, *Weapons and Field Gear of the North Vietnamese Army and Viet Cong* (Atglen, PA: Schiffer Publishing Ltd, 1998), 104, 110–111; SIPRI, *Anti-Personnel Weapons* (New York: Crane, Russak and Company, 1978), 186–187; and

David C. Isby, *Jane's Weapons and Tactics of the Soviet Army* (New York: Jane's, 1981), 335.

24. Kaufmann and Jurga, *Fortress Europe: European Fortifications of World War II*, 200, 209–211.

25. U.S. War Department, *Handbook of the Italian Military Forces*, 286–88. C. E. E. Sloan, *Mine Warfare On Land* (New York: Brassey's Defense Publishers, 1986), 25. Quotation is from U.S. War Department, *Amendments no. 1 to Engineer Intelligence Bulletin Number 3. Comparative Analysis Charts of Allied and Enemy Mines*, Document 172.252-3, United States Air Force Historical Research Center, Maxwell AFB, AL.

26. Alfred Price, *Luftwaffe Handbook 1939–1945* (New York: Charles Scribner's Sons, 1977), 43–45. U.S. War Department, Amendments no. 1 and no. 13. Military Intelligence Division, *Tactical and Technical Trends no. 34* (Washington, DC: War Department, September 23, 1943), 23.

27. American sources during the war went so far as to compare the defenses at Tarawa Atoll to "a small island edition of the German West Wall," though they were quick to point out that the Japanese defenses lacked the depth of the German ones. U.S. War Department, *Japanese Defense Against Amphibious Operations*, Special Series no. 29 (Washington, DC: Military Intelligence Division, February 1945), 15.

28. Type 93 description is from U.S. War Department, "Landmines, Grenades, and Booby Traps,"*Intelligence Bulletin* 1, no. 1 (Washington, DC: Military Intelligence Division, September 1943): 2–5. Type 96 description is from U.S. War Department, *Handbook on Japanese Military Forces, TME-30-480* (Washington, DC: Military Intelligence Service, October 1, 1944; reprint, Baton Rouge: Louisiana State University Press, 1991), 215–16 (page references are to reprint edition). This work is hereafter referred to as *Handbook on Japanese Military, 1944 ed.*

29. U.S. War Department, "Some Data on Enemy Mines and Obstacles," *Intelligence Bulletin* 2, no. 11 (Washington, DC: Military Intelligence Division, July 1944): 55–59.

30. Earthenware mine description is from U.S. War Department, "New Pottery Land Mine Introduced on Leyte Island," *Intelligence Bulletin* 3, no. 4 (Washington, DC: Military Intelligence Division, December 1944): 1–6. Comparison of Model A and Model B is from *Handbook on Japanese Military Forces, 1945 ed.*, VII-A-59.

31. U.S. War Department, "Enemy Mines on Leyte," *Intelligence Bulletin* 3, no. 6 (Washington, DC: Military Intelligence Division, February 1945): 62–63.

32. U.S. War Department, "More Notes on Booby Traps and Firing Devices," *Intelligence Bulletin* 3, no. 8 (Washington, DC: Military Intelligence Division, April 1945): 31–32.

33. For detailed examples of typical Japanese defenses, see *Handbook on Japanese Military Forces, 1944 ed.*, 130–32.

34. The use of *panji* pits, spelled *punji* during the Vietnam War, by Allied and Japanese forces is discussed in U.S. War Department, "Bamboo Spike Jungle Traps," *Intelligence Bulletin* 3, no. 2 (Washington, DC: Military Intelligence Division, October 1944): 88–92.

35. Comment on hiding landmines is from *Handbook on Japanese Military Forces, 1945 ed.,* VII A-57. Development of landmine doctrine is discussed in U.S. War Department, "Japanese Minefield Tactics in the Southwest Pacific," *Intelligence Bulletin* 3, no. 4 (Washington, DC: Military Intelligence Division, December 1944): 7–12.

36. Ibid., 7, 13–15.

37. U.S. War Department, "Minefield Patterns in the Defense of Iwo Jima," *Intelligence Bulletin* 3, no. 10 (Washington, DC: Military Intelligence Division, June 1945): 15–21. Quotation is from Charles Harton, "The Surf Turned Red," in R. T. King, *War Stories: Veterans Remember WW II* (Reno: University of Nevada Oral History Program, 1995), 77.

38. Elizabeth Mullener, *War Stories: Remembering World War II* (Baton Rouge: Louisiana State University Press, 2002), 120.

39. S. W. Roskill, *The War at Sea, 1939–1945,* vol. 1, *The Defensive* (London: Her Majesty's Stationary Office, 1954), 100. Edward P. Von der Porten, *Pictorial History of the German Navy in World War II,* revised ed. (New York: Thomas Y. Crowell Company, 1976), 45, 58.

40. Ibid., 36, 46. Hartmann, *Weapons That Wait, Mine Warfare in the U.S. Navy,* 61. Shipping casualties and quotation are from Martin Gilbert, *The Second World War: A Complete History*(New York: Henry Holt and Company, 1991), 29–30. A similar quotation is used in Levie, *Mine Warfare at Sea,* 78.

41. For first person accounts of defusing the German mine, see Hartmann, *Weapons That Wait, Mine Warfare in the U.S. Navy,* 61–63. Degaussing, sweeping, etc., are discussed in Ibid., 63–65.

42. Franz Kurowski, *Luftwaffe Aces: German Fighter Aces of World War II* (Mechanicsburg, PA: Stackpole Books, 2004), 204, 212–13. Michael I. Handel, *War, Strategy and Intelligence* (London: Frank Cass and Company, Ltd., 1989), 157. The British acoustic mine was first used in September 1941. S. W. Roskill, *The War at Sea, 1939–1945,* vol. 2, *The Period of Balance* (London: Her Majesty's Stationary Office, 1956), 263.

43. Roskill, *The War at Sea, 1939–1945,* 1:95–97, 81, 124–25, 264, 511–12. Roskill provides a table detailing the effectiveness of direct attack versus aerial mining in 1940–41 in Ibid., 512, and one for the first half of 1943 in Roskill, *The War at Sea, 1939–1945,* 2:395. S. W. Roskill, *The War at Sea, 1939–1945,* vol. 3, *The Offensive,* pt. 1 (London: Her Majesty's Stationary Office, 1960), 94. RAF Bomber Command put out 47,307 of these mines and RAF Coastal Command the remaining 841. John Chilstrom, "Mines Away! The Significance of U.S. Army Air Forces Minelaying in World War II" (thesis, School of Advanced Airpower Studies, Air University, 1992), 8, 42.

44. Ellis A. Johnson and David A. Katcher, *Mines Against Japan* (White Oak, MD: Naval Ordnance Laboratory, 1973), 46, 53. This work was originally written in 1947 as a classified report. Ibid., iii.

45. James Sadkovich, *The Italian Navy in World War II* (Westport, CN: Greenwood Press, 1994), 39–40, 142–43.

46. Ibid., 183–84, 206, 216.

47. Ibid., 40, 220–22.

48. Milan N. Vego, *Naval Strategy and Operations in Narrow Seas,* 2nd ed. (London: Frank Cass Publishers, 2003), 170.

49. V. I. Achkasov and N. B. Pavlovich, *Soviet Naval Operations in the Great Patriotic War* (Annapolis, MD: Naval Institute Press, 1981), 12, 23, 61, 64, 72, 302. Von der Porten, *Pictorial History of the German Navy in World War II,* 156.

50. Ibid., 12, 44, 234–35, 248–50, 282, 302. Vego, *Naval Strategy and Operations in Narrow Seas,* 220.

51. Hartmann, *Weapons That Wait, Mine Warfare in the U.S. Navy,* 58–60. Johnson and Katcher, *Mines Against Japan,* 44–45, 53–55.

52. Theodore Roscoe, *United States Submarine Operations in World War II* (Annapolis, MD: Naval Institute Press, 1949), 179–80. *Argonaut* was lost during a depth charge attack in January 1943. Ibid., 193. Johnson and Katcher, *Mines Against Japan,* 90–91. USS *Trigger* incident is discussed in W. J. Holmes, *Undersea Victory: The Influence of Submarine Operations on the War in the Pacific* (New York: Doubleday & Co. Inc., 1966), 191.

53. Japanese casualties are from Samuel E. Morison, *History of United States Naval Operations During World War II* (Boston: Little, Brown and Co., 1953), 6:76. James F. DeRose, *Unrestricted Warfare* (New York: John Wiley & Sons, Inc., 2000), 169–170. For a full list of the American submarines lost during the war, see Keith M. Milton, *Subs Against the Rising Sun* (Las Cruces, NM: Yucca Free Press, 2000), 348. The United States did not have submarines that could go down to 400 feet until the introduction of the Balao Class submarines in 1943. Robert Hargis, *U.S. Submarine Crewman 1941–45* (Oxford: Osprey Publishing Ltd., 2003), 20.

54. Roscoe, *United States Submarine Operations in World War II,* 213. U.S. War Department, *Handbook of Japanese Military Forces,* 215. James F. Dunnigan and Albert A. Nofi, *Victory at Sea: World War II in the Pacific* (New York: William Morrow & Co. Inc., 1995), 187.

55. Holmes, *Undersea Victory: The Influence of Submarine Operations on the War in the Pacific,* 291–92, 345, 459. Roscoe, *United States Submarine Operations in World War II,* 479–80. DeRose, *Unrestricted Warfare,* 186–87, 199, 238.

56. Johnson and Katcher, *Mines Against Japan,* 45, 53–54, 95–97.

57. Ibid., 38, 95–102. Johnson and Katcher provide a nice set of charts listing specific targets and the types of mines used at each.

58. Samuel E. Morison, *History of United States Naval Operations During World War II,* vol. 8, *New Guinea and the Marianas,* March 1944–August 1944 (Boston: Little, Brown and Co., 1953), 32–33. Walter Karig et al., *Battle Report,* vol. 4, *The End of an Empire* (New York: Rinehart and Co., 1948), 180–181. Quotation is from Fred Foisy, *I'm Here to Tell You* (Victoria, B.C.: Trafford, 2003), chap. 4. Patrick Degan, *Flattop Fighting in World War II: The Battles Between American and Japanese Aircraft Carriers* (Jefferson, NC: McFarland & Co., Inc., 2003), 176–77.

59. Johnson and Katcher, *Mines Against Japan,* 137. Bomb payloads are from Jim Winchester, *Aircraft of World War II* (San Diego, CA: Thunder Bay Press, 2004), 43,

57. Frederick M. Sallagar, *Lessons From an Aerial Mining Campaign (Operation "Starvation"): A Report Prepared for United States Air Force Project Rand* (Santa Monica, CA: Rand, 1974), 1, 62–63. Quotation is from Ibid.

60. British mine numbers are from Chilstrom, "Mines Away! The Significance of U.S. Army Air Forces Minelaying in World War II," 9. Overall estimates are from James J. Busuttil, *Naval Weapons Systems and the Contemporary Law of War* (New York: Oxford University Press, 1998), 37. Clearance statistics are from Peter Elliot, *Allied Minesweepers in World War 2* (Annapolis, MD: Naval Institute Press, 1979), 170–81.

Chapter 7

1. Walter Karig et al., *Battle Report: The War in Korea* (New York: Rinehart and Company, Inc., 1952), 310, 332. Hartmann, *Weapons That Wait, Mine Warfare in the U.S. Navy*, 80.

2. Hartmann, *Weapons That Wait, Mine Warfare in the U.S. Navy*, 78–80. For a detailed account of the loss of the South Korean minesweeper, see Karig et al., *Battle Report: The War in Korea*, 324–26. Quotation is from Ibid., 326. Hartmann, *Weapons That Wait, Mine Warfare in the U.S. Navy*, 80–81.

3. Karig et al., *Battle Report: The War in Korea*, 296. Landmine guidelines and quotations are from Department of the Army, *FM 5-15 Field Fortifications* (Washington, DC: Department of the Army, 1949), 244–45. Use of booby traps is discussed in Ibid., 324–31

4. MacArthur, *Military Demolitions*, 30. Robert F. Fuller, *The United States Air Force in Korea 1950–53*, revised ed. (Washington, DC: Office of Air Force History, United States Air Force, 1984), 324, 678. Ibid. United States Army, *Mine and Booby Traps* (Washington, DC: United States Army, n.d.), 108–109. U.S. Army War College Library, Carlisle Barracks, PA.

5. Quotation and problem are from USAF Air Proving Ground Commander, "Operation Doan Brook," Draft of speech for April 7 at Elgin Air Force Base, p. 2 (n.d.). U.S. Army War College, Carlisle Barracks, PA. Other information is from Eric Prokosch, *The Simple Art of Murder, Antipersonnel Weapons and Their Developers* (Philadelphia: NARMIC, December 1972), 54. Douglas Pike Collection Technology File, Vietnam Archive, Texas Tech University, Lubbock, TX (hereafter cited as Pike Collection).

6. The Pusan Perimeter minefields totaled around 520 antitank and antipersonnel mines. The attack discussed was the night of August 31 to September 1, 1950. The Dupuy Institute, *Military Consequences of Landmines Restrictions*, vol. 1, no. 2, *VVAF Monograph Series* (Washington, DC: Vietnam Veterans of America Foundation, Spring 2000), 48.

7. Larry Grupp, "The Claymore Mine," *Military History* 13, no. 2 (June 1996): 17–20.

8. Importance of France as an ally is discussed in George C. Herring, *America's Longest War*, 2nd ed. (New York: Alfred A. Knopf), 8–13. The status of the Republic

of Vietnam and the Democratic Republic of Vietnam are discussed in great detail in Robert F. Randle, *Geneva 1954: The Settlement of the Indochinese War* (Princeton: Princeton University Press, 1969), 409–54. American figures are from Stanley Karnow, *Vietnam: A History* (New York: Viking Press, 1983), 682, 684. Chinese figures are from Xiaoming Zhang, "The Vietnam War, 1964–1969: A Chinese Perspective," *The Journal of Military History* 60, no. 4 (October 1996): 759.

9. Quotation is from Westmoreland's October 14, 1969, speech before the Annual Luncheon Association of the United States Army, Sheraton Park Hotel, Washington, DC. A portion of this speech is quoted in "The Pentagon Plays Electronic Wargames." The text of the speech is included as Exhibit #1 in United States Congress, Senate, *Investigation into Electronic Battlefield Program*, 92nd Cong., 1st sess., *Congressional Record* (July 13, 1970): 23823-4. Congress, Senate, Report of the Electronic Battlefield Committee of the Preparedness Investigating Subcommittee of the Committee on Armed Services, 1971, Committee Print, pp. 1–2 (hereafter referred to as *Electronic Battlefield*). NARMIC, *Background Report on the Automated Battlefield* (December 1971): 2–3. Pike Collection, Technology File, 1971. See also Mike Gravel, *The Pentagon Papers* (Boston: Beacon Press, 1971), 4:114–123.

10. NARMIC, *Background Report on the Automated Battlefield*, 17–18. *Electronic Battlefield*, 2–3.

11. Jacob Van Staaveren, *Interdiction in Southern Laos, 1960–1968* (Washington, DC: Center for Air Force History, 1993), vi, 8, 273–83. Figures are from Ibid., 301. For a detailed history of the Ho Chi Minh Trail, see John Prados, *The Blood Road: The Ho Chi Minh Trail and the Vietnam War* (New York: John Wiley and Sons, 1999). For a more detailed discussion of IGLOO WHITE, see CHECO Southeast Asia Report, "IGLOO WHITE: (Initial Phase)" (July 31, 1968). Vietnam Archive, Texas Tech University, Lubbock, TX.

12. Prokosch, *The Simple Art of Murder, Antipersonnel Weapons and Their Developers,* 54. Charles Snow, First Acceptance Tests of the CBU-42/A Munition ADTC-TR-70-1 (Elgin AFB: Armament Development and Test Center, January 1970), 5–8. U.S. Air Force Historical Research Center, Maxwell AFB, AL. The development cost for the BLU-54 and dispenser totaled $24.0 million. United States Congress, Senate, *Congressional Record* (July 13, 1970): 23828.

13. Van Staaveren, *Interdiction in Southern Laos, 1960–1968,* 259–60, 282, and Prokosch, *The Simple Art of Murder, Antipersonnel Weapons and Their Developers,* 56–59.

14. CHECO Southeast Asia Report, "IGLOO WHITE: July 1968–December 1969" (July 10, 1970): 2. Vietnam Archive, Texas Tech University, Lubbock, TX. Congressional Record (July 13, 1970): 23833–23834.

15. Congressional Record (July 13, 1970): 23833–23834.

16. VC use of improvised munitions is discussed in United States Marine Corps, *Professional Knowledge Gained from Operational Experience in Vietnam, 1967* (Washington, DC: Department of the Navy, 1989), 317. The prevalence of hand grenades and Claymores is discussed in James W. McCoy, *Secrets of the Viet Cong* (New York: Hippocrene Books, 1992), 322, 335, and in Combined Intelligence Center in Vietnam

[CICV], *What A Platoon Leader Should Know about the Enemy's Jungle Tactics* (Vietnam, October 12, 1967), 23. Vietnam Archive, Texas Tech University, Lubbock, TX. For a more complete survey of mines used by VC and North Vietnamese Army forces, see CICV, *VC Employment of Mines and Booby Traps TIS-1* (Vietnam, August 1970), and CICV, *War Material Used By the Viet Cong in South Vietnam or Presumably Available to North Vietnam TIS-3* (Vietnam, February 1969). The latter is the most comprehensive. Both works are from the Vietnam Archive, Texas Tech University, Lubbock, TX. A less complete but more accessible source is McCoy. One of the more interesting documents published by the Combined Intelligence Center is a photo essay on VC weapons production based on 2100 VC negatives captured by the 25th Infantry on September 14, 1966. The study includes photographs of the manufacture of mines, grenades, and booby traps. CICV, *VC [Weapons] Production ST 67-053* (Vietnam, n.d.). Vietnam Archive, Texas Tech University, Lubbock, TX.

17. A description of this technique can be found in a number of sources. Among them are United States Marine Corps, *Professional Knowledge Gained from Operational Experience in Vietnam, 1967* (Washington, DC: Department of the Navy, 1989), 346, and Combined Intelligence Center, *VC Mine Indicators TIS-2* (Vietnam, October 1 and 3, 1970), 2. Vietnam Archive, Texas Tech University, Lubbock, TX.

18. A subsequent investigation of the ambush described above revealed that the unit had not followed recommended procedures, had transmitted plans over unsecured communications lines, had unnecessarily divided forces, and had failed to prepare proper fire support. Donn A. Starry, *Vietnam Studies: Mounted Combat in Vietnam* (Washington, DC: Department of the Army, 1978), 108–110. American armor units had ample reason to fear mines. Between November 1968 and May 1969, mines caused 77 percent of tank losses and 77 percent of Armored Personnel Carrier (APC) losses. Ibid., 79. Supplementary armor and rollers are discussed in Ibid., 82. Mine detector equipped jeeps are discussed in United States Marine Corps, *Professional Knowledge Gained from Operational Experience in Vietnam, 1965–1966* (Washington, DC: Department of the Navy, 1991), 288–89.

19. Route selection and need for caution is discussed in United States Marine Corps, *Professional Knowledge Gained from Operational Experience in Vietnam, 1967*, 350–52. The herringbone pattern is discussed in Starry, *Vietnam Studies*, 85–87.

20. Bounties on land mines can be found in United States Marine Corps, *Professional Knowledge Gained from Operational Experience in Vietnam, 1965–1966*, 286–87.

21. Examples of CICV booklets include CICV, *VC-NVA Employment of Mines and Booby Traps, TIS-1* (Vietnam, August 1970); CICV, *What A Platoon Leader Should Know about the Enemy's Jungle Tactics*; and CICV, *VC Mine Indicators TIS-2* (Vietnam, October 13, 1970). Previous works are all from the Vietnam Archive, Texas Tech University, Lubbock, TX. Postwar analysis is from Julian J. Ewell and Ira A. Hunt, *Vietnam Studies: Sharpening the Edge: The Use of Analysis to Reinforce Military Judgment* (Washington, DC: Department of the Army, 1974), 138.

22. Julian J. Ewell and Ira A. Hunt, *Vietnam Studies: Sharpening the Edge: The Use of Analysis to Reinforce Military Judgment*, 138–41.

23. Lists of common places for VC booby traps can be found in Ibid., 140, which includes a breakdown of the location of mines and booby traps encountered by the 9th Division, and in United States Marine Corps, *Professional Knowledge Gained from Operational Experience in Vietnam, 1965–1966*, 264–65.

24. Richard Pyle, *Schwarzkopf: The Man, The Mission, The Triumph* (New York: Signet Books, 1991), 39–40. The psychological impact of VC warfare can be found in *Investigation of the My Lai Incident: Report of the Armed Services Investigating Subcommittee of the Committee on Armed Services House of Representatives* (Washington, DC: Government Printing Office, 1970), 11. The issue of sanity is discussed in Ibid., 53.

25. The newspaper story incident can be found in Seymour Hersh, *Cover-Up: The Army's Secret Investigation of the Massacre at My Lai 4* (New York: Random House, 1972), 25.

26. Civilians are discussed in John Sack, *Lieutenant Calley: His Own Story* (New York: Viking Press, 1971), 70. Quotation is from Ibid., 74–75. Italics are from original.

27. John H. Hay, *Vietnam Studies: Tactical and Material Innovations* (Washington, DC: Department of the Army, 1974), 10. The use of sheet metal and grenades is discussed in CICV, *Order of Battle Study ST 67-032 VC Anti-Heliborne Operations* (Vietnam: January 6, 1967). Vietnam Archive, Texas Tech University, Lubbock, TX. This document also provides an extensive discussion of other weapons used to thwart heliborne operations.

28. Mine discussion is from Bernard Williams Rodgers, *Vietnam Studies: Cedar Falls–Junction City: A Turning Point* (Washington, DC: Department of the Army, 1974), 137.

29. Military Assistance Command Vietnam, "Significant Problem Areas Report" (May 1971). Vietnam Archive, Texas Tech University, Lubbock, TX. Vietnam figures are from BDM Corporation, *A Study of Strategic Lessons Learned in Vietnam*, vol. 6, *Conduct of the War*, book 2 (Alexandria, VA: Defense Logistics Agency, 1981), 16–25. Vietnam Archive, Texas Tech University, Lubbock, TX. Korean figures are from The Dupuy Institute, *Military Consequences of Landmines Restrictions*, 50.

30. Levie, *Mine Warfare at Sea*, 144. Ambush is detailed in U.S. Navy Department, Naval History Division, *Riverine Warfare: The U.S. Navy's Operations on Inlands Waters* (Washington, DC: GPO, 1969), 41. Tamara Moser Melia, *"Damn the Torpedoes": A Short History of U.S. Naval Countermeasures, 1777–1991* (Washington, DC: Naval History Center, Department of the Navy, 1991), 91–98.

31. Levie, *Mine Warfare at Sea*, 144. Hartmann, *Weapons That Wait, Mine Warfare in the U.S. Navy*, 187–88.

32. Levie, *Mine Warfare at Sea*, 144–45. Quotation is from Hartmann, *Weapons That Wait, Mine Warfare in the U.S. Navy*, 152. The mouths to several rivers were also mined. Robert Morris, *History of the Mining of North Vietnam 8 May 1972–14 January 1973*, ser. 03/C700800, Department of the Navy (June 30, 1975), 3-3, 3-19, 3-41. Vietnam Archive, Texas Tech University, Lubbock, TX.

33. Hartmann, *Weapons That Wait, Mine Warfare in the U.S. Navy*, 148–54.

34. Melia, *"Damn the Torpedoes": A Short History of U.S. Naval Countermeasures, 1777–1991,* 111. Levie, *Mine Warfare at Sea,* 157–58.

35. Figures are from A. Walter Dorn, "Small Arms, Human Security and Development," *CIDA, Development Express* no. 5 (1999–2000): 2.

36. The text of these treaties and examples of similar treaties can be found in *International Humanitarian Law.* CD-ROM.

37. Ibid.

38. Paul Davies, *War of the Mines: Cambodia, Landmines and the Impoverishment of a Nation* (London: Pluto Press, 1994), 10–13.

39. Ibid., 13–14.

40. International Campaign to Ban Landmines (ICBL), *Landmine Monitor Report 2000: Toward a Mine-Free World* (New York: Human Rights Watch, 2000), 387–88, 396. This work is one of the better sources for statistics and general information on the landmine problem worldwide.

41. A brief history of the conflicts in Angola can be found in Human Rights Watch, *Land Mines in Angola: An Africa Watch Report* (New York: Human Rights Watch, 1993), 4–8.

42. Information is from ICBL, *Landmine Monitor Report 2000,* 131–34, 150–51. Landmine estimates from the United Nations are more pessimistic, ranging from 10–15 million. Ibid., 134.

43. ICBL, *Landmine Monitor Report 2000,* 270, 317–18. See also Americas Watch Committee, *Landmines in El Salvador and Nicaragua: The Civilian Victims* (New York: Americas Watch Committee, 1986).

44. ICBL, *Landmine Monitor Report 2000,* 270, 317–18.

45. Croatian figures are from Ibid., 614. Bosnian figures from 1998 are from International Committee of the Red Cross, *The Silent Menace: Landmines in Bosnia and Herzegovina* (Geneva: ICRC, 1998), 14. Bosnian, March 2000 figures are from ICBL, *Landmine Monitor Report 2000,* 592.

46. The similarities mentioned above are not intended to draw a moral parallel.

47. ICBL, *Landmine Monitor Report 2000,* 459–65.

48. Defensive line is described in Michael J. Mazarr, Don M. Snider, and James A. Blackwell, Jr., *Desert Storm: The Gulf War and What We Learned* (Boulder, CO: Westview Press, 1993), 130–31. Quotation is from Phillip Thompson, *Into the Storm: A U.S. Marine in the Persian Gulf War* (Jefferson, NC: McFarland & Co., Inc., 2001), 82. Ten percent of the B-52 strikes flown during the war were on minefields. Results seem to have been mixed at best. James A. Winnefeld, Preston Niblack, and Dana J. Johnson, *A League of Airmen: U.S. Air Power in the Gulf War* (Santa Monica, CA: Rand, 1994), 168.

49. Airfield denial tactics are discussed in Winnefeld, Niblack, and Johnson, *A League of Airmen: U.S. Air Power in the Gulf War,* 165. Description of Gator mine is from C. E. E. Sloan, *Mine Warfare on Land* (London: Brassey's Defense Publishers, 1986), 32. Effectiveness of the Gator mine is discussed in Dupuy Institute, *Landmines in the 1991 Gulf War: A Survey and Assessment* (n.p.: Dupuy Institute, n.d.), 11–13. <http://www.dupuyinstitute.org/pdf/m-4minesgulfwar.pdf>.

50. The ranger mine is described in Sloan, *Mine Warfare on Land,* 38. ADAM description is from William C. Schneck and Malcolm H. Visser, "Advances in Mine Warfare: Antipersonnel Mines," *Engineer* 23, no. 3 (August 1993): 26.

51. Sloan, *Mine Warfare on Land,* 52–53.

52. Casualty figures are from Colonel John F. Troxell, USA, "Landmines: Why the Korea Exception should be the Rule" *Parameters* 20, no. 1 (Spring 2000), reprint on the Internet <http://carlisle-www.army.mil/usawc/Parameters/00spring/troxell.htm>, no page numbers provided (July 8, 2002).

53. Jody Williams and Stephen Goose, "The International Campaign to Ban Landmines," chapter in *To Walk Without Fear: The Global Movement to Ban Land-mines,* eds. Maxwell A. Cameron, Robert J. Lawson, and Brian W. Tomlin (Oxford: Oxford University Press, 1998), 22.

54. Ibid., 22, 24–25, 28.

55. Ibid., 26–27.

56. Ibid., 34–36.

57. The treaty conference is discussed in Ibid., 42–45. The text of the treaty can be found in Ibid., 464–78. Quotation is from Ibid., 465. Figures are from ICBL, "Treaty Members," <http://www.icbl.org/treaty/members> (October 8, 2005). The Nobel Peace Prize is discussed in Jody Williams and Stephen Goose, "The International Campaign to Ban Landmines," 45–46.

58. Figures are from ICBL, "Ratification Updates." Examples of countries concerned with finding an alternative weapon include the United States, Pakistan, and India. ICBL, *Landmine Monitor Report 2000,* 489, 522.

59. Norman Friedman, *The Naval Institutes Guide to World Naval Weapons Systems* (Annapolis, MD: Naval Institute Press, 1989), 430, 450, 456.

60. Levie, *Mine Warfare at Sea,* 162–63. William M. Leogrande, "Making the Economy Scream: US Economic Sanctions Against Sandinista Nicaragua," *Third World Quarterly* 17, no. 2 (June 1996): 330, 340–41. Mine descriptions are from "How to Block a Harbor," *Time* 123 (April 23, 1984): 20. Levie uses this source as well.

61. International Court of Justice, *Case Concerning Military and Paramilitary Activities in and Against Nicaragua (Nicaragua v. United States of America)* 4 (n.p.: United Nations Publications, January, 2001): 1, 5, 122, 133.

62. Christin Marschall, *Iran's Persian Gulf Policy from Khomeini to Khatami* (London: RoutledgeCurzon, 2003), 89–91. Levie, *Mine Warfare at Sea,* 166–70. Fried-man, *The Naval Institutes Guide to World Naval Weapons Systems,* 450. Busuttil, *Naval Weapons Systems and the Contemporary Law of War,* 41–42.

63. Busuttil, *Naval Weapons Systems and the Contemporary Law of War,* 2, 94–97. Levie, *Mine Warfare at Sea,* 135–38. A full copy of the Sea Bed treaty is located on the Nuclear Threat Institute website <http://www.nti.org/e_research/official_docs/inventory/pdfs/.%5Captseabd.pdf>.

64. Capitalization and symbols are in the originals. Dudley, ed., *The Naval War of 1812,*162. Sears, ed., *The Civil War Papers of George B. McClellan,* 254.

65. Discussion of Korea and Gator mines are from Troxell.

66. Clinton quotation is from Ibid., 92. For examples of arguments on security, see Ibid. and David E. Funk, "A Mine is a Terrible Thing to Waste: The Operational Implications of Banning Anti-Personnel Landmines" (monograph, School of Advanced Military Studies, United States Army Command and General Staff College, 1998), 42. Funk comments that "It is doubtful that Barbados or Sweden, for instance, will be called upon to defend democracy in South Korea, or to prevent a third-world dictator from subjugating his neighbors in the deserts of Southwest Asia." Ibid. Casualty figures are from The Dupuy Institute, "Military Consequences of Landmine Restrictions," *VVAF Monograph Series*, vol. 1, no. 2 (Spring 2000): 11.

Selected Bibliography

Military Manuals and Government Documents

Baker, William C. Jr. Subproject SP 220, "Mines and Obstacles for Use Against Mechanized Units," Report No. 571. Fort Belvoir, Virginia: March 31, 1939. Carlisle Barracks, PA: U.S. Army War College Library.

Balck, Hermann. Interview from the U.S. Air Force Oral History Program, transcript. Maxwell AFB, AL: U.S. Air Force Historical Resource Center.

Barnes, J. S. *Submarine Warfare, Offensive and Defensive.* New York: D. Van Nostrand, 1869.

BDM Corporation. *A Study of Strategic Lessons Learned in Vietnam,* Vol. 6. *Conduct of the War,* Book 2. Alexandria, VA: Defense Logistics Agency, 1981. Lubbock, TX: Vietnam Archive, Texas Tech University.

Beach, William Dorance. *A Manual of Military Field Engineering for the Officers and Troops of the Line.* Fort Leavenworth, KS: United States Infantry and Cavalry School, 1894.

———. *A Manual of Military Field Engineering for the Officers and Troops of the Line.* 4th ed. Kansas City, MO: Hanson Kimberly Publishing Company, 1898.

———. *A Manual of Military Field Engineering for the Officers and Troops of the Line.* 5th ed. Kansas City, MO: Hanson Kimberly Publishing Company, 1902.

Bradford, Royal Bird. *History of Torpedo Warfare.* Newport, RI: U.S. Torpedo Station, 1882.

CHECO Southeast Asia Report. "IGLOO WHITE: (Initial Phase)." July 31, 1968. Lubbock, TX: Vietnam Archive, Texas Tech University.

CHECO Southeast Asia Report. "IGLOO WHITE: July 1968–December 1969." July 10, 1970. Lubbock, TX: Vietnam Archive, Texas Tech University.

Chief of Engineers, U.S. Army. *Engineer Field Manual, Parts I–VI.* 4th ed. Washington, DC: Government Printing Office, 1912.

—————. *Engineer Field Manual, Parts I–VI.* 5th ed. Washington, DC: Government Printing Office, 1917.

Cochran, Thomas, ed.*The New American State Papers 1789–1860,* Vol. 8. Wilmington, DE: Scholarly Resources, 1973.

—————. *The New American State Papers 1789–1860,* Vol. 9. Wilmington, DE: Scholarly Resources, 1973.

Combined Intelligence Center Vietnam. *Order of Battle Study ST 67-032 VC Anti-Heliborne Operations.* Vietnam: January 6, 1967.

—————. *ST 67-062 VC Employment of Claymore Mines Against Helicopters.* Vietnam: July 1, 1967.

—————. *VC Employment of Mines and Booby Traps TIS-1.* Vietnam: August 1970.

—————. *VC Mine Indicators TIS-2.* Vietnam: October 13, 1970.

—————. *VC-NVA Employment of Mines and Booby Traps, TIS-1.* Vietnam: August 1970.

—————. *VC [Weapons] Production ST 67-053.* Vietnam: n.d.

—————. *War Material Used by the Viet Cong in South Vietnam or Presumably Available to North Vietnam TIS-3.* Vietnam: February 1969.

—————. *What a Platoon Leader Should Know about the Enemy's Jungle Tactics.* Vietnam: October 12, 1967.

Committee of Imperial Defense. *Official History of the Russo-Japanese War,* Pt. 3, "The Siege of Port Arthur." London: Wyman and Sons, 1909.

Complete United States Infantry Guide for Officers and Non-Commissioned Officers, Reprinted from Government Publications. Philadelphia: J. B. Lippincott Company, 1917.

Department of the Army. *FM 3-51: Land Mine Warfare.* Washington, DC: Government Printing Office, 1949.

—————. *FM 5-15: Field Fortifications.* Washington, DC: Government Printing Office, 1949.

Ernest, O. H. *A Manual of Practical Military Engineering, Prepared for the Use of the Cadets of the United States Military Academy, and for the Engineering Troops.* New York: D. Van Nostrand, 1873.

Fiebeger, G. J. *A Text-book on Field Fortification.* 3rd ed. New York: John Wiley and Sons, 1913.

Gay de Vernon, Simon Francis. *A Treatise on the Science of War and Fortification,* Vol. 2, trans. John Michael O'Conner. New York: J. Seymour, 1817.

German Traps and Mines, E.-in-C. Fieldwork Notes No. 59, September 29, 1918. Carlisle, PA: Institute of Military History.

Gilliespie, Ernest R. *Ammunition Manual for General Training.* Raritan Arsenal, n.p.: Ordnance Department, 1943.

Halleck, Henry Wagner. *Elements of Military Art and Science.* 3rd ed. New York: D. Appleton and Co., 1863.

International Court of Justice. Case Concerning Military and Paramilitary Activities in and Against Nicaragua (*Nicaragua v. United States of America*), Vol. 4. n.p.: United Nations Publications, January 2001.

Investigation of the My Lai Incident: Report of the Armed Services Investigating Subcommittee of the Committee on Armed Services House of Representatives. Washington, DC: Government Printing Office, 1970.

King, W. R. *Torpedoes: Their Invention and Use from the First Application to the Art of War to the Present Time.* Washington, DC: n.p., 1866.

Kuhn, Joseph E. *Reports of Military Observers attached to the armies in Manchuria during the Russo-Japanese War,* Pt. 3, "Report of Major Joseph E. Kuhn, Corps of Engineers." Washington, DC: Government Printing Office, 1906.

MacArthur, Douglas. *Military Demolitions.* n.p.: Staff College Press, 1909.

Mahan, Dennis Hart. *A Complete Treatise on Field Fortifications, with the General Outlines and Principles Regulating the Arrangement, the Attack, and the Defense of Permanent Works.* New York: Wiley and Long, 1836; reprint, New York: Greenwood Press, 1968.

———. *A Complete Treatise on Field Fortifications, with the General Outlines and Principles Regulating the Arrangement, the Attack, and the Defense of Permanent Works.* 3rd ed. New York: Wiley and Sons, 1862.

———. *A Complete Treatise on Field Fortifications, with the General Outlines and Principles Regulating the Arrangement, the Attack, and the Defense of Permanent Works.* 4th ed. New York: Wiley and Sons, 1868.

McCully, Newton A. *The McCully Report: The Russo-Japanese War, 1904–5.* Annapolis: Naval Institute Press, 1977.

Mercur, James. *Military Mining.* West Point, NY: U.S. Military Academy Bindery, 1892.

Military Assistance Command Vietnam. "Significant Problem Areas Report." May 1971.

Mitchell, William Augustus. *Fortification.* 2nd ed. Washington, DC: The Society of American Military Engineers, 1928.

Morris, Robert. *History of the Mining of North Vietnam 8 May 1972–14 Jan 1973,* ser 03/C700800, Department of the Navy. June 30, 1975. Lubbock, TX: Vietnam Archive, Texas Tech University.

Scott, H. L. *Military Dictionary.* New York: D. Van Nostrand, 1861; reprint, Westport, CT: Greenwood Press, 1971.

Snow, Charles. *First Acceptance Tests of the CBU-42/A Munition.* ADTC-TR-70-1. Elgin AFB: Armament Development and Test Center, January 1970. Maxwell AFB, AL: U.S. Air Force Historical Research Center.

United States Army. *Mine and Booby Traps.* Washington, DC: United States Army, n.d. Carlisle Barracks, PA: U.S. Army War College Library.

USAF Air Proving Ground Commander. "Operation Doan Brook," Draft of speech for April 7 at Elgin Air Force Base, p. 2. (n.d.) Carlisle Barracks, PA: U.S. Army War College.

U.S. Congress. *Congressional Record.* 92nd Cong., 1st sess. (July 13, 1970): 23823-4. Congress, Senate, Report of the Electronic Battlefield Committee of the Preparedness Investigating Subcommittee of the Committee on Armed Services, *Investigation into Electronic Battlefield Program,* 1971, Committee Print.

U.S. Department of the Army. *Regulations for Mine Planters.* n.p.: Government Printing Office, 1909.

———. *Significant Landmines and Booby Traps Encountered by U.S. Forces 1940-1970,* Vol. 2. Washington, DC: Engineer Agency for Resources Inventories, 1972.

U.S. Navy Department, Naval History Division. *Riverine Warfare: The U.S. Navy's Operations on Inlands Waters.* Washington, DC: Government Printing Office, 1969.

U.S. War Department. *Amendments No. 1, 13 Military Intelligence Division, Tactical and Technical Trends No. 34.* Washington, DC: War Department, September 23, 1943.

———. *Amendments No. 1 to Engineer Intelligence Bulletin Number 3. Comparative Analysis Charts of Allied and Enemy Mines.* Maxwell AFB, AL: United States Air Force Historical Research Center.

———. "Bamboo Spike Jungle Traps," *Intelligence Bulletin,* Vol. 3, No. 2. Washington, DC: Military Intelligence Division, October 1944.

———. *Enemy Landmines and Booby Traps, TM 5-325.* Washington, DC: Government Printing Office, April 19, 1943.

———. "Enemy Mines on Leyte," *Intelligence Bulletin,* Vol. 3, No. 6. Washington, DC: Military Intelligence Division, February 1945.

———. *Engineer Intelligence Bulletin, Mine Series No. 2.* Washington, DC: Technical Intelligence Branch, August 31, 1944.

———. *German Mine Warfare in Winter.* n.p.: Information Section, Intelligence Division, OCE, HQ., ETOUSA, January 7, 1945.

———. *Handbook of the Italian Military Forces, TME-30-420.* Washington, DC: Military Intelligence Service.

———. *Handbook on German Military Forces, TME-30-451.* Washington, DC: Military Intelligence Service, March 15, 1945; reprint, Baton Rouge: Louisiana State University Press, 1990.

———. *Handbook on Japanese Military Forces, TME-30-480.* Washington, DC: Military Intelligence Service, October 1, 1944; reprint, Baton Rouge: Louisiana State University Press, 1991.

———. *Handbook on Japanese Military Forces, TME-30-480.* Washington, DC: Military Intelligence Service, July 1, 1945.

———. *Handbook on U.S.S.R. Military Forces.* Washington, DC: Government Printing Office, November 1945.

———. *Japanese Defense Against Amphibious Operations,* Special Series No. 29. Washington, DC: Military Intelligence Division, February 1945.

———. "Japanese Minefield Tactics in the Southwest Pacific," *Intelligence Bulletin,* Vol. 3, No. 4. Washington, DC: Military Intelligence Division, December 1944.

———. "Landmines, Grenades, and Booby Traps," *Intelligence Bulletin,* Vol. 1, No. 1. Washington, DC: Military Intelligence Division, September 1943.

———. "Mines in the Spotlight," *Intelligence Bulletin,* Vol. 3, No. 8. Washington, DC: Military Intelligence Division. April 8, 1945.

———. "Minefield Patterns in the Defense of Iwo Jima," *Intelligence Bulletin,* Vol. 3, No. 10. Washington, DC: Military Intelligence Division, June 1945.

———. "More Notes on Booby Traps and Firing Devices," *Intelligence Bulletin,* Vol. 3, No. 8. Washington, DC: Military Intelligence Division, April 1945.

———. "New Pottery Land Mine Introduced on Leyte Island," *Intelligence Bulletin,* Vol. 3, No. 4. Washington, DC: Military Intelligence Division, December 1944.

———. "Some Data on Enemy Mines and Obstacles," *Intelligence Bulletin,* Vol. 2, No. 11. Washington, DC: Military Intelligence Division, July 1944.

de Vauban, Sebastien LePreste. *A Manual of Siege Craft and Fortification,* trans. George A. Rothrock. Ann Arbor: University of Michigan Press, 1968.

Vitruvius, *On Architecture,* Vol. 2, trans. Frank Granger. Cambridge, MA: Harvard University, 1956.

Von Scheliha, Viktor Ernest Karl Rudolph. *A Treatise on Coast-Defense.* London: E. and F. N. Spoon, 1868; reprint, Westport, CT: Greenwood Press, 1971.

Walker, John K. Jr. "Air Scatterable Landmines as an Air Force Munition," 1978 Air University Airpower Symposium, Air War College, Maxwell, AFB, February 13–15, 1978.

Wheeler, Junius Brown. *The Elements of Field Fortification for the use of the Cadets of the United States Military Academy at West Point, New York.* New York: D. Van Nostrand, 1882.

Primary Sources

Books

Alcaraz, Don Ramon et al. *The Other Side,* trans. Albert Ramsey. n.p.: 1850; reprint, New York: Burt Franklin and Co., 1970.

Battlefields of the South, from Bull Run to Fredericksburg. New York: John Bradburn, 1864; reprint, New York: Time-Life Inc., 1984.

Bently, Nicholas, ed. *Russell's Dispatches from the Crimea 1854–1856.* New York: Hill and Wang, 1966.

Bonner-Smith, D., ed. *Russian War, 1855: Baltic Official Correspondence.* n.p.: Navy Records Society, 1944.

Bonner-Smith, D., and A. C. Dewar, eds. *Russian War, 1854: Baltic and Black Sea Official Correspondence.* n.p.: Navy Records Society, 1943.

Burgoyne, John Fox. *The Military Opinions of General John Fox Burgoyne.* London: R. Bently, 1859.

Butler, Benjamin. *Butler's Book.* Boston: A. M. Thayer and Company, 1892.

Caesar, Julius. *The Gallic War,* trans. Carolyn Hammond. Oxford: Oxford University Press, 1996.

Campbell, R. Thomas, ed. *Engineer in Gray: Memoirs of Chief Engineer James H. Tomb, CSN.* Jefferson, NC: McFarland and Company, Inc., 2005.

Cooper, Belton Y. *Death Traps, The Survival of an American Armored Division in World War II.* Novato, CA: Presidio Press, 1998.

Courtney, Richard D. *Normandy to the Bulge: An American Infantry GI in Europe During World War II.* Carbondale: Southern Illinois University Press, 1997.

Davis, Jefferson. *Rise and Fall of the Confederate Government,* Vol. 2. New York: D. Appleton and Company, 1891.

Davis, Nicholas A. *The Campaign from Texas to Maryland with the Battle of Fredericksburg.* Austin, TX: The Steck Company, 1961.

Delafield, Richard. *Report on the Art of War in Europe in 1854, 1855, and 1856.* Washington, DC: George W. Bowman, 1860.

Donald, David Herbert, ed. *Gone for a Soldier: Memoirs of Private Alfred Bellard.* Boston: Little, Brown and Company, 1975.

Gilmore, Q. A. *Engineering and Artillery Operations Against the Defenses of Charleston Harbor in 1863.* New York: D. Van Nostrand, 1865.

Gravel, Mike. *The Pentagon Papers,* Vol. 4. Boston: Beacon Press, 1971.

Guderian, Heinz. *Achtung—Panzer!* trans. Christopher Duffy. London: Arms and Armour Press, 1992.

Jellicoe, John. *The Crisis of the Naval War.* New York: George H. Doran Co., 1920.

Johnston, Joseph E. *Narrative of Military Operations.* Bloomington: Indiana University Press, 1959.

Jones, J. B. *Diary of a Rebel War Clerk,* 2 volumes. New York: Old Hickory Bookshop, 1935.

King, R. T. *War Stories: Veterans Remember WWII.* Reno: University of Nevada Oral History Program, 1995.

Lamb, William. *Colonel Lamb's Story of Fort Fisher.* Carolina Beach, NC: The Blockade Runner Museum, 1966.

Laswell, Mary, ed. *Rags and Hope: The Memoirs of Val C. Giles, Four Years with Hood's Brigade, Fourth Texas Infantry, 1861–1865.* New York: Coward McCann, 1961.

Long, Armistead, ed. *The Memoirs of Robert E. Lee.* New York: J. M. Stoddart & Company, 1886.

Longstreet, James. *From Manassas to Appomattox: Memoirs of the Civil War in America.* Bloomington, IN: Indiana University Press, 1960.

McClellan, George. *Armies of Europe.* Philadelphia: J. B. Lippincott and Co., 1861.

———. *McClellan's Own Story.* New York: C. L. Webster and Co., 1887.

Mordecai, Alfred. *Military Commission to Europe in 1855 and 1856.* Washington, DC: George W. Bowman, 1860.

Morton, James St. Clair. *Letter to the Hon. John B. Floyd, Secretary of War, presenting for his consideration a new plan for the fortification of certain points of the sea coast of the United States.* Washington, DC: William A. Harris, 1858.

———. *Memoir on American Fortification.* Washington, DC: William A. Harris, 1859.

Mullener, Elizabeth. *War Stories: Remembering World War II.* Baton Rouge: Louisiana State University Press, 2002.

Myers, William Star, ed. *The Mexican War Diary of George B. McClellan.* Princeton: Princeton University Press, 1917.

Nevins, Allan, ed. *A Diary of Battle: The Personal Journals of Colonel Charles S. Wainwright 1861–1865.* New York: Harcourt Brace and World Inc., 1962.

Official Records of the Union and Confederate Navies in the War of the Rebellion, Series I, 27 volumes. Washington, DC: Government Printing Office, 1899–1922.

Page, T. E., ed. *Aeneas Tacticus, Asclepiodotus, Onsander,* trans. Illinois Greek Club. Cambridge, MA: Harvard University Press, 1943.

Sakurai, Tadayoshi. *Human Bullets,* trans. Masujiro Honda and Alice Bacon. Tokyo: Teibi Publishing Co., 1907.

Scheer, Reinhard. *Germany's High Sea Fleet in the World War.* New York: Peter Smith, 1934.

Sears, Stephen W., ed. *Civil War Papers of George B. McClellan: Selected Correspondence, 1860–1865.* New York: Ticknor and Fields, 1989.

Siculus, Diodorus. *The Library of History,* trans. C. H. Oldfather, Vol. 10. Cambridge, MA: Harvard University Press, 1950.

Thompson, Phillip. *Into the Storm: A U.S. Marine in the Persian Gulf War.* Jefferson, NC: McFarland & Co., Inc., 2001.

Vegetius Renatus, Publius Flavius, *Epitome of Military Science,* trans. N. P. Miller. Liverpool: Liverpool University Press, 1993.

von Siemens, Werner. *Inventor and Entrepreneur: Recollection.* New York: Augustus M. Kelley, 1968.

War of the Rebellion: Official Records of the Union and Southern Armies, Series IV. 3 volumes. Washington, DC: Government Printing Office, 1897–1900.

Williams, T. Harry, ed. *With Beauregard in Mexico.* Baton Rouge: Louisiana State University Press, 1956.

Zhukov, Georgi. *Marshal Zhukov's Greatest Battles*, trans. Theodore Shabad. New York: Harper and Row, 1969.

Journals and Magazines

Alexander, E. P. "Sketch of Longstreet's Division—Yorktown and Williamsburg." *Southern Historical Society Papers* 10, nos. 1 and 2 (January and February 1982): 32–45.

Beauregard, P. T. "Defense of Charleston." *North American Review* 143 (July 1886): 42–53.

Crowley, R. O. "The Confederate Torpedo Service." *Century Magazine* 51, no. 1 (May 1898): 290–300.

Cunningham, S. A. "More of Gen. Rains and his Torpedoes." *Confederate Veteran* 2, no. 9 (September 1894): 283.

Davis, Jefferson, and Hunter Davidson. "Davis and Davidson, A Chapter of War History Concerning Torpedoes." *Southern Historical Society Papers* 24 (1896): 284–291.

Denson, C. B. "William Henry Chase Whiting, Major-General C. S. Army." *Southern Historical Society Papers* 26 (1898): 129–181.

Minnich, J. W. "Incidents of the Peninsular Campaign." *Confederate Veteran* 30, no. 2 (February 1922): 53–55.

Rains, Gabriel J. "Torpedoes." *Southern Historical Society Papers* 3, nos. 5 and 6 (May and June 1877): 255–260.

Stickney, Joseph L. "With Dewey at Manila." *Harpers's New Monthly Magazine* 98, no. 585 (February 1899): 476–484.

Secondary Sources

Books

Achkasov, V. I., and N. B. Pavlovich. *Soviet Naval Operations in the Great Patriotic War*. Annapolis, MD: Naval Institute Press, 1981.

Ambrose, Stephen E. *Duty, Country, Honor: A History of West Point*. Baltimore: Johns Hopkins Press, 1966.

Americas Watch Committee. *Landmines in El Salvador and Nicaragua: The Civilian Victims*. New York: Americas Watch Committee, 1986.

Bauer, K. Jack. *The Mexican War 1846–1848*. New York: Macmillan Publishing Company, 1974.

Bell, A. C. *A History of the Blockade of Germany*. 1931, reprint, London: Her Majesty's Stationary Office, 1961.

Bishop, William Warner, et al. *A Catalog of Books Represented by Library of Congress Printing Cards,* 152 volumes. Paterson, NJ: Rowman and Littlefield Inc., 1963.

Bradbury, Jim. *The Medieval Siege*. Woodbridge, UK: Boydell Press, 1992.

Brodie, Bernard and Fawn. *From Crossbow to H-Bomb*. Bloomington: Indiana University Press, 1973.

Brooks, Nathan Covington. *A Complete History of the Mexican War 1846–1848*. Baltimore: Hutchinson and Seebold, 1849; reprint, Chicago: The Rio Grande Press Inc., 1965.

Caiden, Martin. *The Tigers are Burning*. New York: Hawthorn Books, 1974.

Cameron, Maxwell A., Robert J. Lawson, and Brian W. Tomlin, eds. *To Walk Without Fear: The Global Movement to Ban Landmines*. Oxford: Oxford University Press, 1998.

Childs, David. A Peripheral Weapon? The Production and Employment of British Tanks in the First World War. London: Greenwood Press, 1999.

Cogar, William B. *Dictionary of Admirals of the U.S. Navy,* Vol. 2. Annapolis, MD: Naval Institute Press, 1991.

Contamine, Philippe. *War in the Middle Ages,* trans. Michael Jones. Cambridge, MA: Blackwell Publishers, 1984.

Cowley, Robert, and Geoffrey Parker, ed. *The Reader's Companion to Military History*. New York: Houghton Mifflin Co., 1996.

Croll, Mike. *The History of Landmines*. Barnsley, UK: Pen & Sword Books Ltd., 1998.

Cullum, George W. *Biographical Register of the Officers and Graduates of the United States Military Academy at West Point, N.Y.: From Its Establishment, in 1802, to 1890. With the Early History of the United States Military Academy*. Boston: Houghton Mifflin and Company, 1891.

Davies, Paul. *War of the Mines: Cambodia, Landmines and the Impoverishment of a Nation*. London: Pluto Press, 1994.

Davis, Burke. *The Civil War: Strange and Fascinating Facts.* New York: The Fairfax Press, 1982.

Degan, Patrick. *Flattop Fighting in World War II: The Battles Between American and Japanese Aircraft Carriers.* Jefferson, NC: McFarland & Co., Inc., 2003.

DeRose, James F. *Unrestricted Warfare.* New York: John Wiley & Sons, Inc., 2000.

Dudley, William, ed. *The Naval War of 1812,* Vol. 2. Washington, DC: Naval Historical Center Department of the Navy, 1992.

Duffy, Christopher. *The Fortress in the Age of Vauban and Fredrick the Great 1660–1789,* Vol. 2. London: Routledge and Kegan Paul, 1988.

Dufour, Charles L. *The Mexican American War.* New York: Hawthorn Books, 1968.

Dunnigan, James F., and Albert A. Nofi. *Victory at Sea: World War II in the Pacific.* New York: William Morrow & Co. Inc., 1995.

Dupuy, Ernest and Trevor. *The Encyclopedia of Military History from 300 B.C. to Present.* New York: Harper and Row, 1970.

The Dupuy Institute. *A Measure of the Real-World Value of Mixed Mine Systems.* McLean, VA: The Dupuy Institute, June 20, 2001.

———. *Landmines in the 1991 Gulf War: A Survey and Assessment.* Washington, DC: Vietnam Veterans of America Foundation, n.d.

Durkin, Joseph T. *Stephen R. Mallory: Confederate Navy Chief.* Chapel Hill, NC: The University of North Carolina Press, 1954.

Elliot, Peter. *Allied Minesweepers in World War 2.* Annapolis, MD: Naval Institute Press, 1979.

Emering, Edward. *Weapons and Field Gear of the North Vietnamese Army and Viet Cong.* Atglen, PA: Schiffer Publishing Ltd., 1998.

Evans, Clement A., ed. *Confederate Military History,* Vol. 4. D. H. Hill Jr., *North Carolina.* Atlanta: Confederate Publishing Company, 1899.

———, ed. *Confederate Military History,* Vol. 6. Joseph T. Derby, *Georgia.* Atlanta: Confederate Publishing Company, 1899.

Evans, David C., and Mark R. Peattie. *Kaigun: Strategy, Tactics, and Technology in the Imperial Japanese Navy, 1887–1941.* Annapolis, MD: Naval Institute Press, 1997.

Ewell, Julian J., and Ira A. Hunt. *Vietnam Studies: Sharpening the Edge: The Use of Analysis to Reinforce Military Judgment.* Washington, DC: Department of the Army, 1974.

Feuer, A. B. *The Spanish American War at Sea: Naval Action in the Atlantic.* Westport, CT: Praeger Publisher, 1995.

Foisy, Fred. *I'm Here to Tell You.* Victoria, B.C.: Trafford, 2003.

Fort McAllister Tour Guide. Richmond Hill, GA: Fort McAllister State Historical Park, [1990].

Friedman, Norman. *The Naval Institutes Guide to World Naval Weapons Systems.* Annapolis, MD: Naval Institute Press, 1989.

Fuller, Robert. *The United States Air Force in Korea 1950–53.* Revised ed. Washington, DC: Office of Air Force History, United States Air Force, 1984.

Gilbert, Martin. *The First World War: A Complete History.* New York: Henry Holt and Company, 1994.

———. *The Second World War: A Complete History.* New York: Henry Holt and Company, 1991.

Glantz, David, and Jonathan House. *The Battle of Kursk.* Lawrence, KS: University of Kansas Press, 1999.

Glatthar, Joseph T. *The March to the Sea and Beyond.* New York: New York University Press, 1985.

Gray, Edwyn. *The Devil's Device: The Story of Robert Whitehead, Inventor of the Torpedo.* London: Seeley, Service and Co. Ltd., 1975.

Green, Constance, Harry Thompson, and Peter Root, *The Ordnance Department: Planning Munitions for War.* The United States Army in World War II. Washington, DC: Office of the Chief of Military History, Department of the Army, 1955.

Guichard, Louis. *The Naval Blockade 1914–1918,* trans. Christopher R. Turner. New York: D. Appleton and Company, 1930.

Hagerman, Edward. *The American Civil War and the Origin of Modern War.* Bloomington: Indiana University Press, 1988.

Halévy, Daniel. *Vauban: Builder of Fortresses,* trans. C. J. C. Street. London: Geoffrey Bles, 1924.

Hall, Bert S. *Weapons and Warfare in Renaissance Europe: Gunpowder, Technology, and Tactics.* Baltimore: Johns Hopkins University Press, 1997.

Halle, Armin. *Tanks: An Illustrated History of Fighting Vehicles.* New York: Crescent Books, 1971.

Halpern, Paul. *A Naval History of World War I.* Annapolis, MD: Naval Institute Press, 1994.

———. *The Naval War in the Mediterranean, 1914–1918.* Annapolis: Naval Institute Press, 1987.

Handel, Michael I. *War, Strategy and Intelligence.* London: Frank Cass and Company, Ltd., 1989.

Hargis, Robert. *U. S. Submarine Crewman 1941–45.* Oxford: Osprey Publishing Ltd., 2003.

Hartmann, Gregory K. *Wait, Mine Warfare in the U.S. Navy.* Annapolis: Naval Institute Press, 1979.

Hawthorne, Hildegarde. *Matthew Fontaine Maury.* New York: Longmans, Green and Co., 1943.

Hay, John H. *Vietnam Studies: Tactical and Material Innovations.* Washington, DC: Department of the Army, 1974.

Henry, Ralph Selph. *The Story of the Mexican War.* New York: The Bobbs-Merrill Company Inc., 1950.

Herring, George C. *America's Longest War.* 2nd ed. New York: Alfred A. Knopf, 1986.

Hersh, Seymour. *Cover-Up: The Army's Secret Investigation of the Massacre at My Lai 4.* New York: Random House, 1972.

Holmes, W. J. *Undersea Victory: The Influence of Submarine Operations on the War in the Pacific.* New York: Doubleday & Co. Inc., 1966.

Hopkins, Albert A. *The Scientific American War Book; The Mechanism and Technique of Warfare.* New York: Munn & Company, Inc., 1916.

Hough, Richard. *The Great War at Sea, 1914–1918.* Oxford: Oxford University Press, 1983.

Human Rights Watch. *Land Mines in Angola: An Africa Watch Report.* New York: Human Rights Watch, 1993.

International Campaign to Ban Landmines. *Landmine Monitor Report 2000: Toward a Mine-Free World.* New York: Human Rights Watch, 2000.

International Military and Defence Encyclopedia, Vol. 4. Washington, DC: Brassey's Inc., 1993.

International Red Cross. *Anti-personnel Landmines—Friend or Foe?* 2nd ed. Geneva: ICRC, 1997.

———. *Overview 1999: Landmines Must Be Stopped.* Geneva: ICRC, 1999.

———. *The Silent Menace: Landmines in Bosnia and Herzegovina.* Geneva: ICRC, 1998.

Isby, David C. *Jane's Weapons and Tactics of the Soviet Army.* New York: Jane's, 1981.

Jahns, Patricia. *Matthew Fontaine Maury and Joseph Henry, Scientists of the Civil War.* New York: Hasting House, 1961.

Johnson, Ellis A., and David A. Katcher, *Mines Against Japan.* White Oak, MD: Naval Ordnance Laboratory, 1973.

Johnson, Underwood, and Clarence Clough Buel. *Battles and Leaders of the Civil War,* 4 volumes. New York: The Century Company, 1884, 1887, 1888.

Liddle, Peter H. *The 1916 Battle of the Somme: A Reappraisal.* Hertfordshire, UK: Wordsworth Editions Ltd., 2001.

Lundelberg, Philip K. *Samuel Colt's Submarine Battery: The Secret and the Enigma.* Washington, DC: Smithsonian Institute Press, 1974.

Kaufmann, J. E., and H. W. Kaufmann. *Fortress America: The Forts that Defended America, 1800 to the Present.* Cambridge, MA: Da Cappo Press, 2004.

———. *Fortress Third Reich: German Fortifications and Defense Systems in World War II.* Cambridge, MA: Da Capo Press, 2003.

Kaufmann, J. E., and Robert M. Jurga. *Fortress Europe: European Fortifications of World War II.* Cambridge, MA: Da Capo Press, 1999.

Karig, Walter, et al. *Battle Report,* Vol. 4, *The End of an Empire.* New York: Rinehart and Co., 1948.

———. *Battle Report: The War in Korea.* New York: Rinehart and Company, Inc., 1952.

Karnow, Stanley. *Vietnam: A History.* New York: Viking Press, 1983.

Kern, Paul. *Ancient Siege Warfare.* Bloomington: Indiana University Press, 1999.

Kurowski, Franz. *Luftwaffe Aces: German Fighter Aces of World War II.* Mechanicsburg, PA: Stackpole Books, 2004.

Lambert, Nicholas. *Sir John Fisher's Naval Revolution.* Columbia, SC: University of South Carolina Press, 1999.

Lambert, Nicholas, ed. *The Submarine Service, 1900–1918.* Hants, UK: Ashgate Publishing Ltd., 2001.

Lawrence, A. W. *Greek Aims in Fortification.* Oxford: Clarendon Press, 1979.

Levie, Howard S. *Mine Warfare at Sea.* Dordrecht, Netherlands: Martinus Nijhoff Publishers, 1992.

Lewis, Charles Lee. *Matthew Fontaine Maury, Pathfinder of the Seas.* Annapolis: United States Naval Institute, 1927.

Lewis, Michael. *The Spanish Armada.* New York: Thomas Y. Crowell Company, 1960.

Mackay, Ruddock F. *Fisher of Kilverstone.* Oxford: Clarendon Press, 1973.

Mahon, John K. *History of the Second Seminole Indian War: 1835–1842.* Gainesville, FL: University of Florida Press, 1967.

Marder, Arthur J. *From the Dreadnought to Scapa Flow,* Vol. 1. Oxford: Oxford University Press, 1961.

———. *From Dreadnaught to Scapa Flow,* Vol. 4. London: Oxford University Press, 1969.

———. *From the Dardanelles to Oran: Studies of the Royal Navy in War and Peace 1915–1940.* London: Oxford University Press, 1974.

Marschall, Christin. *Iran's Persian Gulf Policy from Khomeini to Khatami.* London: RoutledgeCurzon, 2003.

Martin, Colin, and Geoffrey Parker. *The Spanish Armada.* New York: W. W. Norton and Company, 1988.

Massie, Robert K. *Castles of Steel.* New York: Random House, 2003.

Mazarr, Michael J., Don M. Snider, and James A. Blackwell, Jr. *Desert Storm: The Gulf War and What We Learned.* Boulder, CO: Westview Press, 1993.

McCoy, James W. *Secrets of the Viet Cong.* New York: Hippocrene Books, 1992.

McPherson, James. *Battle Cry of Freedom: The Civil War Era.* New York: Oxford University Press, 1988.

Melia, Tamara Moser. *"Damn the Torpedoes": A Short History of U.S. Naval Countermeasures, 1777–1991.* Washington, DC: Naval History Center, Department of the Navy, 1991.

Miller, Francis Trevelyan, ed. *The Photographic History of the Civil War,* Vol. 5. New York: The Review of Reviews Co., 1912.

Millett, Allen, and Peter Maslowski. *For the Common Defense, A Military History of the United States.* New York: The Free Press, 1994.

Milton, Keith M. *Subs Against the Rising Sun.* Las Cruces, NM: Yucca Free Press, 2000.

Morgan, William, ed. *Naval Documents of the American Revolution,* Vol. 6. Washington DC: Naval History Division, Department of the Navy, 1972.

———, ed. *Naval Documents of the American Revolution,* Vol. 8. Washington DC: Naval History Division, Department of the Navy, 1980.

———, ed. *Naval Documents of the American Revolution,* Vol. 9. Washington DC: Naval Historical Center, Department of the Navy, 1986

Morison, Samuel E. *History of United States Naval Operations During World War II,* Vol. 8, *New Guinea and the Marianas, March 1944–August 1944.* Boston: Little, Brown and Co., 1953.

Motley, John Lothrop. *History of the United Netherlands,* Vol. 1. New York: Harper and Brothers Publishers, 1888.

Murphy, W. *Spies, Scouts and Raiders.* Alexandria, VA: Time-Life Books, 1985.

NARMIC. *Background Report on the Automated Battlefield.* Philadelphia: NARMIC, 1971. Douglas Pike Collection, Technology File, 1971. Lubbock, TX: Vietnam Archive, Texas Tech University.

Oldham, Peter. *The Hindenburg Line.* London: Leo Cooper, 1997.

Perry, Milton F. *Infernal Machines.* Kingsport, TN: Louisiana State University Press, 1965.

Prados, John. *The Blood Road: The Ho Chi Minh Trail and the Vietnam War.* New York: John Wiley and Sons, 1999.

Price, Alfred. *Luftwaffe Handbook 1939–1945.* New York: Charles Scribner's Sons, 1977.

Prokosch, Eric. *The Simple Art of Murder, Antipersonnel Weapons and Their Developers.* Philadelphia: NARMIC, December 1972. Douglas Pike Collection Technology File. Lubbock, TX: Vietnam War Archive, Texas Tech University.

Prukhorov, A. M. *Great Soviet Encycolpeadia.* 3rd ed. trans. Lawrence W. Cannon et al. New York: Macmillan Inc., 1977.

Pyle, Richard. *Schwarzkopf: The Man, The Mission, The Triumph.* New York: Signet Books, 1991.

Quick, John. *Dictionary of Weapons and Military Terms.* New York: McGraw-Hill Book Company, 1973.

Randle, Robert. *Geneva 1954: The Settlement of the Indochinese War.* Princeton: Princeton University Press, 1969.

Rickover, H. G. *How the Battleship Maine was Destroyed.* Washington, DC: Government Printing Office, 1976.

Rodgers, Bernard Williams. *Vietnam Studies: Cedar Falls –Junction City: A Turning Point.* Washington, DC: Department of the Army, 1974.

Roland, Alex. *Underwater Warfare in the Age of Sail.* Bloomington: Indiana University Press, 1970.

Roscoe, Theodore. *United States Submarine Operations in World War II.* Annapolis, MD: Naval Institute Press, 1949.

Roskill, S. W. *The War at Sea, 1939–1945,* Vol. 1, *The Defensive.* London: Her Majesty's Stationary Office, 1954.

———. *The War at Sea, 1939–1945,* Vol. 2, *The Period of Balance.* London: Her Majesty's Stationary Office, 1956.

———. *The War at Sea, 1939–1945,* Vol. 3, *The Offensive,* Pt. 1. London: Her Majesty's Stationary Office, 1960.

Royle, Trevor. *Crimea: The Great Crimean War.* New York: St. Martin's Press, 2000.

Sack, John. *Lieutenant Calley: His Own Story.* New York: Viking Press, 1971.

Sadkovich, James. *The Italian Navy in World War II.* Westport, CN: Greenwood Press, 1994.

Sallagar, Frederick M. *Lessons From an Aerial Mining Campaign (Operation "Starvation"): A Report Prepared for United States Air Force Project Rand.* Santa Monica, CA: Rand, 1974.

Scharf, J. Thomas. *History of the Confederate States Navy from its Organization to the Surrender of its Last Vessel.* New York: Rodgers and Sherwood, 1877.

Scott, James Brown. *The Hague Conventions and Declarations of 1899 and 1907.* 3rd ed. New York: Oxford University Press, 1918.

———. *The Hague Peace Conferences of 1899 and 1907: A Series of Lectures Delivered Before the Johns Hopkins University in the Year 1908,* Vol. 1. New York: Garland Publishing, Inc., 1972.

———. *The Hague Peace Conferences of 1899 and 1907: A Series of Lectures Delivered Before the Johns Hopkins University in the Year 1908,* Vol. 2. New York: Garland Publishing, Inc., 1972.

Sears, Stephen W. *George B. McClellan The Young Napoleon.* New York: Ticknor and Fields, 1988.

Sheffy, Yigal. *British Military Intelligence in the Palestine Campaign.* London: Frank Cass Publishers, 1998.

SIPRI. *Anti-Personnel Weapons.* New York: Crane, Russak and Company, 1978.

Sloan, C. E. E. *Mine Warfare On Land.* New York: Brassey's Defense Publishers, 1986.

Smith, Augustine Jr. *Torpedo and Submarine Attacks on the Federal Blockading Fleet off Charleston During the War of Secession.* n.p.: University of Virginia, 1907.

Staaveren, Jacob. *Interdiction in Southern Laos, 1960–1968.* Washington, DC: Center for Air Force History, 1993.

Starry, Donn A. *Vietnam Studies: Mounted Combat in Vietnam.* Washington, DC: Department of the Army, 1978.

Symonds, Craig L. *Navalists and Antinavalists: The Naval Policy Debate in the United States, 1785–1827.* Newark: University of Delaware Press, 1980.

Tolf, Robert W. *The Russian Rockefellers.* Standford, CA: The Hoover Institute Press, 1976.

Trask, David F. *The War with Spain.* Lincoln, NB: University of Nebraska Press, 1996.

United States Marine Corps. *Professional Knowledge Gained from Operational Experience in Vietnam, 1965–1966.* Washington, DC: Department of the Navy, 1991.

United States Marine Corps. *Professional Knowledge Gained from Operational Experience in Vietnam, 1967.* Washington, DC: Department of the Navy, 1989.

Vego, Milan N. *Naval Strategy and Operations in Narrow Seas.* 2nd ed. London: Frank Cass Publishers, 2003.

Von der Porten, Edward P. *Pictorial History of the German Navy in World War II.* Revised ed. New York: Thomas Y. Crowell Company, 1976.

Wayland, John. *The Pathfinder of the Seas.* Richmond: Garret & Massie Inc., 1930.

Winchester, Jim. *Aircraft of World War II.* San Diego, CA: Thunder Bay Press, 2004.

Winnefeld, James A., Preston Niblack, and Dana J. Johnson. *A League of Airmen: U.S. Air Power in the Gulf War.* Santa Monica, CA: Rand, 1994.

Winter, F. E. *Greek Fortifications.* Toronto: University of Toronto Press, 1971.

Yadin, Yigael. *The Art of Warfare in Biblical Lands in the Light of Archeaological Discovery,* trans. M. Pearlman. London: Weidenfeld and Nicolson, 1963.

Yearns, W. Buck, and John G. Barret, ed. *North Carolina Civil War Documentary.* Chapel Hill, NC: University of North Carolina Press, 1980.

Journals and Magazines

Abbott, Jackson M., and Logan Cassedy. "Landmines: Past and Present." *Military Engineer* 54 (September–October 1962): 367–368.

"Anti-Tank Defenses." *Professional Memoirs, Corps of Engineers* 11 (1919): 422–423.

Artillery Inspector, Ministry of War, French Army. "German Mine for Wrecking Tanks." *Professional Memoirs, Corps of Engineers* 11 (1919): 305–307.

"The Barrier Type of Tank Defenses." *Professional Memoirs, Corps of Engineers* 11 (1919): 302–304.

Brock, Darryl E. "Naval Technology from Dixie." *Americas* 46, no. 4 (July/August 1994): 6.

Confederate Ordnance Department, Vertical File, Confederate Research Center, Hill County Junior College, Hillsboro, Texas.

Dorn, A. Walter. "Small Arms, Human Security and Development." *CIDA, Development Express* no. 5 (1999–2000): 1–15.

The Dupuy Institute. "Military Consequences of Landmine Restrictions." *VVAF Monograph Series* 1, no. 2 (Spring 2000): 1–61.

Funk, David E. "A Mine is a Terrible Thing to Waste: The Operational Implications of Banning Anti-Personnel Landmines." Monograph, School of Advanced Military Studies, United States Army Command and General Staff College, 1998.

"German Traps and Land Mines. From a Captured German Document.," *Professional Memoirs, Corps of Engineers* 11 (1919): 277–278.

Greene, F. V. "Our Defenseless Coasts." *Scribner's Magazine* 1 (January–June 1887): 51–66.

Grupp, Larry. "The Claymore Mine." *Military History* 13, no. 2 (June 1996): 17–20.

Halvorsen, Peter F. "The Royal Navy and Mine Warfare, 1868–1914." *The Journal of Strategic Studies* 27, no. 4 (December 2004): 686–688.

"How to Block a Harbor." *Time* 123 (April 23, 1984): 20.

James, Alfred P. "The Battle of the Crater." *Military Affairs* 2, no. 1 (Spring 1938): 3–25.

Krepon, Michael. "Weapons Potentially Inhumane: The Case of Cluster Bombs." *Foreign Affairs* (April 1974): 595–611.

Leogrande, William M. "Making the Economy Scream: US Economic Sanctions Against Sandinista Nicaragua." *Third World Quarterly* 17, no. 2 (June 1996): 329–348.

"The Manufacturers of Anti-Personnel Weapons." *Economic Priorities Report* 1, no. 1 (April 1970): 3, 14–16. Douglas Pike Collection, Technology File, 1970. Lubbock, TX: Vietnam Archive, Texas Tech University.

Newton, Isaac. "Has the Day of the Great Navies Passed?" *The Galaxy* 24, no. 3 (September 1877): 293–304.

Schneck, William C., and Malcolm H. Visser. "Advances in Mine Warfare: Antiper-sonnel Mines." *Engineer* 23, no. 3 (August 1993).

Toepfer, Carl. "Technics in the Russo-Japanese War." *Professional Memoirs. Corps of Engineers* 2, no. 6 (April–June 1910): 196–197.

"Torpedoes and Torpedo Boats." *Harper's New Monthly Magazine* 65 (June–Novem-ber, 1882): 45.

"Torpedoes." *The Manufacturer and Builder* 9 (1877): 181–182.

Troxell, John F. "Landmines: Why the Korea Exception should be the Rule." *Parame-ters* 20, no. 1 (Spring 2000): 82–101. Reprint on the Internet, http://carlisle-www.army.mil/usawc/Parameters/00spring/troxell.htm, no page numbers provided (July 8, 2002).

Zhang, Xiaoming. "The Vietnam War, 1964–1969: A Chinese Perspective." *The Jour-nal of Military History* 60, no. 4 (October 1996): 731–763.

Dissertations and Theses

Bergon, Arthur William Jr. "The Confederate Defense of Mobile, 1861–1865." Ph.D. diss., Louisiana State University and Agricultural and Mechanical College, 1980.

Chilstrom, John. "Mines Away! The Significance of U.S. Army Air Forces Minelaying in World War II." Thesis, School of Advanced Airpower Studies, Air Univer-sity, 1992.

Funk, David E. "A Mine Is A Terrible Thing To Waste: The Operational Implications Of Banning Anti-Personnel Landmines." Monograph, School of Advanced Military Studies, United States Army Command and General Staff College, 1998.

Jamieson, Perry David. "The Development of Civil War Tactics." Ph.D. diss., Wayne State University, 1979.

Osterhoudt, Henry Jerry. "The Evolution of U.S. Army Assault Tactics, 1778–1919. The Search for Sound Doctrine." Ph.D. diss., Duke University, 1986.

Weinert, Richard Peter. "The Confederate Regular Army 1861–1865." M.A. thesis, The American University, 1964.

Web Sites and Electronic Sources

International Campaign to Ban Landmines. "Ratification Updates." http://www.icbl.org/treaty/ (30 October 2002).

———. "States Not Parties." http://www.icbl.org/treaty/snp/ (March 15, 2006).

———. "State Parties." http://www.icbl.org/treaty/members/ (March 15, 2006).

1971 Seabed Treaty. Nuclear Threat Institute Web site. http://www.nti.org/e_research/official_docs/inventory/pdfs/.%5Captseabd.pdf.

Index